Women in
Wonderland

Women in Wonderland

by Dorothy Dohen

SHEED AND WARD - New York

Library of Congress Card Number: 60-12868

Manufactured in the United States of America

In memory of two happy women:
my mother and my grandmother

ACKNOWLEDGMENTS

Grateful acknowledgment is made to the authors and publishers who granted their permission to reprint passages from the following books and periodicals:

Chastity, edited by A. Plé, O. P. from "The Religious Life Series," published by The Newman Press; *The Veil of The Heart,* by Piccarda, published by St. Anthony's Guild; *The Lonely Crowd,* by David Riesman, published by Yale University Press; *Sex and Personality,* by Lewis M. Terman and Catharine Miles, reprinted by permission of McGraw-Hill Book Company, Inc., copyright, 1936; *Love in the Western World,* by Denis de Rougemont, published by Pantheon Books, Inc.; "Toward a Theology of Woman," by Rev. A. Lavaud, published by *The Thomist; Contemplative Life in the World,* by A. M. Goichon, published by B. Herder Book Company; *The Way of All Women,* by Dr. M. Esther Harding, published by Longmans, Green and Company; "What is Happening to the American Family," from *New Emphasis on Cultural Factors,* by Margaret Mead, published by Family Service Association of America; *Women in Marital Conflict,* by Florence Hollis, published by Family Service Association of America; *Woman in the Modern World,* by Eva Firkel, published by Fides Publishers; *Male and Female,* by Margaret Mead, copyright by William Morrow & Company, Inc., Publishers; *Teacher in America,* by Jacques Barzun, published by Little, Brown & Company; "Love and Celibacy," by B. Häring, *C.Ss.R.,* published by *Theology Digest; Modern Woman: The Lost Sex,* by Marynia F. Farnham and Ferdinand Lundberg, published by Harper and Brothers; *The Challenge of Being A Woman,* by Helen Sherman and Marjorie Coe, published by Harper and Brothers; *Women Today,* edited by E. Bragdon, published by Bobbs-Merrill Company, Inc.

Contents

1

The Fascinating Female

WHAT *is a woman?*

"A small man," answered Plato.

"A castrated man," replied Aristotle.

"What a misfortune to be a woman! And yet the worst misfortune is not to understand what a misfortune it is," thought Kierkegaard.

"Anatomy is her destiny," proclaimed Freud. "She is envious of the male, and the only way she can seek compensation for her biological inferiority is by becoming pregnant."

What is a woman? "The superior sex," says Ashley Montagu.

What is an American woman?

A "sex-hungry, spoiled, self-centered, aggressive, clothes-happy, frustrated, neurotic" person, according to one British anthropologist.

"A female with a $5,000 kitchen who cooks least well of any woman in the world," say some.

"A female who is fast losing her femininity, just as the American male is losing his masculinity," say others.

Are American women happy?

No, say two American women writers. "We enjoy the highest standard of living in history: we are the best dressed, best groomed, best housed women anywhere, with the least drudgery; we have the most freedom, the greatest amount of formal education, and the widest opportunities to enrich our lives; and American men are unexcelled in indulgence, generosity, and willingness to give us a chance to do whatever we want to do. Despite all these good things, too many American women are dissatisfied, and even neurotic, finding life one disagreeable task after another, and husband, children and work sources of irritation."[1]

American women are not happy, implied a *Fortune* poll. Twenty-five percent of them, if they could be born over again, would wish to be men.[2]

Do American women know what they want out of life?

There seems to be some confusion on this point. One survey reports that, although seventy-five percent of high school girls want to marry, only twenty-five percent want to be homemakers.[3]

Gimbel's facetiously summarized the American girl's ambivalence in an ad for college clothes. "What's college? That's where girls who are above cooking and sewing go to meet a man so they can spend their lives cooking and sewing."

Do American women know what they want out of life? No, say some observers. "Modern women seem to find the times to be out of joint. So often they feel frustrated and harassed . . . At times they appear to wish for the olden days when women's roles were restricted, but they had a sure, safe place in a man's world."[4]

But others claim that times are changing, and American women are changing with them. Do American girls today know what they want out of life? Yes, replies Margaret Mead. "Marriage, the sooner the better, and children *at once!*"

And the president of Smith College recently pleaded with his students not to succumb to the "prevailing mania for early marriages"!

Does that mean that American women now are going to stay in the home and be content with domestic bliss? No, statistics solemnly tell us, the average American woman is now finished child-bearing when she is 26.1 years of age, and is ready to go back to work when her youngest child starts school and she is approximately thirty-two years old.[5] Already over half the women working are married, and one forecaster predicts that soon ninety percent of all women will be employed outside the home. *Despite the apparent confusion and unhappiness from which they are suffering, are American women managing to survive?*

Very well, thank you. Women have always been noted for their hardihood, but now in the United States they are definitely the long-lived sex. They are outliving their husbands remarkably well. At present the proportion of widowed women between the ages of sixty to sixty-five is double the proportion of widowed men,[6] and it is predicted that the young married woman of today may spend an average of sixteen years in widowhood.

Despite the fact that Dr. Schindler recently warned us that American women beat a path to the doctor's office loaded down with psychosomatic ills, they seem to survive very nicely and there is every indication that—happy or not—they will see a ripe old age.

THE PURSUIT OF HAPPINESS

Why all this interest in women? Margaret Mead replied to this question on an hour-long television show devoted to the issue, "Are American Women Losing Their Femininity?" She answered that we think of the question of femininity because we are preoccupied with the question of happiness. Ours is indeed a society in which self-concern is the chief concern.

In the type of society in which everyone is struggling for survival, practically nobody has the opportunity to worry about whether he is happy or not. Happiness means that you live another day, or get a few ounces of rice for another meal. You manage to survive! In such a society anyone would be likely to give the answer that was given by a couple in Puerto Rico who were managing to live barely on a subsistence level. Asked if they were happy, they first looked surprised, then shrugged their shoulders, and finally they replied, "We survive."

But American women, like American men, are interested in much more than just surviving. They are interested in being positively happy. In what does happiness consist? Of that they are not sure. Somehow or other they feel it must have something to do with their being women, something to do with how they are treated, something to do with what they are doing with their lives, but what exactly they are not sure.

Of course, there are American women who seem content with their lives, and are not overly concerned with whether they are being feminine or not. Yet one wonders if the American women who are un-self-consciously happy, without wondering how they are supposed to be, are typical. For, increasingly, these women seem to be in a minority. A multitude of articles appear in the women's magazines advising how this marriage can be saved, how America lives, how I got over my nervous breakdown, and how I kept my husband's love. The implication always is that the average reader of these periodicals is someone exposed to the dangers of a loosening marriage bond, a fickle husband, financial doom (or sometimes, fortunately, less hazardous budgetary problems), possible hospitalization for mental depression (unless cancer kills her first), and forever looming ahead of her—increased avoirdupois. These magazines deserve much praise for tackling these problems in a realistic way. Often they impress one as having a great deal more sense than their readers, who never seem to tire of finding out again and again that it is possible to make a successful sexual adjustment in marriage and that it is highly probable that at some time in their lives they will resort to spanking their children. The excessive anxiety of American women to do right by their apparently multitudinous obligations is revealed on every one of these periodical pages. The magazine, evidently, is successful in quelling their anxiety to some extent, but, fortunately for the publisher, the anxiety recurs; so next month there is another issue in which once again the war is waged against cancer, mental disease and the incipient breakdown of sex in marriage.

American women are interested in American women because everybody is looking at everybody else to see if anybody has discovered how she can be happy.

The interest in books and articles on women is not of recent origin. Women obviously have always been a fascinating subject —a fact attested to by, among other things, the thirteen drawers containing twenty-thousand index cards on "woman" and "women" in the catalogue room of the New York Public Library. Someone was always on the verge of discovering the mystery of woman and therefore impelled to write a book to explain her, while, since the mystery was never revealed *in toto,* someone else had the privileg of then writing another book. And so it went.

SOME TYPICAL CONFUSIONS

What were Catholics doing meanwhile? Writing books too, of course! What woman is, what woman should be, what woman should do with a man, what woman should do without a man, have engaged Catholic authors of books, magazine articles, and newspaper columns. Speakers, not to be outdone by writers, told in public and private all there is to know about woman's psychology as well as her theology (it being taken for granted in Catholic circles, unlike secular ones, that everybody knows her biology!)

These so-called "Catholic" views are varied, interesting, and—although never written to amuse—often entertaining. Perhaps there are not many like him, but one Catholic husband has openly advocated that it is part of the husband's role to give spiritual direction to his wife. Another American Catholic husband felt that the wife as well as the children should be silent at meals while the father led the conversation. (All of these odd views are, of course, bolstered by the quotation from Saint Paul about women being subject to their husbands.) This past year one Catholic magazine reached a new extreme in the reaction against feminism. In an article advocating that husband and wife vote for the same candidate, it implied that the unity of marriage, the sacredness of the marriage bond, the wife's obedience to her husband, and Catholic theology all demand it! A husband and wife have no moral right, the article solemnly declares, to cast opposing ballots and, as one might suspect, it is up to the wife to change her mind, since "If husband and wife cannot agree, the husband's decision must prevail."[7] (Think of all those hard-working feminists twirling in their graves, as they hear their opponents say "See, we told you it would never do to give women the vote!")

Yes, some of the proposals supposedly deduced from theology are very queer indeed. Take what is written about single women. The single woman, it would seem, has a bad enough time in America anyway since Kinsey and his associates thought they had discovered that if she has preserved her chastity she is in an abnormal condition. But single Catholic women are told by one pamphlet writer that they are not missing anything. There is nothing to sex anyhow; no reason why anybody should want it, or feel frustrated without it. In fact, the priest-author goes on to declare, single women should be glad they are not married since spiritually they are well-circumstanced, and have—even—a slight edge on salvation! The single woman might well be confused by all of this, especially if she heard the Sister President say at the time of her graduation from college that if she remained single she was selfish. No Catholic woman should choose to remain single: she must either go in the convent or get married. Who is right: Father X or Sister Y? It is especially disconcerting since, as usual, they both quote from Saint Paul!

These directives, supposedly derived from theology, are bad. But some of the counsels presented under the guise of a "Catholic" psychology of women are even worse. One apostolic group, quite laudably concerned about the role of Christian woman, categorically declared a few years ago that a woman should not study philosophy: the only way she could learn it was by marrying a philosopher!

Another case in point is the well-known book by Gina Lombroso. Lombroso had a tremendous influence on the Catholic antifeminists. (She had some very good ideas as well.) By implication, however, she reduced woman to one big Intuition. In a book which contains some sound insights, she makes a number of surprising statements; one, for example, that woman has a maternal instinct and it is with the same maternal instinct that she loves her father,

her son, *and* her husband; another, that women cannot be interested in a profession for objective reasons; she chooses it only because someone she loves is involved in it. What proof does she give for these two contentions? None for the first. For the second she gives her own case: she herself became a doctor because her father was one, and when he died lost interest in medicine and ceased to practice. (In all justice to Kinsey and the charge that he and his successors are unscientific in their sampling, it should be noted—even Kinsey had a larger and more representative sampling than Lombroso's single case.)

Even Chesterton has been drawn into the endeavor to prove that there is a "Catholic" psychology of woman. Woman, he is quoted as saying, is a universalist; man is a specialist. Probably this was all very well and true at the time Chesterton wrote it (about 1910), but one doubts that it was true for the ages before him or is true at the present time—for reasons that will be given in detail later on in the book. Moreover, Chesterton, who was a great journalist and who was engaged in the then current political tussle over feminism, probably never expected his words to be taken as Gospel—or even as a timeless statement on the philosophy of the sexes or the psychology of women. The most clever paradoxes get hoary, and writers do Chesterton no service by quoting his as a decisive word on all questions involving the situation of women today.

One of these famous Chestertonian passages concerns the role of the mother: "To be Queen Elizabeth within a definite area, deciding sales, banquets, labors and holidays; to be Whitely within a certain area, providing toys, boots, sheets, cakes and books; to be Aristotle within a certain area, teaching morals, manners, theology and hygiene; I can understand how this might exhaust the mind, but I cannot imagine how it could narrow it.* How can it be a large

* "Hmmph! He can't?" says the mother of a pack of little children. "He should be with seven children all day long and have nothing but infantile talk and he could soon understand how the mind gets narrowed." Is she right or wrong? Let Jacques Barzun take up the cudgels in her behalf. Maintaining that conditions for the homemaker are anti-intellectual, he states, "Whereas the very essence of thought is continuity, the very essence

career to tell other people's children about the Rule of Three, and a small career to tell one's own children about the universe? How can it be broad to be the same thing to everyone, and narrow to be everything to someone? No; a woman's function is laborious, but because it is gigantic, not because it is minute. I will pity Mrs. Jones for the hugeness of her task; I will never pity her for its smallness."[9]

That is certainly an heroic statement of the situation of the busy mother, and swept along by Chesterton's glorious prose, one might overlook that it begs several very important questions. The modern mother is not going to find that it solves all her dilemmas (even intellectually), and several dilemmas have been added to her situation since Chesterton wrote that passage fifty years ago. But there is no need to quarrel with Chesterton. What should be emphasized is the fact that many problems women face today—both within the home and outside of it—deserve careful consideration. They are not going to be solved by quoting another cliché about how woman must be womanly. For there one hits one of the vital questions: What exactly does *womanly* mean?

We are told that as Catholic women we should work to bring into the world feminine values. But what are feminine values? As Dr. Harding remarks: "It is so easy to SAY that woman must bring into life specifically feminine values . . . but it is exceedingly difficult to define with any clarity exactly what these are or where they may be found."[10]

THIS BOOK AND ITS PURPOSE

Certainly there are some values that forever will transcend time and place. But there are other values that belong to particular cultures and appear dated—or even dangerous—if they are transposed too literally into another society or into a different

of domestic life is interruption. If a young woman dared disconnect the doorbell, smash the phone, and gag the baby, she might be able to read a book or think a thought; but with a duty toward everybody but herself, her mind necessarily reverts to the feral state. It is not a matter of intelligence or good will or even energy, but of hourly preoccupation."[8]

era. What these values are the interested woman is anxious to discover.

That is the particular *raison d'être* of this book. There have been several excellent books written concerning the role of the modern Christian woman; the writings of Edith Stein, Gertrud von le Fort, and Eva Firkel come immediately to mind. And there are others. However, all of them are European. Nothing seems to have been written about the specific situation and problems of the *American* Catholic woman. Similarly, while there is much excellent material analyzing the dilemma of the modern American woman from the sociological point of view, and many good books have been written to bring the insights of anthropology and psychology to bear on her problems,* very little has been written, in theological perspective, of the American *Catholic* woman.

This book holds out no promise of giving all the answers. In fact, it will avoid facile solutions. There has been too much disastrous copying of other people's lives on the part of the American woman, and nothing is gained by holding some particular woman up for the reader's admiration with the admonition to go and do in like manner.

Even if it were possible to give a recipe for a happy feminine life, conditions change so rapidly that the recipe would soon be useless. Any woman who knows the slightest thing about cooking will know she has to learn to cook all over again, in a sense, when she switches from a gas to an electric stove. Life, needless to say, is more complicated than cooking, and with her physical, social, and even emotional environment changing rapidly, a woman has to learn to adjust.

Women who desire recipes for living have to realize that even in cooking much of the success depends on the prudence and art of the cook. (As any tearful bride realizes as she laments her first dismal failure after faithfully following the recipe.) How much more, then, does successful living and the realistic solu-

* Several of these works will be quoted in later chapters of this book, since it is important to put at the disposal of Catholic readers the best research and thinking that has been done on the situation of women in America and the role-conflicts women face in the modern world.

tion of one's problems depend on one's personal prudence and the skill (or art, if you will) that has been developed in coping with actual situations. Life has infinite variety, and no two women can lead exactly the same life, for no two women are exactly alike nor have they the same opportunities, circumstances, responsibilities—or husbands. Anyone's life is inextricably entangled in the lives of others; the mature person recognizes this fact and realizes that no one can tell her how she is supposed to cope with these human relations or with the many other facets of her life. People can counsel, inspire, suggest. Books are proverbially food for thought. An author can be an irritant or a goad, causing the reader to take a long look at her life or perhaps simply to do a bit of personal examination.

It is impossible not to sympathize with those readers who would like a definitive answer to their problems, and it is the author's hope that this book will show that the reluctance to give answers is not caused either by a lack of compassion for the crosses of women today or a lack of realization of her opportunities. However, only the immature and the fearful want someone else to tell them what to do; only they run away from freedom. Today women need to be encouraged to grow, to become mature, to face the opportunities and responsibilities of their freedom and not to be afraid.

This book has grown out of several years of thought and study. The author can only hope that it will prove to be of some help to others. For readers who desire to check facts for themselves or to pursue in their own way any of the subjects treated, a list of references is appended to each chapter. This list aims to be suggestive rather than complete, and it includes those sources which the author herself has found most helpful.

The book is the result of research, the author's own experiences, and her observations of the experiences of other women. Much of the material (especially in the later chapters which deal with women in their various roles) is presented through the case-history method. The author has taken pains to present no experience that is unique or that does not have universal implications.

Always the aim has been to explore the actual situation of American women. Emphasis has been placed on the common elements in their lives as they exist in concrete cases.

NOTES

1. Helen Sherman and Marjorie Coe, *The Challenge of Being a Woman* (New York: Harper and Brothers, 1955), p. 6.
2. *Fortune,* August 1946. Interestingly enough, only three percent of the males queried would desire to be women if they could be born over again. It is regrettable that the *Fortune* article does not give information which would enable us to judge the reliability of the survey.
3. Sherman and Coe, *op. cit.,* p. 18.
4. Robert J. Havighurst writing in *Potentialities of Women in the Middle Years,* edited by Gross (Michigan State University, 1956), p. 8.
5. *Ibid.,* p. 20.
6. *Ibid.,* p. 127.
7. We hope we shall be forgiven for not giving the sources of our "horrible examples." Since the authors and speakers quoted often have had excellent things to say along with what we consider their foolish and unfounded statements, we do not wish to ruin their reputations by identifying them.
8. Jacques Barzun, *Teacher in America* (Garden City, New York: Doubleday Anchor Books, 1954), p. 213.
9. Gilbert K. Chesterton, *What's Wrong with the World* (New York: Sheed and Ward, 1942), p. 153. This book was originally published by Dodd, Mead in 1910.
10. M. Esther Harding, M. D., *The Way of All Women* (New York: Longmans, Green, 1937), p. 105.

2

The Theology of Woman

WHEN Saint Thomas Aquinas quoted Aristotle approvingly to the effect that woman is a misbegotten male,[1] it was probably fortunate that there were not too many literate women around. But, perhaps even if more women of the thirteenth century could have read it would have made little difference to them. They would merely have laughed at the pomposity of males and, especially if they were happy to be women, tolerantly allowed Thomas to think what he wished.

Thomas was not the only Doctor of the Church who was inclined to take a dim view of women. His other famous remark, that a woman was made exclusively for procreation, "but she was not fitted to help man except in generation, because another man would have proved a more effective help in anything else,"[2] he borrowed from his equally famous predecessor, Saint Augustine.[3]

Needless to say, these pronouncements are not part of Christian dogma. Saints Thomas and Augustine might speculate on the subject, but their ideas on the female sex never became a part of Christian doctrine. What is a part of Christian doctrine on women (and it is surprisingly little) is eminently sane.

It should be noted at the outset that theologians, even Doctors of the Church, belong to their own times. With all their rationality, they never manage fully to transcend their own cultural prejudices. Ethnocentrism is found in the thinking of theologians as well as other lesser human beings, and, especially on the question of the relationship of the sexes, theologians were (and probably are today) children of their own time and culture. This is, of course, no reason for alarm. The fact that the essentials of theology safely transcend cultural variations (although in practice the *lived* truths of faith reflect the biases of the age or region in that they too have a *cultural accent*) does not mean that the accidentals partake of the same transcendence. And since most of the theological writing on woman concerns accidentals, it is to be expected that it should bear the mark of the culture of the individual writer and not the mark of the transcultural, universal Church.

Even the pronouncements of the recent Popes show the same cultural relativity when they deal with the woman question. Thus, Pius X declared that it was unseemly for a woman to sit in a parliamentary body, and less than fifty years later Pius XII urged that women who had the opportunity and the talent for public life make their special contribution to legislative deliberations.[4] It may be argued, of course, that these two Popes took different stands because society had changed very rapidly in a few decades; and the needs of the early twentieth century differed radically from those of the mid-twentieth century. However that may be, it is obvious that Pius X was a child of his time when he stated that a woman was outside her sphere in a parliamentary body, while Pius XII, when he declared that "Every woman has, then—mark it well—the obligation, the strict obligation in conscience, not to absent herself" from social and political life, showed himself a man of the age when political rights for women had become an accomplished fact. The one Pope spoke in a time of agitated feminism, the other Pope when feminism had already won for women the right to vote.

Sometimes, indeed, it is difficult to separate what is unchangeable in the pronouncements of popes and theologians from what is merely an accidental rule for a special circumstance of a particular time and place. In a most enlightening article concerning the development of a theology of woman, Father Lavaud, the eminent Dominican theologian, writes: "Even in the New Testament there are some cases in which it is difficult to distinguish what is an unchangeable rule made for all times and places, and what is only a prescription dictated by Apostolic prudence in view of historical conditions. There is, for instance, the decision of Saint Paul regarding what should be the part, deportment and head-dress of women in the Christian assemblies. It is not to be denied *a priori* that certain ideas that were specifically Jewish left more traces than they should have in the mind of some Fathers and Doctors."[5]

Certainly the case of the devout German women who today receive Holy Communion with their heads uncovered, apparently with the approval of their pastors, would seem to prove that the Pauline rule concerning a woman's head-covering in Church was without permanent binding force and without any intrinsic connection with Christian doctrine! (And what would St. Paul think of the Christian women of parts of Africa who attend Mass not only with head uncovered but most of their body as well?)

Another cause for the seemingly warped views of some Fathers and Doctors concerning women given by Father Lavaud is the fact that not as "a matter of right or necessity, but of historical fact" most theologians have been "clerics or monks and therefore celibates . . . They run the risk, at the same time, of falling into error by considering it as an aid to virtue to have a rather low opinion of woman, and of paying more attention in reading the Bible to complaints made by the wise man against the wicked woman, the dangerous temptress, than to the beautiful and delicate commendations bestowed on the valiant and chaste woman . . ."[6]

In interpreting the writing of Saint Augustine on women it should be remembered that he himself may have been understandably reacting against the part women had played in his rather loose moral life before his conversion. Further, he was writing at a time when pagan excesses of immorality were not yet past history. It is a proof of his wisdom and grace that he wrote as favorably about women and procreation as he did, and gave the exalted explanation concerning marriage which has become part of the Church's traditional teaching on that Sacrament.

As for Saint Thomas, he took over much of his teaching on woman from Saint Augustine and Aristotle. Aristotle, it would seem, had a very low opinion of woman and saw her role as limited to procreation. The Greek man, if we are to believe some Greek literature, sought love from another man and used relations with his wife only for the purpose of having children.[7] Saint Thomas, while he, of course, purged the thought of Aristotle of its homosexual overtones, nevertheless seems to have been influenced by that thought to the extent of limiting a woman's role in a man's life only to her childbearing function.

However, neither Saint Augustine nor Saint Thomas fell into the error of some of the other Doctors of the Church, namely Saints Athanasius, Gregory of Nyssa, and Ambrose, that the distinction of the sexes was intended and realized by God only in view of sin (or that He made male and female before sin because He foreknew the mode of generation which would take place after sin). Neither did they concur with the even stranger opinion of Saint John Chrysostom according to which God had provided for procreation of the race in the state of innocence otherwise than by sex relations and generative functions.[8] Saint Thomas reaffirmed the goodness of sex in marriage by holding fast to the opinion that, even if there had never been a fall, intercourse would have been the same as it is today.

Even Saint Thomas' remark about woman being a misbegotten male ("as being a product outside the purpose of nature considered in the individual case: but not against the purpose of universal nature"[9]) may have been the result of his faulty knowledge of biology rather than of any inherent prejudice against women. And women, as well as men, owe him a debt of gratitude that in his theology as a whole he stressed the goodness of the body and of human nature in general.

Except in the notable case of the doctrine concerning the Sacrament of Holy Orders, the dogmatic and moral theology that applies to men applies equally to women. The fact that there is a scarcity of references to women in the writings of theologians does not mean that they are not considered as having the same responsibilities, opportunities, and destiny as the rest of humanity, but it is precisely because women have never been considered a separate species by the Church that no specific theological mention is made of them. What holds true for men in the life of grace holds true equally for women. What is held up to men for their belief is held up also to women. What are sins for men are sins also for women, and while vice and virtue in practice may be conditioned by sex, in speculative theology the evil that must be avoided and the good that must be embraced is the same for either sex.*[10]

It would be acknowledging, or at any rate implying, that women are essentially different if one desired to build up a special "theology of woman," for the main body of the "theology of woman" is already included in the "theology of man." There are indeed very few points of Biblical history and Christian doctrine that deal specifically with women.

ADAM AND EVE

Genesis describes the creation of Eve. "And God created man to his own image: to the image of God he created him. Male and female he created them. And God blessed them, saying: Increase and multiply, and fill the earth . . ." (Gen. 1, 27-28).

In the second account of the creation of man, in Chapter 2, we read: "And the Lord God said: It is not good for man to be alone; let us make him a help like unto himself. And the Lord God having formed out of the ground all the beasts of the earth, and all the fowls of the air, brought them to Adam to see what he would call them: for whatsoever Adam called any living creature the same is its name. And Adam called all the beasts by their names, and all the fowls of the air, and all the cattle of the field: but for Adam there was not found a helper like himself. Then the Lord God cast a deep sleep upon Adam: and when he

* St. Jerome sums this up in these words: "With us Christians what is unlawful for women is equally unlawful for men, and as both serve the same God both are bound by the same obligation."

was fast asleep, he took one of his ribs, and filled up flesh for it. And the Lord God built the rib which he took from Adam into a woman: and brought her to Adam. And Adam said: This now is bone of my bone, and flesh of my flesh; she shall be called woman, because she was taken out of man. Wherefore a man shall leave father and mother, and shall cleave to his wife: and they shall be two in one flesh. And they were both naked, to wit, Adam and his wife: and were not ashamed." (Gen. 2, 18-25).

This account of the creation of Eve is beautiful in its simplicity. There is the poignancy of the plight of Adam: he looks around at all the beasts and calls them by name, but he looks in vain for someone resembling himself. God sees his plight and considers how it should be remedied. "All exegetes agree that this divine deliberation is a delightful touch, and that, although it is a literary device, its purpose is to glorify the creation of woman."[11] For Eve is created because Adam is aware of his loneliness and yearns for someone to complete him. Woman is not someone foisted on man, but someone man needs.

The literary device which the writer of Genesis used at a time when woman was a depressed class, deified in her grossly sexual aspects, but not respected as a living human being, pointed up the contrast between woman as God made her and woman as she existed in the ancient semitic world. As one exegete, Father McKenzie, remarks: "In Hebrew society also woman was a depressed class; the storyteller was not attempting a feminist reform, but he wished to state that in the beginning it was not so . . ." In contrast to the goddess of fertility of the primitive world whose cult was surrounded by all manner of immorality degrading to woman, "the Hebrew story describes the 'helper meet for man': his partner and, in the context of the story, his equal. She is made to share his life and not merely his sexual experience; it is not good for the man to be alone. What could be more directly contrasted to the image of the goddess than the description of this couple as naked and unashamed?"[12]

The certain teaching of the Church interpreting these passages from Genesis is as follows:

Despite the difference in sex, both the man and the woman are like unto God. (Woman was made from man but she, as well as he, is in the Divine image.)

Man was created male and female by God in order that the human race might be procreated as He had commanded. ("Increase and multiply.")

In the conjugal society—in other words, in marriage—the woman is physically and morally dependent upon the man.

Human nature is total neither in the man alone nor in the woman alone, but in them both.[13]

What is uncertain, according to most exegetes, is the exact manner of the formation of woman by God.[14] It is not certain whether the rib of Adam is mentioned by way of symbol or because it was the actual material used.* Saint Thomas wrote: "It was right for the woman to be made from a rib of man. First, to signify the social union of man and woman, for the woman should neither *use authority over man,* and so she was not made from his head; nor was it right for her to be subject to man's contempt as his slave, and so she was not made from his feet. Secondly, for the sacramental significations; for from the side of Christ sleeping on the Cross the Sacraments flowed—namely, blood and water—on which the Church was established."[16] The fact of woman's being taken from the side of man shows at the same time her dependence and her dignity; thus she becomes an expressive figure of the Church born "from the open side of Christ as He slept on the Cross, the sleep of love and death, of death out of love . . ."[17]

ON WOMAN'S SUBJECTION TO HER HUSBAND

It would seem that the relationship of man and woman in marriage is already clearly indicated in Genesis. This relationship

* "The term used in describing the creation of Eve, namely, 'rib' or 'side' is certainly one of the most obscure words in Genesis . . . The Biblical Commission has formally stated that Eve was drawn in some way from Adam . . . Adam was at least the exemplary cause of Eve in so far as her body and her nature were fashioned after his. The exact manner in which her body is formed is uncertain from the text, nor has tradition clarified it with any certainty."[15]

was later spelled out by Saint Paul for Christian couples: "Husbands, love your wives, just as Christ also loved the Church, and delivered himself up for her" (Eph. 5, 25). "Let wives be subject to their husbands as to the Lord"* (Eph. 5, 22). "Let each one of you also love his wife just as he loves himself; and let the wife respect her husband" (Eph. 5, 33). "The wife has not authority over her body, but the husband; the husband likewise has not authority over his body, but the wife." (I Cor. 7, 4). From these passages it is clear that the woman's subjection to her husband is one of dignity and honor; that his love for her is expected to be cherishing and protecting, as is Christ's love for the Church; that the husband loving his wife is loving himself, since they are two in one flesh; and that marital rights in no sense are a masculine prerogative: the wife has a right to intercourse with her husband just as he has a right to request it with her.

What is the nature of this subjection of the wife to her husband? Pope Pius XI, in his encyclical *On Christian Marriage,* explains it thus: "This subjection, however, does not deny or take away the liberty which fully belongs to the woman both in view of her dignity as a human person, and in view of her most noble office as wife and mother and companion; nor does it bid her obey her husband's every request if not in harmony with right reason or with the dignity due to a wife; nor, in fine, does it imply that the wife should be put on a level with those persons who in law are called minors, to whom it is not customary to allow free exercise of their rights because of their lack of mature judgment, or of their ignorance of human affairs. But it forbids that exaggerated liberty which cares not for the good of the family; it forbids that in the body which is the family, the heart be separated from the head to the great detriment of the whole body and the proximate

* Father Fitzsimons writes: "It has been suggested that while St. Paul conceded the equality of women with men in the eyes of God, at the same time he still maintained that they should remain subject to men. In other words they were given equality but not freedom. This is based mainly on his exhortation to women to be subject to their husbands, a command particularly resented in these later days by emancipated woman. However, it should be made clear that St. Paul was talking of the relationship between husband and wife, and not between men and women in general . . ."[18]

danger of ruin. For if the man is the head, the woman is the heart, and as he occupies the chief place in ruling, so she may and ought to claim for herself the chief place in love." (Part 1, Paragraph 17)

It is obvious that the idea of the Christian subjection of wife to husband allows for considerable latitude. The interpretation of Pius XI's words as they apply in practice would be marked by consideration of custom and cultural relativities. Those who would interpret the proper relationship of husband and wife as exacting a definite set of rules and customs would reveal themselves only as victims of their own ethnocentrism. For who is to say who embodies more clearly the spirit of the conjugal relationship: the woman in countries of Latin culture who bustles around waiting on her husband while he eats, or the American husband who waits until his wife also is seated before he begins his meal? Both couples in both cultures may be expressing the love and honor due to each other, and only an extremely opinionated, intolerant person would hazard a definitive judgment as to which couple best reveal an understanding of Christian marriage. (That a person in a particular culture has the right to prefer his way of doing things as "best" goes without saying, but that is not the point here.) Moreover, it is patently ridiculous to interpret the theology of Christian marriage as necessitating a oneness on political matters, tastes in art, or baseball teams! (Although certainly it may be more pleasant if husband and wife are in agreement.) The subjection of the wife is limited to matters pertaining to the good of the family, and, since Pius XI, by implication, acknowledged that the wife is in possession of mature judgment and knowledge of human affairs, she has the right to her own opinions.

For the subjection of the wife is always balanced by the love which brings about equality between wife and husband. As Denis de Rougemont writes: "Christianity has asserted the complete equality of the sexes, and this as plainly as possible. Saint Paul says: 'The wife hath no power of her own body, but the husband; and likewise also the husband hath not power of his own body, but the wife.' Once she is man's equal, woman cannot be man's goal. Yet at the same time she is spared the bestial abasement that sooner or later must be the price of divinizing a creature. But her equality is not to be understood in the contemporary sense of giving rise to rights. It belongs to the mystery of love . . . For a truly mutual love exacts and creates the equality of those loving one another. God showed His love for man by exacting that man should be holy even as God is holy. And a man gives evidence of his love for a woman by treating her as a completely human person, not as if she were the spirit of the legend—half-goddess, half bacchante, a compound of dreams and sex."[19]

The love between husband and wife, tending toward that perfect love which casts out fear, "renders precepts superfluous and in a high degree supplies for obedience."[20] The Christian couple, loving each other in the love of Christ for His Church, need not be concerned unduly about the subjection of the wife, for the love of the husband frees her at the same time as it renders her honor and dignity.

Perhaps it is unnecessary to return to a consideration of Saint Thomas' argument that a woman was made only for procreation. It seems clear from the text in Genesis that Eve was made for Adam to dispel his loneliness, to complete him, and to make his happiness in Paradise perfect. Eve was made obviously for procreation, but, when the writer of Genesis describes the subjective disposition of Adam before Eve was made, it is not the future generation that appears uppermost in Adam's mind, but his present loneliness because in all creation there was no being who resembled him. Eve was made to be his help in procreation and in so much else besides. While Father Lavaud remarks that "it would be a manifest absurdity to deny that the Creator of all good things prepared woman for childbirth," he reminds us that man's sexual organs are ordained for procreation too. "It is one thing to recognize and affirm the evident orientation of the sexes to procreation . . . another to say that the distinction of the sexes" is "no more than means for the attainment of the end which is procreation."[21] Saint Thomas to the contrary, there *are* some things which a woman can help a man with better than another man can! (But what these things are belongs to the order of experimental science and not of theology.)

One other question: it is obvious that Eve was created for the sake of Adam, but does that mean woman exists *only* for the sake of man? In practice the Church has always given a negative answer to that question. By affirming the right of a woman to consecrate her virginity in direct service of God, the Church has always claimed for her a meaning and a purpose in her own being, separated from her evident role as a helpmate of man in marriage. When it is said that woman was created for the sake of man, "for his sake" means that he requires her to attain the meaning of his existence. "Never could it mean that woman was created merely for the sake of man; every creature has its proper meaning, that is, to portray, to body forth, each in its own way, God's Being."[22] Woman, as a human person, exists ultimately to glorify God.

EVE AND HER DAUGHTERS

Genesis recounts how the serpent tempted Eve and how she in turn tempted Adam. When he fell and God decreed their punishment He said to Eve: "I will multiply thy sorrows, and thy conceptions. In sorrow shalt thou bring forth children, and thou shalt be under thy husband's power, and he shall have dominion over thee." (Gen. 3, 16). Such is the curse of Eve. This is the penalty of her sin. This passage of Genesis is not meant to condone man's abuse of power over his wife; exegetes do not interpret it to mean that since the fall he has the right to abuse her. Rather, it would seem, that it is a prophecy of what is to come. In the family, between husband and wife, there would exist domestic tension.[23] "The husband has not acquired the right to govern his wife without love or according to his caprice and to satisfy his ego. But he often does, and his sin is an aspect of the woman's punishment."[24]

And what about the curse of the pain of childbirth? In this

aspect of Eve's punishment, we see how the blessing peculiar to woman was, by the fall, changed into sorrow. As man's blessing in creation was changed by the fall, so that in the future all his joy in creative effort would become embittered by the necessary toil which would have to accompany it, woman's joy in bringing forth her children would be accompanied by the pain and anguish of delivery. Her blessing was not taken away, but what should have been unclouded joy for her became the source of anguish. There is no justification for interpreting this passage of Genesis to mean that it is not right or laudable to seek to mitigate the pains of woman in childbirth (just as it is both right and laudable to lessen the harshness of man's dominion over her). The Christian woman bringing forth her children has the added joy of knowing that at the baptismal font they will be made children of God; so, in reality, the fruits of her pain are destined to become brothers of Christ. But, since the fall and Eve's curse, pain accompanies childbirth, and in spite of the advances in medical science which have greatly mitigated the pain, it will probably be always true, that woman will be left with an ambivalent attitude toward bearing children. "A woman about to give birth has sorrow, because her hour has come. But when she has brought forth the child, she no longer remembers the anguish for her joy that a man is born into the world" (John 16, 21).

The single woman, too, participates in the curse of Eve. Is it far-fetched to see in her monthly reminder that she is not going to bear a child her personal participation in the anguish of the fall? Her empty womb, as her empty arms without a child, would seem to be evidence that sin brought frustration into the world. She has faculties that will remain unused, potentialities that will not have their fulfillment. As Father Lavaud remarks, theologians who propose that in the state of innocence there would have been an equal number of men and women, and no sterility, nor perpetual virginity, have nothing but conjecture for their assertions.[25] But certainly in Paradise (since everyone would have been perfectly happy) if there would have been perpetual virginity, it would not have been reluctant virginity. The childless woman would not have had to lament her fate and, even if everybody did not get married because she did not want to get married, evidently Providence would see to it that every woman who did want a husband would get one! (How this would have been accomplished is anybody's guess, but it certainly makes an interesting subject for speculation.)

Adam and Eve, after they were driven out of Paradise, had to live in the promise of a Redeemer. They had repented but their punishment remained. Yet Eve, accepting her punishment, also received her blessing. There is something poignantly beautiful about her words after she had brought forth a child: "I have gotten a man through God" (Gen. 4, 1).* Thanks to God's intervention, Eve has ceased to be Satan's ally and has become his enemy. The hostility between mankind and the devil will pass on from Eve to her posterity, and finally through the New Eve—Mary—the devil will be completely vanquished. The seed of the woman will triumph. "I will put enmities between thee and the woman, and thy seed and her seed: she shall crush thy head, and thou shalt lie in wait for his heel" (Gen. 3, 15).[26]

In the childbirth of Mary all women are blessed. The repentance of Eve is made perfect in Mary, and, because of the fruit of her womb, the sin of Adam and Eve can be dismissed as a "happy fault"!

That is the happy ending. But what about woman? Is the fact that Eve fell first proof that woman is the weaker sex morally? Father Lavaud asserts: "Not a single word of the sacred text suggests the idea that Eve, less strong by nature, was proportionally less full of supernatural grace than her husband . . . Neither the experience nor the sacred text describing the fall . . . suggests the idea of a greater capacity for resistance to a proposed evil in man than in woman." Father Lavaud points out that "some of the great theologians, doctors and saints accepted

* Eve in the Eastern Church is venerated as Saint Eve. Perhaps it is unfortunate that this custom is not followed in the West. For certainly the repentant Eve could understand the plight of her daughters and would be happy to intercede for them.

the then current medieval idea of woman's greater weakness not only in the physical but also in the spiritual, intellectual and moral orders."[27] Evidently this was the result of what could be called a cultural prejudice, and not the result of theological certitude.

It is consoling to realize that not only did the sacrifice of Christ on the Cross repair the sin of Adam and Eve, but it won for us some tremendous privileges as well. The Christian wife can rejoice that the dignity of her marriage surpasses the dignity of the marriage which Eve would have enjoyed even if she had not sinned. "Marriage between Christians is as much superior to marriage between the couple of Paradise as the Christian is superior to Adam in Paradise." The holiness of Christian marriage is greater and more excellent than the holiness of marriage in the Garden of Eden, "in the same measure that a member of Christ is superior to a man simply endowed with grace." Christian marriage, the mystery of the union of Christ and His Church, "would be far more fitted to transmit grace than marriage as in Paradise. In the latter, grace had a very precarious connection with nature; in Christian marriage the fruit issuing from flesh belonging to the body of the God-man stands by its very nature in close relationship to the God-man and His grace."[28] Woman today, the wife today, thus enjoys a privilege and a dignity never granted to Eve, even in her Paradisial days.

There remains one question: will sex, which has such significance in time, also have significance in eternity? While there will be neither marrying nor giving in marriage in Heaven, the normal woman cannot conceive herself as being other than woman, just as the normal man cannot imagine himself being other than man. As we shall only be complete as human persons in Heaven when our souls are united with our bodies on the last day, our sex, physical though it may be in origin, marks us forever. In Mary assumed bodily into Heaven—the New Eve standing beside the New Adam—we see proof that the duality of sex has significance and value not only for time but for eternity.

NOTES

1. *Summa Theologica,* I, Q. 92, a. 1.
2. *Ibid.,* I, Q. 98, a. 2.
3. *De Genesi ad literam,* IX, 3.
4. Cf. William B. Faherty, *The Destiny of Modern Woman* (Westminster, Maryland: Newman, 1950).
5. B. Lavaud, O. P., "Toward a Theology of Women," *The Thomist,* Vol. II (October 1940), p. 465.
6. *Ibid.,* pp. 467, 468.
7. Cf. Carle C. Zimmerman and Lucius F. Cervantes, S. J., *Marriage and the Family* (Chicago: Regnery, 1956), Chapter XII.
8. Lavaud, *op. cit.,* p. 477.
9. *Summa Theologica,* I, Q. 92, a. 1.
10. The double standard of morality which had been practiced by the pagans was condemned by St. Gregory Nazianzus in the following words: ". . . For what was the reason why they restrained the woman, but indulged the man, and that a woman who practices evil against her husband is an adulteress and the penalties of the law for this are very severe: but if the husband commits fornication against the wife he has no account to give? I do not accept this legislation: I do not approve this custom. They who made the law were men, and therefore their legislation is hard on women, since they have placed children also under the authority of their fathers while leaving the weaker sex uncared for. God doth not so: but said of them 'Honour thy father and thy mother," which is the first commandent with promise . . . There is one Maker of man and woman; one debt is owed by children to both their parents.

    "How then dost thou demand chastity while you do not yourself observe it? How is it that you demand that which you yourself do not give? How is it that though you are but equally a person, you legislate unequally? If you enquire into the worst—the woman sinned, and so did Adam. The serpent deceived them both, and one was not to be found stronger and the other weaker. But do you consider yourself better? Christ saves both by His passion. Was He made flesh for man? So He was also for the woman. Did He die for the man? The woman also is saved by His death. He is called of the seed of David: and so perhaps you think the man is honoured: but He is born of a Virgin and this is on the woman's side. 'They two,' He says, 'shall be one flesh';

so let the one flesh have equal honour." Zimmerman and Cervantes, *op. cit.,* p. 501.

11. Charles Haret, *Beginnings: Genesis and Modern Science* (Dubuque: The Priory Press, 1955), p. 115.
12. John L. McKenzie, S. J., *The Two-Edged Sword,* (Milwaukee; Bruce, 1956), p. 95.
13. Summarized from Haret, *op. cit.*
14. Cf. Haret, *op. cit.*
15. Robert W. Gleason, S. J., "A Note on Theology and Evolution," *Thought,* Vol. XXXIV, No. 133 (Summer 1959), pp. 256, 257.
16. *Summa Theologica,* I, Q. 92, a. 4.
17. Lavaud, *op. cit.,* p. 485.
18. John Fitzsimons, *Woman Today* (New York: Sheed and Ward, 1952), p. 51.
19. Denis de Rougemont, *Love in the Western World* (New York: Pantheon, 1956), p. 312.
20. Lavaud, *op. cit.,* p. 491.
21. *Ibid.,* p. 479.
22. John M. Oesterreicher, "Edith Stein on Womanhood," *Integrity,* Vol. VII, No. 12 (September 1953), p. 22.
23. Cf. Haret, *op. cit.,* p. 211.
24. Lavaud, *op. cit.,* p. 515.
25. *Ibid.,* p. 483.
26. Cf. Haret, *op. cit.,* p. 219.
27. Lavaud, *op. cit.,* pp. 499, 497.
28. Matthias Joseph Scheeben, *The Mysteries of Christianity* (St. Louis: B. Herder, 1947), pp. 599-604.

3

Man and Woman: The Biological and Cultural Differences

How different are men and women? And what causes them to be different?

To understand the situation of the modern American woman, it is necessary to look first at her relationship to the modern American man. As has been noted, theology tells us little about women: it tells us that God created man—male and female; that men and women are equal before God; that woman was created to be man's helpmate in procreation; and that in marriage, the wife is subject to the husband. But whether woman is as illogical as she is supposed to be and man as untidy as his wife says he is; whether girls are better pupils in school than their brothers, and men better drivers than women; whether women are unsuited for jobs requiring a knowledge of mathematics and men unsuited for jobs involving aesthetic appreciation, are all questions that theology does not answer. There is, for instance, a beautiful collect giving thanks to God that He has given the grace of martyrdom even to the weaker sex; presumably the author of this prayer meant by the weaker sex woman, but he failed (possibly through tact) to specify in what respect this sex is weaker. All these questions are quite obviously outside the realm of theology. They belong in the realm of common sense and a person's own informal observations, if they are to be treated on an amateur level, and in the realm of experimental science, if they are to be given professional and scholarly attention.

The sciences that deal with man are fascinating, and it is remarkable that they are still comparatively new. Biology is an old study, but experimental psychology, sociology, and anthropology are relative youngsters. Possibly they got a late start because men were always rather smug in thinking that man was one subject they knew all about. The realization that you can miss the obvious and that knowledge of human beings does not always yield itself to common sense but needs careful, systematic observation and research was late in coming. We cannot pretend that the sciences which deal with man—the behavioral sciences—are far advanced; they are only at their beginning. They have added greatly to our knowledge of man, but they have not answered every question which puzzles us about him.

The scientists who have investigated sex differences, for instance, have been exceedingly tentative in their conclusions. What is surprising is that with the immense amount of research which has been done on the personality differences of men and women very few differences have been discovered. Men and women, at least in American culture, seem more alike than different.

Are men and women then the same? Obviously not! That is, if we speak about their physical make-up. Quite evidently they do not look alike. Men are on the whole taller than women; at least, if we are referring to men and women of the same racial group. American women are taller than Vietnamese men, but we do not need formal science to tell us that the average American woman is shorter than the average American man. The human male averages five percent heavier than the female at birth and twenty percent heavier by age twenty; while the boy child is only about two percent taller than the girl, by the time they are both twenty, he is approximately ten percent taller. The male at all ages shows greater muscular strength, and, even taking his greater body weight into consideration, he consumes more fuel and produces more energy than does the female.[1]

Physiologically girls are ahead, however, in their developmental acceleration. They not only reach physical maturity earlier, but throughout childhood they are also further advanced toward their adult status. In fact, this developmental acceleration begins even before birth, so that at the time of birth the average girl is more mature than the average boy. (This may seem a rather insignificant fact, but the greater physical developmental acceleration of females has important ramifications on their personality and their relationship with males. Some investigators have suggested that girls may be accelerated in intellectual as well as in physical development. This, however, has not been directly demonstrated.)[2]

Females, it would seem, not only grow up faster, but spend more time as grown-ups than males do. For, weak as woman may perhaps be in other ways, she is tough, and at all ages she demonstrates greater hardihood in clinging to life. Even during the prenatal period, males have a more difficult time surviving: while it is estimated that twenty to fifty percent more boys than girls are conceived, only five to six percent more boys than girls are born. The greater longevity of a woman makes her the insurance company's delight, at the same time that she is the hostess' problem; unfortunately there is always an "extra" woman. Since there is a proportional scarcity of males, women have more competition for a husband and at the same time less choice. The difference in "viability" of males and females, then, has important ramifications on the social situation, and one can safely surmise that it makes for different personality development in the sexes.

Women seem able to stay alive longer, but men seem steadier while they are maintaining life. Thus, men show less fluctuation in body temperature, basal metabolism, level of blood sugar, and females are more subject to flushing, fainting, and various glandular disturbances. How these physiological differences in stability may affect personality differences will be discussed later.

A principal and exceedingly evident difference between males and females is the fact that physically women are made for motherhood as men are made for fatherhood. Besides the difference in sex organs, males and females secrete different amounts of the respective sex hormones. All males secrete some of the female sex hormone (estrogen) as well as some of the male sex hormone (androgen), and females likewise secrete both sex hormones. The relative proportion of the two hormones secreted by the individual determines the degree to which he develops masculine or feminine characteristics.

Males and females differ, too, in the chromosomes each of their body cells contains. In the female, each body cell contains twenty-two pairs of chromosomes plus an XX pair; in the male, each body cell contains the same twenty-two pairs plus an XY pair. In this respect, therefore, the two sexes differ *in every cell of the body.** "This does not mean, of course, that every body cell must necessarily develop differently in men and women, since not all genes may be active in the development of every cell. But these sex differences in gene constitution, repeated in every body cell, may provide a mechanism which accounts for many of the physical differences between the sexes."[4]

The physical diversities between the sexes are so great that they perhaps seem to answer the two questions: "How different are men and women?" "Very different!" "Why are they different?" "Because God saw to it that biology would make them so!"

But the answer is not at all that simple. Obviously biology accounts for a good deal. But not all differences are biological, and not all sex differences can be explained by biology. Women, for example, cry more than men; women often dissolve into tears at the slightest provocation, while the weeping man is extremely rare, and this has been explained by the unsteadiness of the female physiological mechanism. Weeping among men, however, was quite common in the Middle Ages. And if biology explains every-

* Dr. Carrel pointed up the important biological differences between the sexes in the following words: "The differences between man and woman do not come from the particular form of the sexual organs, the presence of the uterus, from gestation or education. They are of a more fundamental nature. They are caused by the very structure of the tissues and by the impregnation of the entire organism with specific chemical substances secreted by the ovary. . . . In reality, woman differs profoundly from man. Every one of the cells of her body bears the mark of her sex. The same is true of her organs, and above all of her nervous system."[3]

thing, how do we account for all those variations in the roles and attitudes of the sexes in certain tribes studied by anthropologists? It is "the convention of one Philippine tribe that no man can keep a secret, the Manu assumption that only men enjoy playing with babies, the Toda proscription of almost all domestic work as too sacred for women," and "the Arapesh insistence that women's heads are stronger than men's."[5]

That there are personality differences between the sexes is evident, but these differences are not always consistent, and they do not seem always to conform to the biological expectation. A factor other than the biological comes into the picture here. What is it?

THE PSYCHOANALYST'S VIEW

Freud, the founder of psychiatry, was apparently satisfied with a biological explanation of sex differences. Woman, he held, is man's biological inferior, and it is her realization of this biological inferiority that explains her feminine personality. Freud saw what he termed "penis-envy" as a seemingly inevitable psychological experience of the little girl. The recognition of her organic incompleteness, he felt, had necessary repercussions on her future psychological life. According to his theory the wish with which a girl turns to her father is ultimately the wish for the penis. If a girl's sexual development is normal, penis-envy develops into a wish for a child as compensation for her bodily defect, and a woman's happiness during pregnancy is attributable to symbolic gratification in the possession of a penis. Particularly is the wish for a male child based on the female's desire to compensate for her own organic inferiority.[6]

In classic Freudianism it has been assumed that any character trait of a woman had its essential root in penis-envy. Thus, passivism, masochism, eroticism, and narcissism found in the female were considered traceable to psychological sex differences which themselves had anatomical and physiological causes. However, no competent psychoanalytic worker any longer believes that it is the mere sight of the male organ that causes penis-envy in a girl; rather they use the term to refer to the little girl's envy of the boy, whatever its cause, or the adult female's jealousy of the male.*

Even psychiatrists who acknowledge themselves to be deeply indebted to Freud have severely criticized his theory. Thus, Karen Horney pointed out the fact that the phenomenon of penis-envy is found only in neurotic women, in contradistinction to Freud who saw it as basic to the psychological development of *all* women. She wrote: "It would require tremendous evidence to make it plausible that woman, physically built for specifically female functions, should be psychically determined by a wish for attributes of the other sex."[7] Dr. Horney claimed further that the apparent mass of case-history material on penis-envy recorded by the psychoanalysts resulted, in the first place, from their own theoretical bias, since they were inclined to ascribe ambition and dictatorial behavior in females to penis-envy without bothering to seek other, possibly more realistic explanations as they would if they were dealing with male patients; and, in the second place, it resulted from a tendency on the part of neurotic women themselves who find an explanation of their difficulties posited on penis-envy easier to take. "It is much easier for a patient to think that nature has given her an unfair deal than to realize she actually makes excessive demands on the environment."[8] Woman, she continued, has the tendency which is present in every person of a minority group to use that status as a cover for inferiority feelings whatever their source.

Karen Horney noted that the phenomenon of the "tomboy," of the girl who wants to be a boy, is less frequent since girls have been brought up with greater freedom. (Freud, it should be noted, was doing his research and writing at a time when women were subjected to the excessive restrictions of the Victorian era.) Where masochistic trends are found today in neurotic women, Horney believed that one had to look not for biological reasons

* It is interesting to compare Freud's view of the female with that of Aristotle and St. Thomas: that she is a misbegotten male. They all seem to agree that woman is biologically inferior.

but for cultural ones. The traditionally greater dependence of women, the ideology that her life is given content only through others, and the fact that woman lived for centuries under conditions which restricted her to a private emotional sphere tended to make her overvalue love and thus to dread losing it. Although these cultural realities do not in themselves bring about masochistic attitudes, they account for the fact that in neurotic women aberrations develop in a masochistic direction. Dr. Horney remarked that as long as homemaking was a really big task for a woman and the number of her children was unrestricted, she had the feeling of being a constructive factor in the economic process and thus escaped a feeling of inferiority in comparison with the male; today if the emotional basis of a woman's self-confidence is exclusively dependent on giving or receiving love the foundation is too small and too shaky.

Another psychiatrist, Clara Thompson, pointed out that recognition of biological sex differences and of the fact that a woman has to encounter certain hazards (menstruation, pregnancy, menopause) that a man does not, does not seem to be the same thing as saying a woman is biologically inferior or suffering from an anatomical lack, as Freud implied.[9] Like Dr. Horney, Dr. Thompson noted that the attitude of women in the competitive pattern of our culture is not qualitatively different from that found in any minority group. Envy, she wrote, is characteristic of any competitive culture, and in our culture today there are two situations which tend to stimulate envy in woman. The first is competition with the male; the second is the tendency to place an inferior evaluation on woman's specific biological role in bearing children.[10] Although today it would seem that there is less actual reason to envy the male, sexual freedom for women has not necessarily brought emotional freedom. Women in our culture still labor under social handicaps, the more so perhaps since certain social changes, adding an element of ambiguity to their position, have only increased their conflicts.[11]

Dr. Zilboorg has added a rather sensible remark to this discussion of penis-envy. Commenting that it is curious that Freud should theorize that man attains his sexual destiny directly, but woman only indirectly, Zilboorg asked, why cannot there be a maternal instinct? Why must the female's desire for a child be satisfaction of penis-envy?* However, Zilboorg cautioned against a too hard-pressed attempt to account for hostility between the sexes on the basis of recent cultural development and asserted that hostility between men and women is a very ancient phenomenon.[12]

One further example of a psychoanalytic theory of sex difference which shows significant departure from the classic Freudian theory is that of Dr. Suttie, who criticized Freud for his antifeminism and suggested that masculine jealousy of women may be more basic than penis-envy. The fundamental jealousy, Suttie insisted, may be that of the man for the woman's reproductive and lactational powers. The lack of these satisfactions in man's own life may account for his more intense creative and cultural interest, possibly for his more aggressive temperament, and conceivably even for the gradual political and economic predominance of the male sex. (Suttie gives as an example of male jealousy of women the case of the Aranda tribe of Australian aborigines who say men can bear children!)[13] Whether Dr. Suttie is right or not about male envy of the female, the idea that greater cultural achievement on the part of men is their compensation for not being able to bear children has been independently advanced by other experts.

The various psychoanalytic explorations of female envy (which —if one is to judge from the *Fortune* survey—is quite common in America) have been considered for whatever light they might shed upon the basic differences between the sexes. While Freud accounted for sex differences purely on the basis of biology, his

* In the same article, Zilboorg remarked that involving women more actively in spheres of life other than the fulfillment of their maternal role does not necessarily mean a diminishing of motherhood. France, where the role of women is most traditional, has a low birthrate; Soviet Russia, where women participate in most phases of social, political, economic, and professional life, has a high birthrate.

successors have tended to discard his explanation as being over-simplified, and have turned to the consideration of the influence of culture to explain the apparent difference in the personalities of men and women.

THE ANTHROPOLOGIST'S VIEW

Under the influence of cultural anthropologists, the emphasis, for a time, was on the relativity of sex roles in different cultures. Particularly relevant are the field work and the theories of Margaret Mead, whose study of three primitive societies on the island of New Guinea attracted much attention during the 1930's. To test the theory that the temperaments of males and females are the same everywhere, Margaret Mead studied differentiation in the personalities of the sexes and in the social roles of men and women among the tribes of the Arapesh, Mundugumor and Tchambuli. Among the Arapesh, she found both sexes gentle, responsive, unaggressive and "maternal," both men and women participating in child care; among the Mundugumor, both men and women are aggressive, harsh and violent; among the Tchambuli, sharply divergent roles are prescribed for the sexes and are accompanied by marked temperamental differences, but the roles reverse Western notions about what is naturally male and female; economic life is supervised by the women and the men devote themselves to art and ceremony. While the women are noted for their bantering camaraderie, the men are anxious, distrustful of each other, and given to "catty" remarks.[14]

Margaret Mead's research seemed to prove once and for all that biology is not determining and that it is culture which accounts for the different personalities of men and women. One popular book reviewer, taking this conclusion with a grain of salt, pointed out that Margaret Mead had not yet discovered a society where the men bear the babies! Biology is here to stay. Other critics of Margaret Mead noted that the societies she studied in which there is a reversal of sex roles or a complete lack of differentiation are rare exceptions to the rule and are most artificially conditioned.[15]

It would seem that Margaret Mead did too urgently fit her facts to her theory. At times her thesis seemed to be rather emotional and rather unscientific, to say the least. This was certainly true of her contention that personality and social role could be classified as well by eye-color as by sex. One wondered if she was simply being facetious or if she really believed that sex and eye-color have the same degree of biological unimportance and psychological irrelevance.[16]

This tendency on the part of cultural anthropologists to ignore biological differences caused Johnson and Terman to write: "The physiologist has long known that woman is something other than a wombed man; the social psychologist is beginning to suspect it; and one dares to look forward to a change in the present-day bias of the cultural anthropologist."[17]*

THE PSYCHOLOGIST'S VIEW

Numerous psychoanalysts and anthropologists have offered their answers to the two questions: how different are men and women, and what makes them different. Extensive material on sex differences has also been presented by experimental psychologists. On the whole they have not been able to check the theories of clinical psychologists, since the latter usually describe a cluster of the personality traits which they find in the individual, and this cluster cannot be separated easily to be checked by the research of experimental psychologists.

Experimental psychology offers considerable material on sex differences in personality, but it must be evaluated with a basic reservation in mind. When psychologists have compared large

* In all justice to Margaret Mead, it should be noted that she has exercised the woman's proverbial privilege and, in a book written approximately fourteen years after her study of the three tribes, she has conceded the importance of sex in differentiating personalities and social roles. "We know of no culture that has said, articulately, that there is no difference between men and women except in the way they contribute to the creation of the next generation; that otherwise in all respects they are simply human beings with varying gifts, no one of which can be exclusively assigned to either sex."[18]

groups of males and females and discovered a significant sex difference in some personality trait, aptitude or interest, they have almost always noted a large overlap. Overlapping means that within each of the two groups compared there are wide individual differences. Since in any psychological trait women differ widely from one another, and men similarly differ widely among themselves, any relationship found between group averages will not necessarily hold true for individual cases. Even where divergences between the sexes are great some overlapping exists. Take, for example, the scores obtained by boys and girls on the College Entrance physics examination. Physics is known as a "masculine" subject, and, as one would expect, boys on the whole do better than girls on the physics examination; that is, the average boy does better than the average girl. But even here there is considerable overlapping: fifty-four percent of the boys fall below the scores made by the top third of the girls.[19] In any discussion of the sex differences of tested groups, this fact of overlapping warns us against falling into the common error of excessive generalization. In fact, it is true that in any test of personality traits or aptitudes there is a greater difference among the individual women tested than there is between the average man and the average woman. *Women differ more widely among themselves than they differ as a group compared with men.*

Here are some of the aptitudes in which a marked sex difference has been consistently demonstrated. Boys surpass girls not only in muscular strength, but also in speed and co-ordination of gross bodily movements. That baseball is a masculine sport seems no mere matter of chance, since even among preschool children boys can throw a ball more accurately and for a greater distance than girls. But while males excel in gross bodily movements, females, from early childhood, excel in manual dexterity. The little girl dresses herself more efficiently and at an earlier age than the boy, and the woman is often the preferred worker in a factory because she performs certain manipulatory tasks more quickly and accurately than the man.

Women have always been known as the loquacious sex and probably with good cause since female superiority in verbal or linguistic functions exists from infancy. On the average, girls begin to talk earlier than boys and during the preschool years have a larger vocabulary than boys. They likewise begin to use senences earlier and use a more mature language structure. When they get to school and learn to read, girls continue to advance more rapidly than boys. While the verbal superiority of the female, like her superiority in tasks involving manual dexterity, is probably explained by a biological cause (the acceleration in physical development) the girl may learn to talk earlier and better because of her greater contact with her mother, who serves as the principal source of early language training.

As would be expected, boys excel in mechanical aptitudes. But the possibility that this difference has a predominantly cultural cause is suggested by the fact that male superiority is more pronounced on tests of mechanical information than in the more abstract tests of spatial relationships which are equally unfamiliar to both sexes. In the extensive research conducted by Gesell, no significant sex differences were found during the first five years in tests involving block building.[20] By school age, however, the mechanical aptitude tests reveal males as superior, and this superiority is continued throughout adult life. The stereotype of the woman who cannot tell the plyers from the screwdriver probably arose, however, not from any innate mechanical inaptitude in females but from the fact that from babyhood on the girl is not expected to take an interest in mechanics. And since knowledge is cumulative and the woman has not been given the foundations in elementary mechanical principles, the glazed look that comes over her eyes when a problem in advanced mechanics is under discussion is not to be wondered at.*

Jack coming home with a report card showing a high mark in

* The swapping of the traditional roles in the upkeep of the home may perhaps cause a reversal of the stereotype of the unmechanical female. Women in the suburbs today who paint their homes may be found in a few more years fixing the plumbing and installing the electric wiring as well.

arithmetic while Jill exhibits a report card with a high mark in spelling illustrates what the experimental psychologists have found: boys have a greater aptitude for numerical reasoning. One psychologist working with college students found males superior in solving problems that call for "restructuring," that is, discarding the first approach and rearranging the facts a new way in view of eventual solution.[21] Boys have also been shown to be superior in their ability to transfer the knowledge and skill they have acquired to meet the demands of new situations.[22] How much this is the result of an innate sex difference and how much the result of the cultural situation (since males are encouraged to be more independent right from the start and to strike out and think for themselves, while girls are expected to be more docile and receptive to the traditional answers) is hard to judge.

The fact that women excel in musical and artistic appreciation seems to have a clearer cultural base. Girls are given piano lessons more frequently than boys. Although women tend to excel in tests of musical appreciation in general, when, in one test, only subjects who had received no musical training were compared, the sex difference disappeared.[23]

What about sex differences in personality? Do men and women have the same interests and like the same things? Little boys seem to like different games from little girls; while girls prefer more sedentary play, boys engage more often in lively, rough-and-tumble play and in competitive games. Evidently there is a physical basis for their choice of activities, but undoubtedly there is also a cultural basis: they play with the toys that are given them —boys with soldiers, trucks and tanks, girls with dolls and doll-houses. An experimental study in which young children were asked to pick the toys they wanted showed that three-year-old boys and girls did not choose what our culture considers "appropriate" toys for the respective sexes.[24] It seems fairly obvious that boys and girls are educated to like the toys they are supposed to like, just as they are educated to like what is considered the appropriate activity in the particular society in which they are living.*

The difference in activity and interests of the respective sexes continues into adult life. Men talk about money, business affairs, and sports, while women tend to talk about clothes and other women.[25] Women seem to talk about other people to a significantly greater degree than do men. This may be accounted for by what is considered the female's more "social nature." The greater sociability of females, which appears at the nursery school level and continues through old age, is noted by Johnson and Terman: "Sociability (in persons seventy to ninety years of age) still correlates pronouncedly with happiness in females and insignificantly so in males."[26] What explanation can be given for the greater social orientation of women? Although there is no scientific proof of the contention, sometimes found in writings for popular consumption, that female sociability is the outcome of a biological "maternal instinct," there is some evidence available for a physiological explanation. The superior verbal ability of little girls, already noted, certainly gives them a head start in communicating with other children and with adults; it makes it possible for them to be socially oriented before males of the same age. However, there is probably here an interplay of cultural and social influences which arose from—but now operate with—biological facts. The stereotype of the girl, sociable, chatty, pleasing guests with her cute remarks, operates from her earliest childhood and influences her to assume that role which, even if biology has not ordained it, society expects from her.

This greater social orientation of woman is in line with the observations of Doctors Horney and Thompson that she appears to care more about loving and being loved than does man, and that

* Parents sometimes seem unaware of the influence they themselves have in the development of the likes and interests of their children, and often resort to an explanation that boys and girls "come completely different." Thus, one father, after having experience with a son, commented about the difference in the personality of his baby daughter. Said the wife: "But, darling, Johnny was hardly home from the hospital when you were roughing him up and calling him Butch. Anne you've treated like a lady right from the start."

she seems to have her own self-confidence grounded in her ability successfully to maintain a love relationship. If "love is a woman's entire existence" perhaps her role in our culture—and even economic necessity—has made it so. This would go far to explain the fact, noted by Johnson and Terman in the study referred to previously, that while women have a more marked social orientation than men they are more anxious than men about their human relationships and more hesitant in their free expression of their social impulses. Johnson and Terman feel that this can be explained more adequately on the basis of a physiological sex difference, rather than by the alternative explanation that women are more anxious about human relationships than men because in our culture they are more dependent upon them and have more to lose if they do not work out as desired. It seems that in any culture woman, biological facts being what they are, has more to lose in a love relationship than a man; sex for a man can be a passing moment, but for a woman the possible resulting pregnancy represents a radical change in her life.

The Kinsey studies* have documented the differences in attitudes and orientation of men and women toward sex. The major and best-established finding of the Kinsey research is that males are sexually aroused by a wider variety of symbolic stimuli than females. A later study made by Ehrmann agrees with the Kinsey data that lack of sexual responsiveness on the part of the female is one of the most significant deterrents to premarital intercourse. However, the Ehrmann study reveals that while the lack of female responsiveness is the primary reason for sexual restraint with a *non-lover* it is not the reason for restraint with a lover or future husband.[27] In other words, it restates a primary difference between

* The Kinsey studies, besides being criticized from an ethical point of view, have been subjected to the criticism of scientists who pointed out that they depended for their data on the subject's memory and honesty in reporting (a hazardous business!) and that they did not get a fair sampling of American males or females, since only persons who volunteered to give information were included in the study and thus persons whose religious, moral or aesthetic sensibilities would be offended by an interview in this delicate area were excluded from the report.

man and woman long ago recorded in folk wisdom: a woman has to be already in love to be sexually responsive: she cannot divorce love and sex as readily as can a man.

"COY, UNCERTAIN AND HARD TO PLEASE"

Are women more emotionally unstable than men? Johnson and Terman[28] answer yes, and present evidence to show that it has been repeatedly demonstrated that women have less emotional balance. They go on to note that greater psychoneurotic behavior in the female appears not to have decreased in our time when girls are treated more than ever like boys and remark that in tests made of the blind in institutions where there is even less differentiation in treatment of boys and girls, psychoneurotic behavior is still greater in girls than in boys. However, even in our day, and even in institutionalized populations, cultural sex differentiations do persist, and sex stereotypes remain. Still, the physiological basis for the more marked emotional instability of the female cannot be dismissed lightly. The greater bodily fluctuation of the female, and feminine physiological changes, such as the onset of menstruation and the menopause, would seem to incline women to greater "nervous" behavior.*

Another study, this one of high school boys and girls and of college girls,[30] would seem to substantiate the positing of greater neuroticism on the part of the female. Girls of both ages were found to be characteristically more depressed, hysterical, and neurotic than the boys. The girls were noted to be more agreeable, the boys more belligerent and dominating. Although these findings would

* While women may be more "nervous" in their day-to-day behavior, they survive crises with fewer mental breakdowns than do males. Moreover the nervous behavior of women is sometimes greatly exaggerated. Especially is this so in the old wives' tales concerning the so-called "change of life." Not only does the average woman go through the menopause without going to pieces, but Harry E. August, M.D., argues that 85% of women handle it well. He writes that what psychological manifestations during menopause do occur "are reactions to it and not components of it." Such abnormal reactions "usually have existed to some degree before the onset of menopause; in fact they are typical expressions of lifelong patterns of reaction."[29]

not preclude an explanation based at least in part on the different sex hormones, they would lend themselves to the alternative explanation that here cultural factors are important: boys are permitted by the culture to act out their emotional conflicts on others; girls are encouraged to inhibit their emotions and turn their aggression against themselves. In this connection the greater number of boys referred to child guidance clinics as behavior problems, the greater proportion of juvenile delinquents who are males, and the fact that men sent to federal and state prisons outnumber women by twenty-five to one, should be kept in mind.*[31]

Tests of men and women to determine how their attitudes conform to the characteristic responses of each sex in our culture have shed light on sex differences in personality. The most famous of them, the "masculinity-femininity" test developed by Terman and Miles, has been successful in selecting those behavior characteristics which indicate the most clear-cut distinctions between the sexes. Terman and Miles summarize these differences thus:

"From whatever angle we have examined them the males included in the standardization groups evinced a distinctive interest in exploit and adventure, in outdoor and physically strenuous occupations, in machinery and tools, in science, physical phenomena, and inventions; and, from rather occasional evidence, in business and commerce. On the other hand, the females of our groups have evinced a distinctive interest in domestic affairs and in aesthetic objects and occupations; they have distinctly preferred more sedentary and indoor occupations, and occupations more directly administrative, particularly to the young, the helpless, the distressed. Supporting and supplementing these are the more subjective differences—those in emotional disposition and direction. The males directly or indirectly manifest the greater self-assertion and

* These facts do not prove, however, that men are naturally more dishonest, given to crime and law-breaking, and less "moral" than women. Although women are less prone to violent crimes, a recent book on "white-collar" criminality points out that in this area men and women participate equally when the opportunity to sin is equal. (See *The Thief in the White Collar,* by Norman Jaspan with Hillel Black, Philadelphia: J.B. Lippincott, 1960).

aggressiveness; they express more hardihood and fearlessness, and more roughness of manners, language, and sentiments. The females express themselves as more compassionate and sympathetic, more timid, more fastidious, and aesthetically sensitive, more emotional in general (or at least more expressive of the four emotions considered), severer moralists, yet admit in themselves weaknesses in emotional control and (less noticeably) in physique."[32]

Within the groups of men and women tested there is a wide range of scores. An individual's "masculinity-feminity" index shows definite association with his or her education and occupation as well as with the familial surrounding in which the man or woman was raised. Thus, engineers and architects have a higher masculine score than artists or clergymen, and in the female group college teachers have a lower feminine score than do housewives or stenographers. The fact that cultural influences rather than biological causes appear largely to determine the M-F score of an individual is reinforced by the discovery that there seems to be no significant relationship between a male's physique (and his degree of visible "maleness") and the masculinity score he achieves.

That differences in sex role develop under the influence of culture and that personality differentiation takes place in the atmosphere of what society expects from a person according to his sex, was indicated vividly when the Terman-Miles M-F test failed to reveal significantly different responses among men and women in the Netherlands.[33] Needless to say, this does not mean that there are no significant differences between the sexes in Holland; rather it means that sex differences which are clearly marked in this country are not noticeable among the Dutch.*

* The cultural patterns determining sex differences in personality are too frequently overlooked. Those who would transfer apostolic groups from one country to another must beware lest unwittingly they try to make American girls behave like Dutch or Belgian Christian women rather than like *American* Christian women. Similarly the missionary going from the United States to Latin America has to beware lest he carry with him an ideal of masculine or feminine behavior which is quite irrelevant to Latin American culture and has no necessary connection with Christianity—or biology.

WHERE ARE THE FEMALE GENIUSES?

This review of the psychological differences between the sexes should include the question of achievement. Are there—or have there been—as many eminent women as eminent men? Practically everyone would agree that there have not been, although several valiant efforts have been made to prove that female geniuses abound and reach fame as frequently as men. One of these efforts, recorded in a book written by a man in 1917, compared four hundred women whom the author considered had made an exceptional contribution to society with four hundred similar men, whose names, however, he did not give.[34] This study seems particularly amusing today since except for a few women like Joan of Arc, Queen Victoria, Jane Austen, Teresa of Avila, and perhaps a dozen more, the remainder of the famous four hundred are now quite unknown.

And yet there is no clear-cut evidence that women are less intelligent or gifted than men. In fact, what studies have been made of intelligence show the sexes to be fairly equal. Although it was once thought that the female had less of a range in intelligence than the male—and that among the males there were at the same time more geniuses and more idiots—today this theory has been quite definitely discarded.[35] Why then have women not achieved the fame of men?

It is interesting to note that the male's achievement comes relatively late. The girl is the much more successful student in elementary school and through the high-school grades. She gets better marks on the average even in those school subjects, like mathematics, in which the boy does better on aptitude tests. But when the girl graduates and gets out in the world her superior achievement does not continue. The follow-up studies of gifted children[36] have revealed that the adult occupations of the women were on the whole quite undistinguished. Although initial IQ showed a fairly close relationship to occupational level among men, it showed no such relationship among women. Two-thirds of the women with IQ's of 170 or above were housewives or office workers.

Why haven't women achieved eminence? Anastasi contends[37] that the recorded differences in achievement could be fully accounted for in terms of environmental conditions. Until recently a great many occupations have been closed to women. In the past, at least, educational opportunities were quite dissimilar. The sex roles and stereotypes which operated from earliest childhood made the man strive for achievements which the woman was not even supposed to consider. Society did not feel she could square her traditional domestic duties as wife and mother with occupations and interests outside the home. It is not surprising, then, that the one pursuit in which women have achieved fame, literature (notably novel-writing), was one that could be carried on without detriment to the traditional feminine role.

The fact that there are only thirty-two women listed in Cattell's compilation of the thousand most eminent persons in the world[38] is certainly not going to make women feel inferior! Only a woman suffering from the "penis-envy" encountered by psychoanalysts would feel that her stature and sense of adequacy depend on proving that her sex has achieved as much in an external fashion as has the male. The happy, satisfied woman knows full well that even geniuses of the male variety needed women to give them birth. The woman today, who takes advantage of the opportunities given her by society to develop her personal gifts and use them as best she can, does so, if she is content with being a woman, not to prove she is as good as a man, nor to compete with him, but because she enjoys being herself and she sees the gifts she is developing and the work she is producing as part of herself.

Most women find Simone de Beauvoir's tirades against biological facts[39] (in *The Second Sex*) rather ludicrous. De Beauvoir contends that women today are treated like Negroes—*separate but equal*—and argues feverishly that society must do away with the separation which to her is the sign of the woman's inferiority. And yet she cannot do away with biology; thus she is left in the position of having to make a retreat when she argues that women should not be held down by the chains of marriage and motherhood and should be permitted to enjoy her sexual urges exactly like a man. For, having considered the idea that there should be houses of prostitution (in reverse) to which a woman could go for sexual relief and that a woman should feel free to take home a man, it is as if she suddenly sees that this is all too risky for a woman, and she is once more—even though she hates it—back with biology.

But while biological facts in the formation of the personality of the two sexes cannot be dismissed, neither can one forget the reality of culture. The combination of biological and cultural factors is complex; specific differences in personality between the sexes, although they may be rooted in physical sex differences, are largely the result of cultural conditioning. Biology imposes certain limitations on the development of the feminine personality and social roles, but these limitations still permit the wide range of feminine personalities which are apparent in different cultures. Women in various societies may act in different ways and still be true to their nature.

Any theory of sex differences in personality which ignores the reality of culture and seeks to explain differentiation simply on the grounds of biological facts is inadequate. Also inadequate would be any theory that would try to explain the different personalities of men and women completely on cultural lines and neglect to take into consideration the physiological realities which either directly, or indirectly through their social effects, have influenced behavior and the roles men and women have adopted in society.

NOTES

1. Amram Scheinfeld, *Women and Men* (New York: Harcourt, Brace, 1943). This book gives in a palatable way an account of the sex differences as revealed by the behavioral sciences as well as by studies of anatomy and physiology.
2. Anne Anastasi, *Differential Psychology* (New York: Macmillan, 1958). To Chapter 14, "Sex Differences," which summarizes the psychological research that has been conducted on sex differences, we refer those readers who are interested in further knowledge of

this subject. My presentation of the psychological material follows Anastasi's chapter, to which I am heavily indebted.

3. Alexis Carrel, *Man, the Unknown* (New York: Harper and Brothers, 1935), pp. 89f.
4. Anastasi, *op. cit.*, p. 462.
5. Margaret Mead, *Sex and Temperament in Three Primitive Societies* (New York: Morrow, 1935), p. xix.
6. Sigmund Freud, *New Introductory Lectures on Psychoanalysis* (New York: Norton, 1933).
7. Karen Horney, *New Ways in Psychoanalysis* (New York: Norton, 1939), p. 104.
8. *Ibid.*, p. 109.
9. Clara Thompson, "Cultural Pressures in the Psychology of Women," *Psychiatry*, 1942, Vol. 5, pp. 331-339.
10. Clara Thompson, "'Penis Envy' in Women," *Psychiatry*, 1943, Vol. 6, pp. 123-125.
11. Clara Thompson, "The Role of Women in this Culture," *Psychiatry*, 1941, Vol. 4, pp. 1-8.
12. Gregory Zilboorg, "Masculine and Feminine," *Psychiatry*, 1944, Vol. 7, pp. 257-296.
13. Ian D. Suttie, *Origins of Love and Hate* (London: Kegan Paul, Trench, Trubner, 1935), p. 108.
14. Mead, *op. cit.*
15. Willard Waller, *The Family* (New York: Dryden, 1938), p. 45. See also Viola Klein, *The Feminine Character* (London: Internat. Univers. Press, 1946).
16. Mead, *op. cit.*, p. 319.
17. Winifred B. Johnson and L. M. Terman, "Some Highlights in the Literature of Psychological Sex Differences Published Since 1920," *Journal of Psychology*, 1944, Vol. 9, p. 331.
18. Margaret Mead, *Male and Female*, (New York: Morrow, 1949), p. 8.
19. Mirra Komarovsky, *Women in the Modern World: Their Education and Their Dilemmas* (Boston: Little Brown, 1953), p. 22.
20. Arnold Gesell et al., *The First Five Years of Life* (New York: Harper, 1940).
21. E. J. Sweeney, "Sex Differences in Problem Solving," *Stanford Univer., Dept. Psychol., Tech. Rep.*, No. 1, Dec. 1, 1953.
22. M. M. Kostick, "A Study of Transfer: Sex Differences in the Reasoning Process," *Journal of Educational Psychology*, 1954, Vol. 45, pp. 449-458.

23. G. M. Gilbert, "Sex Differences in Musical Aptitude and Training," *Journal of Genetic Psychology,* 1942, Vol. 26, pp. 19-33.
24. Myer Rabban, "Sex Role Identification in Young Children in Two Diverse Social Groups," *Genetic Psychology Monographs,* 1950, Vol. 42.
25. Anastasi, *op. cit.,* p. 479, reports on the investigations which systematically analyzed the conversation by men and women overheard in different locales in New York City, in a midwestern town, and in London.
26. Johnson and Terman, *op. cit.*
27. As reported by Winston W. Ehrmann at the convention of the American Sociological Society, September 4, 1959.
28. Johnson and Terman, *op. cit.*
29. Richard Trumbull, "A Study of Relationships between Factors of Personality and Intelligence," *Journal of Social Psychology,* 1953, Vol. 38, pp. 161-178.
30. *Potentialities of Women in the Middle Years* (Michigan State University, 1956), p. 93.
31. Anastasi, *op. cit.,* p. 488.
32. L. M. Terman and Catherine C. Miles, *Sex and Personality: Studies in Masculinity and Feminity* (New York: McGraw-Hill, 1936), pp. 447-448.
33. Anastasi, *op. cit.,* p. 492.
34. W. A. Newman Dorland, *The Sum of Feminine Achievement* (Boston: Stratford, 1917).
35. Anastasi, *op. cit.,* pp. 456-457.
36. L. M. Terman and Melita H. Oden, *The Gifted Child Grows Up* (Stanford, California: Stanford University Press, 1947).
37. Anastasi, *op. cit.,* p. 495.
38. J. McK. Cattell, "A Statistical Study of Eminent Men," *Popular Science Monograph,* 1903, 62, pp. 359-377.
39. Simone de Beauvoir, *The Second Sex* (New York: Knopf, 1953).

4

Background of the American Woman

In what year did Miss America become an intellectual? Or perhaps it did not happen suddenly in one year. Perhaps a gradual change brought about the contests of the last few years in which candidates for the title are expected to use a subdued form of cheesecake and at the same time demonstrate an ability to compete with the eggheads. And while television viewers watching the selection of Miss America of 1960 might have found the display of brains and talents less than spectacular, even the conservative *New York Times,* in the small space it allotted to her victory, reported dryly: "The new Miss America said that she was very serious about world affairs, that she was keenly interested in matters of state, that she read numerous magazines and newspapers . . ."

Perhaps Miss America is serious about world affairs, though one is cynical enough to suggest that the publicists who run the contest have not really been converted to the intellectual life. But they and the public they serve evidently feel that sex and beauty are no longer the only assets of an attractive young woman—or, if they are, they are not supposed to be. Whether or not intellectuality has really become a new American value under the impetus of scientific competition with the Russians, one is at least expected to pay outward respect to brains, however much one still adheres to the more traditional norm for Miss America contestants, namely, sex appeal.

From the ballyhoo of the contest to the problems of a working wife, everything involving modern American women reflects and can only be judged in the context of American society. The conflicts of American women and the discontent they may experience can only be understood viewed against the background of American life; at least a general impression of American society with its characteristic organization, strains, values, and goals is indispensable if we are to evaluate the complaints of women in the United States. Certain of these complaints arise from difficulties to which all women are heiresses, and certain other difficulties—while they cannot be divorced from the social background in which they occur—are chiefly the result of the personal weaknesses and particular family situations of the individual woman. These two categories are not our concern here. Rather, since we are concerned with the situation of American women, we must examine the problems peculiar to American life.

Analyzing American society is not an easy task. It is a society in which changes take place so rapidly that social scientists insist that by the time they are able to do adequate research into the contemporary American social situation, this situation has already become history and society presents a new series of problems. For, American society does not stand still while the sociologist analyzes it. Worse yet, the data he gathers becames dated while he is still in the field of research. Of course, this phenomenon of change is characteristic of all societies in the mid-twentieth-century world. Perhaps it is especially typical of societies like China or sections of Africa which for centuries adhered to age-old norms and values and remained in a comparatively static state. In such countries change today may be more radical and more marked than in the United States, but it seems true, nonetheless, that the United States is unique in making *change* itself a value. Change here, of course, can be identified with the typical American mobility. The American is expected to change his status; he is supposed to move. Upward mobility has for years been one of the stable values of American life, and the young American in medical school—whose father is a brick-layer and whose immigrant grandfather was a day-laborer—epitomizes by his ambition and his effort the characteristic drive that carries Americans "onward and upward."

With upward mobility goes an increasing degree of geographic mobility. It is estimated that about twenty to thirty percent of the American people move annually. In *The Organization Man,* Whyte's research on Park Forest gives a graphic picture of suburbanites who follow the trail of the Big Corporation, who are anxious to make friends in the community into which they move, but who know full well that their friendships cannot be lifelong since in a few years time they will be transferred by the corporation and on the move again to another community composed of semi-transients like themselves.[1]

BUSINESS SHAPES THE PATTERN

America, of course, has always been a nation on the move. The movement across the ocean from Europe was paralleled by a movement across the American continent itself as new frontiers were opened up. The frontier days are over, but movement keeps on. And it is movement dictated by economics.

The economic institution has been called the primary and characteristic institution of American society. Even today, when it is argued that the typical, successful American has changed, that he is no longer the "inner-directed" entrepreneur, motivated by the Protestant ethic of individualism, it is yet to be proven that it is not the economic institution and the values of business that dominate American life. Americans today, like "the man in the gray flannel suit" may be unwilling to sacrifice everything to their business success; they may consider it vulgar to be as obvious about devotion to money as was the old-time capitalist; they may be more polite and less pushy; but that is not because they are no longer concerned about their financial position. The desire for security may have partially replaced the drive to get ahead, but—if

William Whyte's interpretation of *The Man In the Gray Flannel Suit* is correct[2]—that is not because they have settled for less or because they are particularly enamoured of poverty, but because they want to have their cake and eat it. They want to be a success in business, but they do not want to pay the price that seemed necessary to the old-fashioned businessman. They want money and all it can buy, but they want time to enjoy it. Perhaps the consumer has replaced the producer as the typical American, but they are both devoted to money, and the consumer's life revolves around business as the primary institution of American life as surely as did the producer's.*

Riesman's modern "other-directed" man[4] may look to his social peers to see how he should plan his life; he may get his values from them rather than from within himself, but the values are still, to a large degree, integrated around the economic institution. The modern American may not want to get conspicuously ahead of the Joneses—he values the security of being part of his group too much to find the idea of being a solitary tycoon very attractive—but it is still true to say that he wants to keep up with the Joneses. Like the Joneses, he wants to continue moving upward, to enjoy an even higher standard of living, to exploit to the utmost all the consumer goods he can obtain; and he needs money to do all this. No longer the rough individualist, he cultivates the social graces; he is trained, if he is an employer, to be considerate of his workers and to use the latest human-relations techniques in industry, just as he uses the latest technological methods. America in 1960 would

* For most Americans life revolves around business so naturally that it does not occur to them that this is not the characteristic pattern of all societies. In ancient Jewish society, as well as in medieval society, it was the religious institution that was dominant, and in the Middle Ages it was not accidental but reflective of the values of society that the merchant had a low status. The fact that the desire for profit and the drive to compete for business success is not instinctive to man is further shown by an interesting study, *Cooperation and Competition Among Primitive Peoples,* in which several authors collaborate to analyze these two elements in various societies.[3] That there are primitive societies where everything is organized on a co-operative basis and where any desire to compete or to excel is systematically educated out of the youth may surprise Americans who look upon the competitive state as being the only "natural" human one.

seem to bear little resemblance to the America of 1900 if we regard the portraits of the businessmen of these two eras as reflective of their times. But nonetheless the businessman—not the priest, the educator, or the mother of a large family—retains the leading role in America. And even if the scientist has recently achieved great prestige in the United States, it is not because the contemplation of truth or the pursuit of knowledge for its own sake has become an important value for Americans, but because science is now viewed as being indispensable for the preservation of the "American way of life."*

This primary position that business takes in American life has important ramifications for the family and, as a consequence, for the position and the happiness of women. Obviously, if business is primary, the family has to be secondary. One may well ponder how far this fact influences the woman's evaluation of herself. The mother busy with household tasks replies if she is queried that she is "just a housewife." As someone recently remarked, "Great status is attached to being paid for work. Even though a housewife works hard, she cannot claim the prestige of a salary."[8] Being involved in business has a prestige that is no longer attached to the management of a household, and the woman at home is put on the defensive, even though she may be accomplishing work that demands much more skill and creativity than is required of the woman with a routine office or factory job, who nevertheless, feels herself sharing the prestige and glamor of the business world.

Business provides the model for American life, and the American family has had to adapt itself to the requirements of business. But there are certain standards arising from business which the family cannot copy. Business is concerned with production; it is geared to the goal of achievement—achievement not in terms of the intangibles (the quality of life, the emotional satisfactions, the

* The reader who wants to give more serious consideration to the economic institution as the core institution of American society is referred to the masterly analysis of Talcott Parsons,[5] a difficult but rewarding book. Any good text in sociology—such as the recent one of Joseph H. Fichter[6] or the more comprehensive text by Arnold M. Rose[7]—will help the interested reader to see the place of business in the American social structure.

ministering to the needs of man's spiritual nature) which are pre-eminently and traditionally the concern of the wife and mother, but in terms of products which can be classified and weighed and counted. As David Reisman writes: "Our definitions of work also mean that the housewife, though producing a social work-product, does not find her work explicitly defined and totaled, either as an hour product or a dollar product, in the national census or in people's minds. And since her work is not defined as work, she is exhausted at the end of the day without feeling any right to be, insult thus being added to injury. In contrast, the workers in the Detroit plant who finish their day's production goal in three hours and take the rest of the day off in factory loafing, are defined as eight-hour-per-day workers by themselves, by their wives, by the census."[9]

Various futile attempts have been made to measure, and thereby justify, the housewife's task in the manner of business. It has been calculated how many miles she walks a day doing her various tasks, how many hours she works a day or a week, and so on. But these calculations have failed to get at the heart of her task or to make it understandable and valuable to a society which uses as its norm the production of the business world. The woman's work in the family must necessarily be different: in contrast to the specialization which prevails in business, she fulfills a multiplicity of roles and performs a multiplicity of functions for her husband and children. The measure of her success is uncertain to herself and to others; neither the inner satisfaction of knowing that she achieved her goal—thirty letters typed, work quota filled—nor the exterior approval of society—the pay envelope—sanctions her efforts. She has not proved her capacity for the job over fifty other applicants: she is John's wife and Jimmy's mother because she married the one and bore the other. She takes care of them because she is emotionally involved with them, not because she is particularly fitted for the task in the spirit of the impersonal efficiency of business. Whatever comparison is made of the housewife's role with the typical business role reveals their difference. Evidently, in a society where quality of life was valued more than quantity of production, the woman in the family would not suffer from the comparison, but in a society where business provides the pattern of living the housewife is relegated to inferior status.

The fact that business is the core institution of American life has other effects. It not only makes the family of secondary importance, but it influences the form the family takes. It may be argued that the traditional form of the family was modified in the process of migration from Europe. The immigrant often left the security of a small village where he was probably related by rather distant kinship ties to many of the other residents. But usually, even if he did not bring most of his relatives with him and had to migrate simply with his immediate family, his wife and children, he brought with him the pattern of what is termed "the extended family." He had found his emotional security as well as his material well-being in being part of an extended family which encompassed not only wife and children, parents and grandparents, but uncles and aunts, nephews and cousins as well. After he came to our shores he kept up his feeling for the extended family, at least for a time. But under the pressure and the influence of American business, his descendents found the extended family to be a practical impossibility as a value and a reality to be preserved in their lives. The extended family was replaced by what is called "the nuclear family" which is increasingly the typical family institution in the United States. The nuclear family consists of a husband and his wife and children. That is all.

The extended family could not coexist with business as we know it. The man who is on the move upward cannot be hindered by kinship ties. The grandson of the immigrant, if he is to be successful in American society, cannot worry or feel responsible for his less able relatives. If in business the norm for getting ahead is competence and not family ties, family ties are not only no help, but they would be a positive hindrance.

In the United States upward mobility is individual. True, as he achieves status himself the man takes his wife and children with him. But keeping up with the Joneses would be an impossible task if he had to move upward and keep moving not only himself "but his sisters and his cousins—whom he reckons by the dozens—and his aunts!"

THE FAMILY LEFT TO ITSELF

The geographic mobility promoted under the aegis of business represents another loosening of extended kinship ties. The man transferred around the country has a difficult enough time moving his wife and children without having to worry about other relatives. Usually if he and his wife manage to remain in touch with their parents, they have done all they can do. They gradually lose contact with their other relatives.

The weakening of extended family ties is not due to ill-will or lack of affection; it is simply a sign of the way American life is organized. It reveals itself in little ways: for instance, in the words of the woman who remarks, "I don't have much of a Christmas list. I have to get something special for my husband and the children, and a gift for his mother and my own, but we don't bother about anybody else."

But how does this radically or basically affect the family and how does it make for difficulties in the position of women in the home? Obviously, the fact that a great group of relatives do not exchange gifts at Christmastime is not a deep deprivation, at least materially, for the American child who probably gets more than enough presents from his parents and usually has everything he needs in a material way. It can be argued, of course, that the warmth and love expressed by presents from aunts and cousins as well as grandparents provide an important source of emotional security for the child. He knows without thinking consciously about it that there are in the world a number of people besides his parents on whom he can count. And that is an important point: the woman, as well as the children, in the nuclear family today has few people on whom she can count. Often her own mother lives a thousand miles away and she has nobody she can call on when there is illness or a new baby. The young wife has to cope with the whole household without the physical aid and the psychological support of another woman. Even if her mother or her sister do live nearby, society has decreed that if they are not hampered by family responsibilities themselves (and sometimes even if they are) they should be out working *for money.*

The nuclear family is then in an ironic position. Because the center of American life has moved outside the home, the home can do less and less for the family. The family performs fewer and fewer functions for itself and consequently is weakened.* The less the family is capable of doing for itself and the more its functions are taken over by outside agencies, the more dispensable the family apparently becomes and the more inadequate and unnecessary the woman dedicated solely to her family feels. Practically every vital function once performed by the family has now become the specialized task of professional people, and the woman in the home who says she feels aimless and unproductive keeping house may not simply be giving in to self-pity or manifesting a neurotic trait; she may really be trying to voice a half-obscure realization of what has happened to the family and consequently to her role.

Her husband, returning home from his business environment, often cannot understand her complaint, try as he might. And, if, like an increasing number of American husbands, he thinks her problem is that she is overburdened with work, he good-naturedly pitches in and helps her with dishes and putting the children to bed. He may well wonder why, when he has provided her with every possible labor-saving device he can afford and tries himself to be for her the "extra pair of hands" which are so obviously missing in today's home, she is still dissatisfied.

The present-day sharing of household tasks by husband and wife may give them opportunities for a kind of rapport their

* "In other cultures, the thing that made the family strong was the fact that people could not get along without it. The child was born in the midst of the family with the care of relatives; economic support came from the family; if one was sick he would have perished if he had no family to care for him; recreation, religious practice, care in old age were provided by the family. Men simply had to hold on to the family. Without it, they would have perished."[10]

parents never envisioned, but it is fairly safe to predict that it will not keep a wife from leaving the home to work, nor will it give the husband an identity with his wife. The separation of the home and economic life and consequent separation of husband and wife are a part of industrial society; both men and women are caught in a situation which is apparently irreversible.

THE WORLD MOVED OUT OF THE HOME

This was not always so.* In the agricultural and commercial societies of the ages which preceded the Industrial Revolution, much of the creative work, both by men and by women, was done in the home and virtually every job which was performed by men was also performed by women.[12] Men and women worked side by side. The weaver's wife helped him with his craft, and the merchant's wife helped him with his trade. Woman's place in the Middle Ages might have been in the home, but industry was in the home as well. The fact that seventy-two out of the eighty-five guilds existing in England were open to women during the Middle Ages[13] provides some reflection of the way women were involved in production.

"While the home was the producing unit of society, there was no conflict between the woman's role as a producer and creator and her role as a mother, nurturer and educator of the young."[14] But the Industrial Revolution, by moving production out of the home, took away one of a woman's important functions in society.

* So short is the memory of man that even some of the most perceptive authors forget historical events. Thus G. K. Chesterton when he noted[11] that men are specialists while women are universalists—meaning that men have one function to perform while women must play in the home a multiplicity of roles—forgot that this depends upon the society. In the days prior to the Industrial Revolution both men and women were universalists, performing a wide variety of tasks in a household that filled an economic function as well as a nurturing function. While gradually after the Industrial Revolution men lost their multiple role and became specialized in one task for which they received their pay, women for a longer time kept their universalist role. However, since 1910 (the year Chesterton made this comment) even the role of woman has become more specialized, with many of the tasks she used to perform within the home moved outside it, and it becomes increasingly evident that the trend toward specialism has affected men and women alike.

The consequent dissatisfaction has never been resolved. Now a woman seems to face these alternatives: either she must stay in the home and care for the children and feel herself shut off from the production of society, or, if she desires to participate in what she may feel is the larger work, she must leave the home and thereby fulfill inadequately her duty to her offspring. The roles of producer and mother can no longer be combined without strain.

When production was removed from the home what did women do about it? For a time apparently nothing. But the Industrial Revolution and its effects are certainly related to the genesis of the feminist movement. Various social commentators have explained the background of feminism in various ways, but Thorstein Veblen, writing at the end of the nineteenth and the beginning of the twentieth century, had some particularly interesting theories. He noted, "So long as the woman's place is consistently that of a drudge, she is, in the average of cases, fairly contented with her lot. She not only has something tangible and purposeful to do, but she has also no time or thought to spare for a rebellious assertion of such human propensity to self-direction as she has inherited."[15] But, he went on to say, the woman who no longer is a drudge, whose husband has achieved enough wealth and status that her chief concern—following his desire—is to show off his prosperity to society, is the one who becomes discontented. Unhappy that her life is "an expression of man's life at the second remove," she wants to assert herself, and she discovers anew what Veblen calls ironically "the ancient habit of purposeful activity."[16] Thus feminism is born. Veblen's theory is supported by the fact that it was the women of the leisure classes who first enrolled themselves under the banner of feminism. Women of the working class were evidently too busy working both in the home and out of it—as scrubwomen and in sweatshops—to be bothered about asserting their rights.

But if the early feminists felt that they could continue their role within the family circle and at the same time take on professional responsibilities outside they were to find themselves sadly mistaken. The two roles, once they had become separated, could not be integrated with ease. Marynia Farnham, outstanding psychoanalyst and no friend of the feminists, has pointed out the conflicts which straddling both worlds has brought into a woman's life. She believes that woman, if she is to enjoy the sexual act as a wife and if she is to bear children happily, has certain needs which "can be designated as a wish for dependence, inwardness, a wish to be protected and made secure, a strong desire for passivity and compliance," but if she is to succeed in the cultural requirements of business and professional life, she must have "a great deal of drive, self-assertion, competitiveness, and aggression." To perform one role effectively she has to cultivate precisely the opposite qualities she needs for the other.[17]

The woman who finds herself playing two or more roles that conflict with each other not only in the demands they make for her time and energy but in their contradictory requirements on her own personality may well wonder from time to time if she would be happier if society expected her to fill only one role and that one well. Authors and lecturers on the situation of the modern American woman have stated repeatedly that much of her difficulty comes from the fact that she does not really know what she expects of herself or what society expects of her. In more stable, traditional societies men and women know what to expect of one another. The girl, by observing her mother, imitating her, and joining in her tasks, prepares herself to assume the normal feminine role as it is defined in that particular culture. But in our fast-moving culture that is not possible. The role her mother assumed may have become out-dated even before the girl reaches adulthood. A recent news clipping points out that working wives are no longer on the defensive but housewives are,[18] a reversal which exemplifies the fact that the requirements of femininity and the agreed-upon feminine role change so rapidly that a woman has to keep adjusting and readjusting if she is to do what society expects of her. And since the expectations of society are usually not communicated to her by her parents or by some recognized hierarchical authority, but by her peers, she is one of a group of anxious females all scrutinizing one another to find out what they should do.

THE SEXES: FREE AND EQUAL?

The complaint is also voiced that in American society a woman does not know how to fulfill a feminine role because during her childhood and adolescence she is educated as a boy. The same expectations are given her along with the same education. But even if through college she studies along with the boy, she finds upon graduation that society does not treat men and women in the same way. Their adult roles are different. The brilliant co-ed may find herself relegated to a secretarial job if she enters the business world, while her male friend—who may be considerably less than a genius—finds himself as an executive trainee with opportunities for advancement.* The girl going to graduate school often finds the same discrimination existing in the matter of scholarships and fellowships. With equal intelligence and as good a scholastic record, she cannot always compete with men for the scholarly plums.

Even in college itself young girls find themselves caught between the fact that similar education has given them more or less the same interests and aptitudes as boys and the fact that the old-time stereotype persists that a woman is not supposed to be as bright as a man. Mirra Komarovsky in her book *Women in the Modern World: Their Education and Their Dilemmas* writes: "some 40 percent of women undergraduates have confessed (the proportion was confirmed in two studies on widely separated campuses) that they have occasionally 'played dumb' on dates; that is, concealed some academic honor, pretended ignorance of a subject, 'threw games,' played down certain skills in obedience to the unwritten law that the man must be superior in those particular areas."[19] The college girl may find herself confused by the

* This is done usually with the awareness that the man's business career is for life while even the most devoted business girl may marry and retire. On this situation we are not making a value judgment. Whether or not this discrimination should exist, it does. The girl who is led to expect that in her professional or business career she can get ahead just like a man is due for a rude shock. While some states have laws exacting equal pay for men and women, in practice sex discrimination continues.

conflicting directives of her parents that she should get good marks and make them proud, while at the same time they urge her not to put all her time into study since she must be sure to get a man, "like all the other girls in your crowd."

The conflicts a girl experiences in college and on dates may well prefigure what she may experience in later life. Especially if she is by nature or training independent, self-confident, and extremely competent she may find it difficult to play the accepted feminine role. Particularly if she is very much aware of her capabilities she faces the risk of bending backward to conceal her competence from a man in order to make him feel that she relies on his supposedly superior intellect and better judgment. Some girls find this situation upsetting and feel that it would be insincere to pretend to be less intelligent and capable than they are.

The reactions of women to the idea of "playing dumb" are revealing. I remember one woman, a person of great competence and considerable independence, who was dating an eligible man whom she very much wanted to marry. One morning she came into her office and told a group of women friends that the night before she and her friend were about to go out when he found he could not start his car. He tried in vain to get it started and could not discover what was wrong; the girl had noticed that he had neglected to turn the key in the ignition, but she kept quiet and never revealed what the trouble was. Most of her friends felt she had been right in playing dumb. But one girl was vehement in her feeling that the young woman concerned had been insincere and that her action was pointless. Ten years later in this same group of women the episode of the ignition key was brought up. The woman concerned had married the man and was asked what she would do if her husband made the same mistake. Without hesitation she replied, "Why now I'd tell him right off: 'You stupid idiot, you forgot to turn the key in the ignition!' "

Of course it can be argued that women have always concealed their intelligence from men. Maggie, the heroine in the Barrie play *What Every Woman Knows,* kept hidden from her husband the fact that it was her brilliance and wit upon which he depended for his successful speeches. But American women no longer have the simple life of Scottish Maggie; they are expected to achieve on their own, and not simply to be the power behind the scene of a man's success. On the other hand it still seems true that to get married and stay married a woman cannot outshine her man. He still wants her to be moon to his sun. The result is that the American girl feels uncertain as to her role, and men as well as women are never sure what to expect of each other.

Would women be happier if they had fewer choices to make, if they were trained from babyhood on to think only in terms of marriage, and were married at an early age without having to bother about college or a possible career? There is a certain insecurity that arises from the freedom to choose one's role. As Robert J. Havighurst noted: "No doubt many women would be happier if they had fewer choices to make. The same thing is true with men. When life is structured for us into a routine of work and family roles most of us adjust fairly well to the routine and call this adjustment happiness. When life is presented to us less structured, and when we are given the chance to use leisure time and material goods in quantity to make life better for ourselves and others, we do not easily measure up to the challenge."[20]

It is indeed true that American women have more "leisure time and material goods" than have been possessed by any other women in history. But these riches involve risks. The very opportunities women have weigh heavily upon them.

Men, needless to say, have also been affected by the developments in American life. Every change in the role of woman has modified somewhat the role of man. However, it still seems true that the role a man plays in the world determines his wife's status. The girl who marries a boy who did not complete high school and is content with an unskilled job in the community has a far different standing in the community from the girl who marries a boy attending an Ivy League college who later goes on to law school. The occupation of the husband not only plays a large part in determining his social rank, but also is the major determinant of his wife's prestige. Whether this will gradually change as more married women work and make their own mark in the world one cannot say. Today it is still true that a girl marries a man "for better or for worse," as far as both her position in the community and her personal happiness are concerned.

One of the chief modifications in masculinity in the United States which has accompanied the rapidly changing feminine role is the attitude men take toward women. No one has to be told that there has been a decrease in responsible protectiveness on the part of the male. Men today do not take responsibility for women in general. The values of chivalry are apparently outmoded, and while a man may help his wife in the home and still follow the norms of a gentleman in helping her into the car and in rising when women enter the room, he no longer takes the responsibility for the welfare of his sisters or other female relatives. Women are apparently no longer the sex to be cherished and protected. They drive their own cars and they can shift for themselves. So, evidently, reasons the man who will drive by a woman stranded on a lonely road as her car boils over. The changing values in American life are accurately reflected in the behavior of the two sexes. When a young woman meets a gentleman of the old school who does worry about her safety and security she probably suspects his motives, so dated is the idea that a gentleman has a responsibility to protect all ladies whether or not he has a personal interest in them.

SHIFTING VALUES

It is to be expected that changing values would precede as well as follow changing behavior in our society. The exchange of tasks and of roles reflects as well as encourages these shifting values. Some values, of course, are of secondary importance and they can be lost without harming society in even a minor way. But other values which are losing importance in American life have more than a transitory importance and seem more directly related to our heritage as a Christian nation. Even people who have forsaken all allegiance to a Christian religion, or to any religion at all, formerly recognized the values embodied in the Ten Commandments and the Golden Rule; and such values as honesty, loyalty, responsibility, generosity, and charity—especially to the poor, the weak, the aged and the young—were at least subscribed to until fairly recently. They were values which were generally accepted in American society and although the norms derived from these values were not always faithfully followed, their claims were at least recognized in theory. Most important of all, the fact that there are absolute values was admitted.

Now, however, the question of values has become more complicated. As an expert on child development wrote recently: "The newer attitude sees practically every value as 'relative,' to be decided in terms of each situation and to be 'enforced,' not by an inner conscience, but by 'the group.'"[21] This question of values, emphasized again by the furor created by the television quiz scandals, caused this same writer to point out that during the time some of the quiz contestants were growing up, in the years between 1925 and 1950, parents in *avant-garde* circles were often being told not to impose their own values on their children. Now there has been a swing in the opposite direction since "specialists have seen enough young people who are miserable for lack of any personal standards to recognize that the *laissez-faire* approach has its own shortcomings."[22]

The lack of any clear goal has had tragic effects on the lives of many modern women. The lack of any allegiance to ultimate values has brought personal havoc into the lives of not a few. Failure to recognize the values connected with pre-marital chastity and the sanctity of marriage, in particular, has not only caused personal unhappiness to many women but also has resulted in broken homes, plentiful divorces, emotional disturbance, and delinquency in children. Indeed, confusion over values may wreck more homes than confusion over roles.

To a Catholic woman, who has received with her faith a number of values which she sees as flowing from ultimate truth and as having an absolute importance, the spectacle of a society in which values are regarded as impermanent and to be changed at will may be disturbing. To a Catholic woman who is brought up by religious parents and educated in Catholic schools, the clash with secular norms may be delayed a long time. Sometimes the realization that there is a clash—resulting from the diametric opposition of Christian and secular values*—may come to her as a sudden shock. One young woman educated in a Catholic college suddenly realized one day that if she was not going to practice birth control she and her husband would have to live a life quite different from the secular ideal. "Why didn't somebody tell us," she asked, "that we can't have everything that we're supposed to have as a part of the American way of life and still have a big family?"

Obviously the question of birth control touches the heart of the conflict between Catholic norms and those of non-Catholic America. But there are norms and values in the contemporary situation whose opposition to Catholic standards is a great deal more subtle. If one took, for instance, the ads in a typical woman's magazine and evaluated them with the beatitudes as one's criteria, one would discover that they reflect a way of life that is a negation of Christian ideals. Fortunately for the tranquillity of most Catholic women—as well as of most Catholic men—this opposition is only imperfectly recognized. Most Catholic women achieve some sort of a working compromise with the standards of the secular world so that the clash of values is kept hidden and only reappears starkly at certain times when, what is called "a question of mortal sin" arises.

But there are many Catholic women who do not manage to achieve or maintain some sort of uneasy balance between Christion and worldly values. They may be the Catholic single women who continue alliances with married men, or the Catholic women who are involved in the eighteen percent of the marriages in a fairly typical parish that are invalid.[23] Their adaptation to the ways of modern America has involved some form of serious compromise with Christian values and norms. The large number of

* A representative sociology text can make the statement that pre-marital virginity is no longer considered a value for either sex in American society without its author (Arnold Rose) feeling the need to give references or to cite proof, so far have values shifted from the traditional Christian pattern.

Catholic married women habitually using artificial contraceptives (how many one can only guess) are among the Catholics who have relinquished their adherence to the moral law as it is interpreted by the Church.

There is a very small minority of Catholics who see quite clearly the conflict between Christian and secular values and who try to resolve this conflict for themselves by attempting to ignore the world and refusing to countenance any good that does not flow directly from a Christian source. They run the risk of confusing what is "contemporary" with what is "secularistic." Whether their distrust of things modern is connected with a personal problem of emotional insecurity or not, they are influenced by their distrust to latch onto the vision of an age that is past, but an age which, they have been assured, was Christian. Not seeing that some of the values of this former age were not necessarily absolute, they try as best they can to transpose the transitory cultural values as well as the pattern of living in this previous era into their own lives. Their chief error lies in making every value absolute, every dictum of transcendent importance. Thus, the question of how Christianity is to be lived in our age seems to them already settled. Their solution to the difficulties of women, quite consistently, is a return to the feminine pattern of years ago. Not realizing that such matters as women working outside the home, participation of women in political parties, etc., are to be left to the enlightened prudence of the modern Christian, who has to figure out many things for herself, they want answers on every small question.

But it is important that Catholic women, who like other American women suffer some confusion over their roles in our society, who wonder what they should expect from themselves and what other people (especially men) have the right to expect from them, should face a fundamental task. It is their obligation to assess Christian values and the values of their own society, and to fulfill in their personal lives a feminine role adapted to contemporary needs.

NOTES

1. William H. Whyte, Jr., *The Organization Man* (New York: Simon and Schuster, 1956), Chapters 22 through 28.
2. *Ibid.*, p. 132 and following.
3. Margaret Mead, Editor, *Cooperation and Competition Among Primitive Peoples* (New York: McGraw-Hill, 1937).
4. David Riesman, Nathan Glazer, and Reuel Denney, *The Lonely Crowd* (Garden City, New York: Doubleday Anchor Books, 1955).
5. Talcott Parsons, *Essays in Sociological Theory, Pure and Applied* (Glencoe, Illinois: Free Press, 1954). Particularly relevant to this discussion of women in American society is the chapter on "Age and Sex in the Social Structure of the United States."
6. Joseph H. Fichter, *Sociology* (Chicago: University of Chicago Press, 1957).
7. Arnold M. Rose, *Sociology: the Study of Human Relations* (New York: Knopf, 1956).
8. Mrs. Mary Osborne speaking on "The Married Woman at Home," at the New School for Social Research. Address reported in the *New York Times,* November 5, 1959.
9. Riesman *et. al., op. cit.,* p. 300.
10. Joseph P. Fitzpatrick, S. J., in an address on "The Layman's Role in the Family," at the First Family Institute, Archdiocese of New York, October 31, 1958.
11. Gilbert Keith Chesterton, *What's Wrong With the World* (New York: Dodd, Mead, 1910).
12. Cf. Viola Klein, *The Feminine Character* (London: International University Press, 1946).
13. Doris F. Bernays, *A Wife Is Many Women* (New York: Crown, 1955). For the social position and economic function of women in the Middle Ages see also Ferdinand Lundberg and Marynia F. Farnham, *Modern Woman: the Lost Sex* (New York: Harper, 1947).
14. Marynia F. Farnham writing in *Women's Opportunities and Responsibilities.* The Annals of the American Academy of Political and Social Science, May 1947, Vol. 251, p. 113.
15. Thorstein Veblen, *The Theory of the Leisure Class* (New York: Mentor Books, 1953), p. 232.
16. *Ibid.,* pp. 232-233.
17. Farnham, *op. cit.,* pp. 118-119.
18. Osborne, *op. cit.*

19. Mirra Komarovsky, *Women in the Modern World: Their Education and Their Dilemmas* (Boston: Little, Brown, 1953), p. 77.
20. Robert J. Havighurst writing in *The Potentialities of Women in the Middle Years,* edited by Gross (Michigan: Michigan State University, 1956), p. 8.
21. Dorothy Barclay, writing in the *New York Times,* November 5, 1959.
22. *Ibid.*
23. Joseph H. Fichter, *Parochial School* (Notre Dame, Indiana: University of Notre Dame Press, 1958), p. 382.

5

Women in Marriage

WHEN Ralph Linton wrote that "the ideal marriage for most humans is one in which a good provider is mated to a good housekeeper,"[1] he probably knew he would shock most Americans. So wedded are we to the notion of romantic love that the possibility of a happy marriage existing in a society where such love is unknown is unimaginable to us.

Romantic love seems to be the dominant value which overshadows all else in the minds of most of our fellow citizens when they consider courtship and marriage. And while anthropologists, psychiatrists and marriage counsellors may point out that a happy marriage can exist without romantic love, it is doubtful that many persons will change their minds and seek marital partners on a completely rational basis. As a people we pride ourselves that we do not marry for money or for position or because we need a woman for a housekeeper or a man to bring home the bacon; we marry for *love*.

The girl who is canny enough to consider the future prospects of the young man who begs her to marry him, and the man who coldly considers the qualifications of a young woman for domestic life are sometimes even looked upon as being disloyal to the notion of love. If such considerations do enter into the thinking of people who are choosing a mate they keep them well hidden. Parents and other older people may caution a girl to be sure that the man she marries is responsible and willing to support her, and they may tell the man that he should investigate his fiancée's home-making abilities, while they tell both parties that similarity of interests, of cultural background, of intelligence, of religion, of values, is important and that any major disparity in any one of these important areas will make for future troubles. But the couple themselves are not expected to hold these considerations paramount. Being in love is what is important. Is it then a proof of the direct intervention of Providence or of good upbringing and adequate education, that so many young couples do have the important things in common and that so many men do turn out to be good providers who are mated to good housekeepers?

Of course, the statistics on divorce would seem to prove the failure of romantic love. Still, the pessimist in a society where romantic love appears to be regarded as one of the few absolute values has to pause and consider that if this is really the case a surprising number of marriages do work out well. Even if the young people involved do not give lip service to values other than romantic love, they nevertheless seem to have assimilated these values successfully. In spite of the fact that this may seem incredible to non-Americans who scoff at romantic love there are emotionally balanced, upright young men who fortunately for themselves and their future children fall in love with young women who have as much common sense as they have beauty. Young people who come from happy homes usually make happy marriages, and usually they are guided by their good sense to contract a marriage with a person who is similar to them in background, values, and interests. They indeed have an edge on the young people in some other societies who enter into arranged marriages, since they not only have selected partners for themselves who meet the standards of even the most finicky parents, but are in love with them besides. Romantic love for such Americans is the icing on the cake; what underlies it is rich and substantial.*

* The values inherent in romantic love are obvious to Americans and need not be pointed out here. What is not obvious at all to us, however, is that there can be any good in any other system of mating. Santha Rama Rau in writing about the arranged marriages of her native India sees them as preventing the anxiety and competitiveness which enfold the American girl

But unfortunately the young man or woman who happens to fall in love with someone who coincides with the choice that would have been made if the marriage had been wisely arranged is, seemingly, increasingly rare. As Margaret Mead points out, especially since the second World War the conflict between two notions—marriage for love and marriage for suitability—is more obvious. Formerly, "it did little harm for a man to feel that he could choose from the whole world when he almost always married the girl next door, when what romantic love really meant was that he looked at the ten eligible girls in the community and decided that he loved Susy best . . . Young people thought theirs was a marriage of free choice and of romance, while actually they were contracting a marriage within the same class, the same religious group, the same general occupational picture, and supported by all the old supports that had held up marriage before."[2] Since divorce was rare, it seemed that marriages based on romantic love were succeeding, when in reality these successful marriages were based on something quite different. For, since the second World War, we have come to see what actually happens when marriages are based on this kind of love and little or nothing else. "The extensive mobility in this country has finally torn people so far from their roots that we now have probably the largest number of marriages that history has ever known of couples who have no visible reason for ever getting on together, who share no common background whatsoever, who have no common friends, no common past, not even a dog they can both remember, who married each other sometimes after an acquaintance of only four or five days, and then tried to correspond for two years about two dances and the pattern of the wallpaper in a boarding house. It is incredible that so many marriages have stayed together. We have suddenly come right up against the actual realization of an ideal that we cherished without knowing

seeking her husband, since the Indian girl feels secure in following the judgment of her parents in whom she has confidence. Most important of all, this Indian author sees the arranged marriage system as based on the idea that every person is lovable and therefore marriageable.

its significance."[3] For young people now are actually following the ideal held up to them "that the thing to do was to find someone with whom you fell in love hard, and marry him no matter what his religion, no matter what his economic background, and no matter what all the future in-laws might say."[4] With the ideal a reality, "We are now in the position of having to do some pretty firm re-evaluating to keep our marriages steady at all."[5]

The marriages that are the subject of the famous monthly article "Can This Marriage Be Saved?" in the *Ladies Home Journal* provide graphic illustration of the inevitable failures in marriages based solely on the notion of romantic love. However, it is doubtful that romantic love as a paramount value is going to lose its hold on Americans or that personal choice of the parties concerned is going to yield to a more rational method of marital selection. "When marriage was established on social conventions, and, hence, from the individual standpoint, on chance, it had at least as much likelihood of success as marriage based on 'love' alone. But the whole of western evolution goes from tribal wisdom to individual risk, it is irreversible, and it must be approved to the extent it tends to make collective and native destiny depend on personal decision."[6] The idea of using a mechanical brain to select men and women who would be suited to each other was tried as a joke a few years ago. But as far as we know those chosen for each other in this manner were not particularly responsive, and there is no fear that automation is going to assume the function formerly the province of parents in arranging marriages that would be good for the family, clan, or larger community. Unless there is a radical change in American society freedom of choice in following the dictates of romantic love will remain the method of mate selection, and what parents, educators and priests must do is to help young people to use this freedom well.

Unalloyed romantic love can often place a strain on marriage. The couple who marry only because they have fallen in love may, in a sense, have already reached the high point of their relationship emotionally; whereas the couple in an arranged marriage may perhaps in the future "fall in love," but at least have the opportunity to look forward to a growing toward love to replace the probable neutrality with which they enter matrimony. The parties in a purely romantic love match hope that their love will overcome all differences: the third-generation Irish girl will probably learn to cook spaghetti for her second-generation Italian husband; the Baptist husband will dutifully drive his Catholic wife to Mass every Sunday. But differences like the latter are not readily bridged. The barriers to communication and understanding are at once deeper and more complex, extending as they do not only into the realm of external behavior and activities, but also of interior motivation and emotional reaction.

MARRIAGE IS FOR HAPPY PEOPLE

The situation of married women has to be understood in the social context of romantic love. And, paradoxically enough, the more romantic love has failed us as a nation, the more we are attracted to it, the more our young people rush into marriage, or remarriage. The fact that more American girls today marry at eighteen than at any other age—at an age when they cannot usually be expected to have the maturity to select a partner on a rational basis—shows that romantic love is carrying the day. Is this quest for love in marriage a reflection of the quest for happiness? As has already been noted, our particular society is preoccupied with the question of happiness. Is the rush to enter matrimony a reflection of this phenomenon? It seems to be the case that a great many women—and not just girls of eighteen, for this is true of older women as well—feel that marriage is the solution to the problem of happiness. Marriage is felt to be capable of answering the individual's perplexities, bringing her peace of mind, and emotional as well as physical completeness. Yet a psychiatrist writes: "Theoretically no one should get married who is unhappy as a single person, is marrying from emotional hunger or sexual despair. We don't marry in order to become happy. We marry in order to be happier, which is different."[7]

Mindful of the fact that marriage is the normal destiny of a human being, there are too many advisers of young people who forget that marriage will not automatically render an unhappy person happy. Marrying in order to be happier is quite different from marrying in order to become happy. If persons are disturbed and neurotic in the single state, there is generally no reason to think that they will become less disturbed and neurotic if they marry. There are, of course, exceptions to this rule. Two emotionally immature or neurotic individuals sometimes achieve a happy marriage, if their emotional needs complement each other.[8] A woman who is really seeking a child, not a husband, in a man may enter into a happy relationship with a man who is looking for a mother, rather than a wife. But usually these marriages in which the abnormal emotional needs of the couple are satisfied remain happy only under rather special conditions, notably the absence of children. But in general it is safe to say that marriage itself does not make an emotionally abnormal person normal, nor does it make an unhappy person happy. Marriage—perhaps especially in the insecure, less patterned circumstances of American society—imposes a strain on the normal individual. Even the happy person in a particularly happy marriage knows times of perplexity and anguish. It would seem foolish, then, to hold marriage up as a remedy for maladjustment or as the solution to immaturity. (This is not to say that marriage does not help mature the personality. But the personality must be potentially mature, not retarded.)

The excessively dependent woman who suffers from an inability to be generous in love, who needs to be given affection before she can offer it, and tends to withdraw her love at the slightest hint of betrayal, is going to find adjustment to a marital relationship difficult. The woman who is so insecure that she cannot take any criticism or who cannot admit that any fault in the relationship is hers will likewise find marriage a strain. The woman who, as a result of early childhood experience, has an underlying aggression toward men while at the same time she has rejected her femininity may combine ineptness and discontent in the usual responsibilities and roles of a wife with hostility toward her husband. Even though the emotionally immature or disturbed woman may be helped through some type of therapy to make an adjustment to marriage, marriage itself does not make the adjustment. While marriage may be therapeutic for the healthy personality, it does not cure the emotionally ill, and young women who sense that their unhappiness stems from a disorder within themselves should not be encouraged to seek in marriage an answer to their problem.

In a society preoccupied with sex, it is not surprising that the sexual fulfillment which marriage brings should sometimes be thought to be synonymous with happiness; nor is it surprising that marriages should be considered unhappy if the couple are not sexually compatible. But here it would seem that there is a confusion of cause and effect. As a psychiatrist, George Lawton, writes: "From the cases I have seen in my practice, I conclude that a bad sex adjustment is seldom the cause of a bad marriage. But a bad marriage is generally the cause of a bad sex adjustment."[9] And Florence Hollis in *Women in Marital Conflict* remarks: "When we studied the sex adjustment in our [cases of] unhappy marriages, we found, as might be expected, that for the most part dissatisfaction rather than satisfaction was the rule. While physical factors, early education, and attitudes toward contraception may have contributed, repeatedly the poor sex adjustment appeared to be a symptom primarily of one or more of the personality factors earlier discussed [excessive dependence, rejection of femininity, masochism, etc.]. While we would not say that sexual maladjustment never comes from educational or cultural determinants, our cases would lend support to the thesis that at least when it is associated with marital disharmony it is usually just another way in which basic personality difficulties reveal themselves."[10]

Lack of knowledge on the part of the bride of a few generations ago may have been a deterrent to a ready sex adjustment, though even the shock of intercourse (a shock which, incidentally, Lundberg and Farnham[11] insist has been grossly exaggerated) could be overcome if a woman was normally loving, trusted her husband,

and possessed a spirit of feminine self-surrender. But the fact that knowledge of sex is almost the least part in a satisfactory adjustment to marriage is pointed up by the maladjustment that exists in an era when the number of sex manuals, pamphlets, and articles on sex is phenomenally high.

Bad sex adjustment in marriage is certainly the result of personality disturbances, but these disturbances themselves frequently have social causes. Let us look at the social setting in which boys and girls in this country reach sexual maturity. A recent pamphlet[12] informs us that in our culture at present children between the ages of nine and eleven (the time of childhood when, traditionally, they are not supposed to be interested in the opposite sex) are beginning to date; "going steady" and the use of lipstick are becoming commonplace in this age group. This pre-adolescent interest in sex would seem to be part of the general American preoccupation with the subject. Margaret Mead, however, suggests that it is not so much sex, as the desire for popularity and achievement, that is at the root of the heterosexual game our adolescents are given tacit encouragement to play. Commenting that the prevalent adolescent commitment to physical glamor and attractiveness sometimes gives people of other cultures the impression that Americans are tremendously interested in sex, that our primary occupation in life is physical love, Margaret Mead protests that such is not the case. Success and popularity at the sexual game are more important than sex itself.[13] In this opinion David Riesman seems to concur. "The other-directed person looks to sex not for display but for a test of his or her ability to attract, his or her place in the 'rating-dating' scale—and beyond that, in order to experience life and love . . . Today, millions of women, freed by technology from many household tasks, given by technology many 'aids to romance,' have become pioneers, with men, on the frontiers of sex. As they become knowing consumers, the anxiety of men lest they fail to satisfy the woman also grows—but at the same time this is another test that attracts men who, in their character, want to be judged by others."[14]

THE CURIOUS AMERICAN ADJUSTMENT

Our cultural attitude toward the pre-marital behavior of adolescents and young adults is contradictory. We have no chaperonage. "We permit and even encourage situations in which young people can indulge in any sort of sex behavior they elect. At the same time we have not relaxed one whit our disapproval of the girl who becomes pregnant . . . We actually place our young people in a virtually intolerable situation, giving them the entire setting for behavior for which we then punish them whenever it occurs. The curious adjustment that American culture has made to this situation is petting. . . . Petting requires very special adjustment in both male and female. The first rule of petting is the need for complete control of just how far the physical behavior is to go. . . . The controls are in the hands of the girl . . . From this game . . . arises the later picture of married life in America, in which it is the wife who sets the pattern of sex relations. From it comes the inability of many American women to make complete sexual surrenders,"[15] so used have they become to being careful and on guard and never giving in. Petting has made them wary of the complete surrender requisite for happy marital love.

Complicating their inability to make a total surrender of themselves to their husbands is the fact that they have been told that they too—not just their husbands—are supposed to enjoy sex. Commenting on the ironic situation in which the more some women are told they are supposed to get pleasure out of marriage the more anxious they become that they are not achieving all the pleasure that should be theirs, one married woman remarked, "It seems we're back with the old paradox: it is in giving that you receive. If you give yourself totally and selflessly to your husband you're bound to enjoy marriage. Whereas if you are concerned merely with what you get out of it yourself, you're not going to be satisfied. I think that's why many women today find marriage unsatisfactory. They've never learned to love nor to give."

To this may be added the difficulty mentioned in the discussion of women's conflicting roles: a woman who has emphasized the side of her personality which is concerned with leadership, aggression and initiative, may find it hard to adjust to her role in marital intercourse in which she must be passive and allow her husband to dominate.

The problem of sex in marriage is complicated for a Catholic woman by the fact that Christian values of sex are quite different from those of the secular value system. While Christian theology has always held that sex in marriage is good, but that sexual activity can be disordered and dangerous, various theologians and popular preachers have tended to emphasize either one or the other of these complementary truths. Thus, under the influence of Jansenism, especially of the Irish variety,[16] there are still Catholics who believe that sex in marriage is essentially shameful and only allowed for the purpose of conceiving a child. There are still some Catholics who believe that they should not go to Communion after marital intercourse without going to confession first. On the other hand, under the influence of the American social climate in which they move and breathe, a large number of Catholics are inclined to assent to the belief of many of their fellows that the chief purpose of marriage is pleasure. They miss the personal and spiritual connotations of sex, and the fact that their being "two in one flesh" makes them the living sign of the union of Christ and His Church completely eludes them.

Cana and Pre-Cana Conferences and the Christian Family Movement have done much to educate married couples to the beauty and dignity of sex in marriage, and with renewed emphasis on marital spirituality, engaged and married couples are finding in retreats and prayer together the way to integrate marital intercourse into their total spiritual life. "For the act of sex should be at once the sign and the source, the manifestation and the nourishment of an interior personal love."[17]

MARRIED LOVE

Gustave Thibon writes: "According as the sexual instinct is *lived,* as it is employed by the personality, it can be the strongest manifestation of spiritual love or it can be the worst of its obstacles."[18] Sex in marriage can be an expression of the charity the spouses bear to God and to each other or it can be an expression of lust and selfishness. Strangely enough, it is often thought that it is sexual pleasure itself which is wrong and dangerous, whereas only sex which is disordered, which is separated from its real end and allowed to run wild, constitutes sin. Father Plé, who writes that "What matters is not the vehemence of the pleasure but the way in which the capacity for love is used," notes that "To be chaste is to love and to love passionately."[19] The married woman who rejoices in marital ecstasy need not fear the pleasure of union with her husband as long as it is motivated by and united to charity.

In an age when too often sex is identified with smut, too often love is sullied. While many women still go into marriage as physical virgins, too often there is missing the radiant innocence which can set on fire their love for their husbands. In an age in which marriage is snickered at and smirked over, it would seem that only the rare person can be completely untouched by this common degrading attitude and accept sex in marriage as it is, pure and holy in the sight of God. As Catholics we exclaim over the glory of virginity consecrated to God, but perhaps we underplay the glory of marital chastity, and underrate the virtue of the married woman who has sacrificed her virginity to her husband's love in order that love might bear fruit. As the consecrated virgin's chastity is not holy unless it is rooted in charity, married love cannot be holy unless it is rooted in fidelity and chastity. "To be chaste is to love, and to love passionately." Is it any wonder then that we sometimes see in a holy married woman, who perhaps has lived with her husband for many years, a translucent purity that—more than any treatise on the holiness of marriage—reminds us that matrimony is indeed a great sacrament?

To find readily and simply in the act of marriage itself an expression of charity for God and one's spouse would, it seems, presuppose a will already rooted in God and passions that are controlled and purified. But marriage is a way to holiness as well as an expression of holy love, and in marriage itself love is purified and transfigured. The woman who said that she never feels as close to God as when she is one with her husband may be exceptional, yet in reality she is simply expressing the end of the vocation of marriage, which is union with God. Marriage is for the saint indeed, but it is also for the saint in the making. In our age especially the connection between holiness and sex may not be easy to make, but matrimony is the Christian sacrament which assures us that such a connection is possible. " 'With my body I thee worship': not 'My body worships thy body'—the isolated pleasure-seeking; not 'I worship thee'—the ideal-projection, the fantasy figure; not 'With my body I seize thee, I subjugate thee, I possess thee'—the lust for power that can be stronger even than the lust for lust; but 'With my body I worship thee': I approach thee with wonder and awe and tenderness and humility, for 'Thou' is a mystery, and love is a mystery, and human sex is a mystery, and the body is a mystery; and so they all have to be learnt slowly, gradually, lovingly, patiently . . ."[20]

Marriage is indeed the normal way to sanctity. Woman made for man finds in man her way to God. "To seek God alone in the darkness might well be a terrifying thing; to embark on the journey hand in hand with one you love is to rob the journey of many at least of its terrors."[21] But Father Vann, who wrote that passage, added in a necessary footnote: "To say that such a way to God is easier is not to say that it is simpler. There will be difficulties to overcome which do not confront the man who 'goes out from all things' and has no other thought but the God he is seeking. There will be tensions between the human love and the divine; temptations to forget the latter for the sake of the former. St. Paul makes this clear (I Cor. VII, 32-34). But against all that, given the *will*-to-achieve, there will be the constant support, the mutual strengthening, the sustaining arms . . ."[22]

But husband and wife may get out of step. Especially at a time when couples marry at an early age there is danger that as they mature they may outgrow each other. The husband may achieve a status that puts him in a social circle in which the wife finds herself unpoised and unable to keep up with the conversation. Or what is yet more heart-rending, one of the spouses may travel to God at a faster rate and with greater yearning. A woman can know in marriage greater spiritual loneliness than is possible in any other vocation. For the very fact that they are two in one flesh reveals to them that they are not one before God, and the wife who has spiritual insight and apparently more grace than has been given her husband knows a terrible anguish which is coupled with her loneliness as she yearns to be able to communicate to him her understanding and love of God.

A few years ago, there was among eager young people anxious to make the most of the spirituality of marriage what could be called a false mysticism of marriage. They proclaimed that their two souls had become one, and while they may have meant this as a figure of speech to convey an otherwise inexpressible reality, the expression itself is unfortunate and holds up an unrealizable hope. Not even in marriage, not even in a marriage where the husband and wife are holy and happy, can they become as one soul. For, the nearer they get to God the more they will see their "aloneness" before Him, the more they will suffer the separation, the loneliness that has existed since Paradise was closed, especially between the two persons who love each other most. This is part of the agony of life to be endured, and it is only in eternity, when each will be perfectly united with God, that the at-one-ment of husband and wife will be complete.

Here, love each other as deeply and as ardently as they may, there must be the inevitable gulf between them. Only a person without perception, or one who has not been married for very long, will deny the existence of the gulf. But the woman who accepts it, and at the same time allows her love to bridge it as far as it is able, is happy and at peace.

The importance of developing a spirituality of married love on a firm basis is all the more important since our culture has placed upon the married couple a heavy burden of responsibility and self-reliance. Neither the structure of the society as a whole nor the help of an extended family group gives the couple the moral support and the spiritual help they need to maintain their marriage in dignity and stability. It would seem that today especially husband and wife have to look within themselves for the moral and spiritual resources which in previous ages society would have given them. While this fact puts a tremendous responsibility for maturity on the married couple, it can have a good effect since it causes them to work hard at making a go of their marriage. Successful marriage today evokes the fulfillment of all their potentialities, and the wise couple are aware that they cannot simply drift along: they have to co-operate with the grace of God to assure themselves and their children of a stable, happy, rewarding home life.

That marriage, even on the natural level, is a source of strength for the two persons who have given their lives over to each other is brought out rather well in these words of Jessamyn West: "Marriage, after the first few years, becomes more than the two people involved in it. Something emerges from their effort to live together, even from their misunderstandings and bickerings and failures, something that transcends the particular husband and wife. For a while, when you're first married, you have to protect your marriage, believe in it, even when it appears to wither, to shed all its first tender leaves. Then, if you care for it, it will take root, begin to grow, and finally, and perhaps in spite of you, outstrip you, arch over your head, and become a protection. You two small ones will find refuge and solace in it."[23]

If marriage is to succeed, the woman indeed must be the heart of the home as the husband is the head of the family. Some Catholics feel that St. Paul, in saying to the wife that she must be subject to her husband, put an impossible burden upon her. But this yoke is only unreasonable and degrading when it is separated from the love that the husband bears the wife. The exact form, however, that the conjugal subjection of woman to man should take in our day is not without its perplexities. Some of the efforts to restore order to the Christian home in the face of the excessive emancipation of women have been rather absurd. Thus, as more and more men help their wives with the dishes, some people have argued that any such "womanly" work done by the man is against the order that is supposed to prevail in the Christian home. The article which argued that in the Christian family neither wife nor children are supposed to speak at table without the permission of the husband is another example of this extreme reaction to emancipation!

These examples, of course, are ridiculous and quite miss the point of the headship of the husband. Numerous psychological studies have shown that there are exceedingly few aptitudes that are not shared by both sexes; there is nothing innately "feminine" about dishwashing. (Though there does not seem to be any test that has investigated the relative dishwashing potential of the two sexes!) The parents of a big family may well agree that unless the husband helps his wife put the children to bed and clear away the dishes they will not be able to share any leisure hours together in the evening. Common sense tells them that they can arrive at this decision without upsetting the authority of the husband or the order which should prevail in the home. And as for regulating conversation, it is revealing that in the families in which the husbands have tried to exercise prerogatives which seem abnormal in American life or to demonstrate their authority in minute matters, the wives are usually in reality the stronger personalities; while the husbands scurry around asserting their masculinity over trivialities, often the wives are making the decisions that count. Most happily married couples talk over all major decisions; a husband who is secure in his masculinity and his headship of the family will listen to his wife's ideas, and following her suggestions when they seem better than his own will not disturb him.

But when there is disagreement and the matter is of major importance to the welfare of the family, it would seem that the husband's decision should prevail. For example, wives who take an unnecessary outside job even though their husbands disapprove of women who decide they want no more children and take measures accordingly (whether or not the measures are "moral" in themselves is not the point here) seem to be usurping the headship of the husband. Unless there is a serious reason—such as an incapacitating illness affecting the husband—the wife's subjection entails acquiescing to his considered judgments as they refer to the welfare of the family. The husband's authority implies responsibility for the protection of his wife and children. If it is one of the severest crosses of a wife to be married to a man who is irresponsible, who does not provide either her or their children with financial or emotional support, it is one of the gravest trials for a husband to have a wife who has rejected her feminine role, who countermands his decisions at every step, or who, while she refuses to make a home for the family, runs around directing community affairs.

The roles of husband and wife are in a state of flux in the United States and there are very few clearly defined tasks or functions assigned specifically to either one. That the husband should take the major responsibility for supporting the wife and children, and that the wife should take the greater part in the care of the home and children, still seem to be implied in their roles of "father" and "mother." The Christian husband and wife who are seriously trying to fulfill their duties in marriage have neither to return to a conjugal pattern that is past nor rush to meet a secularistic pattern that is in the process of evolving. The modern pattern which today tries to stress complete equality in the home and interprets it to mean identity of function usually can only work with the premise of birth control. To the Catholic couple with a large family it is apparent that the wife cannot share the financial burden of the husband and still give the children the care they need; she is completely occupied with the nurturing function which began in her womb, continues through the lactation period, and can only end when her children have completed childhood.

This chapter is concerned only with the relationship of the woman with her husband within the home; the changing role of the wife outside the home—particularly the question of the working wife—is left for another chapter.

BIRTH CONTROL

It is significant today that with the great emphasis on sex, this area of married life is no longer considered private or sacred. The most casual acquaintance feels free to tell husband or wife how many children he or she should have. The housepainter who told a woman pregnant with her fifth child that she was having too many kids is matched by the cleaning woman (by no means an old family retainer) who said that her employer's married sisters were having too many babies, and asked "When are they going to stop?" People who would not presume to ask personal questions of a financial nature do not hesitate to voice their opinion on the most intimate area in married life.* Married couples are the subjects of gossip if they have too many children, but Catholic couples are also criticized if they have none or what their peer group considers too few. There is the case of a Catholic wife who had a baby within a year of marriage, but who—through no fault of her own or her husband—did not become pregnant again. She was gossiped about by her neighbors unmercifully: "and her such a good Catholic," was their line. It is no wonder that childless Catholic wives or mothers of only children are forced to talk about their condition a great deal. They seem to feel a continual need to explain to their relatives and friends that they are going to the doctor and trying to remedy their sterility. What once was considered nobody's business but the married couple's is now considered everybody's business. In a climate of birth control everybody is preoccupied with planned parenthood, and the Catholic wife has to become resigned to a situation in which she and her husband will be criticized whether they "do" or they "don't."

That a large percentage of Catholic women do approve of and use contraceptives was indicated in the *Reader's Digest* poll of a few years ago, as well as by the Kinsey Report.† While probably

* This lack of delicacy does not confine itself to married people. Casual acquaintances have no qualms about asking a single woman why she is not married, and another aspect of the problem is revealed in Marjorie Hillis' advice to girls on the subject of extra-marital affairs. She concludes that "probably you shouldn't, but don't let anybody know you don't [have a sex life]."[24]

† In 1955 the Michigan-Scripps study of a national sample of wives aged eighteen to thirty-nine found that 85% of the Protestants and 45% of the Catholics approved of deliberate family limitation. Of the Catholic wives capable of conceiving, four-fifths had used some means of birth control, over half of them a method considered immoral by the Church.

no competent research worker would trust the accuracy of their figures, no one—be he professional or amateur commentator on the social scene—would deny that there are a great many Catholics using artificial means of birth control. Father Fichter, in his recent study of a parish, found that the age group which had the largest number of Catholics who did not receive the Sacraments was the group between thirty and forty years of age.[25] He inferred that it was this group who were most involved in the practice of birth control and who, therefore, stayed away from the Sacraments.

The fact that according to the moral law as it is interpreted by the Church any interference with the normal use and natural outcome of the marital act is a mortal sin means that Catholic married couples are limited in the means they may use to space the births of their children. The Rhythm method and continence are at present the only means recognized as lawful.* In order for the use of Rhythm to be lawful there must be a serious reason present—such as economic inability to care for more children, the poor health of the wife, hereditary disease, or unusual fertility on the part of the wife. Although theologians seem to give the interpretation of sufficient reason for the use of Rhythm a wide latitude, and although the judgment that there is a sufficient reason to limit the number of children or to space conceptions must always ultimately be made by the couple themselves, there are, unfortunately, Catholic couples who practice Rhythm without good cause, out of selfishness or to escape the sacrifice having children entails.

On the other hand, not every Catholic couple is able to raise and educate properly all the children they are biologically able

* The use of the so-called "anti-fertility" pills is allowed when they are taken for the purpose of regularizing the woman's menstrual cycle, but while the Church has not thus far taken an official stand on them, most theologians seem to feel that they cannot be used for the direct effect of rendering the woman sterile, either temporarily or permanently. For further discussion of these pills, see the article by William Gibbons, S.J., in *America,* "What About Anti-Fertility Drugs?" (Dec. 14, 1957); and the article "Contraceptive Pills" by Robert B. McCready, M.D., and John L. Thomas, S.J., in *Marriage* (Vol. XLI, No. 10, October 1959).

to produce. The Church has never held as a norm that a married couple must have as many children as are biologically possible. As Father Joseph Buckley, S.M., writes in *Christian Design for Sex:* "The absolute ideal would seem to be that parents have as many children as they can reasonably afford a decent opportunity to get to heaven. Children are born to earth only that they may one day people heaven."[26]

What this ideal is in practice depends, of course, on the economic and social conditions in which a couple find themselves, as well as on their own health, ability, and subjective dispositions. There are couples who are in the position of being able to cope with an annual baby and being able to raise successfully a dozen or so children, but there are not too many of them. It is all very well to counsel married couples to relax and to "accept all the children God sends." But this advice sometimes begs the question and gives the erroneous idea that the conception of children is exclusively dependent on God—that there is no human act or human decision involved. On the contrary, today's Christian cannot escape responsibility for his use of marriage. While certainly it is laudable for parents to accept the children their intercourse has brought into being, they cannot evade the responsibility for the intercourse in the first place.

While Americans enjoy the highest living standard in the world, it is nonetheless true that this standard is geared to the two-child family. Labor unions, when they seek a living wage, think in terms of a family with four members. A couple with four or five children are therefore already in the position of having to make sacrifices beyond what is expected of their social and economic peers. Another difficulty, already mentioned, stems from the present-day nuclear family: busy mothers do not have the help of relatives. And, ironically, those parents who most need household help can least afford it, while most houseworkers prefer to work for the childless couple or the one-child family.

Medical advances have further changed the situation of the fertile couple. The reduction of infant mortality usually means the raising and educating of all the children brought into the world. Many of our ancestors' children died soon after they reached the baptismal font, but an annual pregnancy now means a baby every year to care for, support, and raise to adulthood.

Other complications have arisen with medical advances. A woman, for example, who in a past century would have died with her first or second child, can now be saved, but is often warned to avoid the danger of future pregnancies, thus forcing a Catholic couple to make a difficult decision. A woman whose frail health makes bed-rest during pregnancy imperative may well wonder what will happen to her other children if she conceives again. As a mother of six children, who had been warned by medical advisors that another pregnancy would be fatal, said: "Priests sometimes misunderstand. They think I'm afraid of dying. But that's not the problem. What would happen to my children if I do die? And what would my husband do? Don't I have a responsibility to him and to them?"

Paul Revere of American Revolutionary War fame had eight children with his first wife who died in childbirth with the eighth; he thereupon married again and his second wife bore him eight more. While not every eighteenth-century family was that large, his case was not atypical. When, recently, two fathers of large families jokingly said that they should take out a big insurance policy on their wives, they were pointing out a basic reality. They couldn't imagine, in view of all their children, that anyone would consent to marry them if they became widowers, and it would take several hundred dollars a week to employ help to replace their wives.

Of course, human prudence must leave something to Providence. A couple who would feel able to cope with any future eventuality might indeed be tempting God. But the Christian wife and husband, abandoning themselves as they should to the arms of Providence, do not forget that God expects them to use their heads. Imploring the guidance of the Holy Spirit, they have to think out their problems and arrive at—what well may be—an extremely difficult decision as to the use they will make of their marital rights.

To couples who have a grave reason for practicing Rhythm, the uncertainty of the method can be a real cross. When Pope Pius XII a few years ago expressed the hope that a more secure method of Rhythm would be discovered, he was probably thinking of those couples who have serious reason to avoid conception. From our human point of view (but then who can know the mind of the Lord or why He permits certain things?) it seems difficult to understand why sometimes the people who have the most reason for using Rhythm are least able to practice it. A woman who uses Rhythm simply for the reason that she wants to keep working when her husband is well able to support her seems to have no difficulty at all, and a wife who already has a number of children and a serious medical problem finds that her condition of spontaneous ovulation makes even an attempt to use Rhythm ridiculous.*

Even when Rhythm is biologically possible, it can remain psychologically difficult. As one married couple wrote: "We live in a sensate culture in which the sex element is hardly absent from the illustration or interpretation of the most ordinary human action. We also live in a mobile, industrial and commercial civilization in which few men enjoy the dignity of a profession or a lay vocation which is fully satisfying; and in which the work of the woman in the home has become sterile, lonely and devoid of traditional meaning. Probably the normal state of twentieth century urban man is a condition of psychological frustration in his work and sexual stimulation by his entire environment . . .

"This then is the setting in which most Catholic married couples

* Why does God will this? We do not know. Well-meaning Catholics who sometimes say that married couples would have no difficulty bearing and raising a large family "if they have enough faith" put themselves in the position of the friends of Job. For there are today people leading lives of radiant holiness who nevertheless experience all sorts of difficulties having children. Grace can, of course, help them to bear these difficulties and turn them to spiritual advantage both for themselves and their children; but to say that faith does away with the difficulties is analogous to the old-time Calvinist view that prosperity is a sign of virtue. That one woman can have ten children with ease and that someone else cannot may not mean that the first person's faith is any greater, but simply that she has better health, more money, and a larger house.

must work out the solution to their problems—an environment hardly conducive to sexual inactivity in or out of marriage. It would be ridiculous to assume that Catholic married couples trying to be prudent in the exercise of conjugal love by the practice of Rhythm or continence are not affected by these influences of the environment about them. The net result of these pressures, together with the romantic tradition of marriage to which we are all heirs, is to make the sexual element in marriage play a more dominant role than it might play in other cultures, or civilizations. And its voluntary regulation is therefore more difficult."[27]

How then can Rhythm be practiced successfully? Separate rooms are fine in Buckingham Palace but they are not feasible in Levittown. Marriage being subordinate to business, a husband who is out of town a great deal because of his job may find that his infrequent week-ends at home do not coincide with his wife's "safe period."

But in spite of these difficulties there are married couples who are able to practice Rhythm successfully without detriment to their emotional or spiritual life. "The greatest natural support during the periods of sacrifice is the friendship and mutual understanding of husband and wife, a bond which is built up during the years in which the family is being established and growing up."[28] In a successful Christian marriage in which the couple have many vital interests in common, in which together they give their attention to rearing well the children they have brought into the world, and in which both of them realize as the years go on that the "deeper, wider life they have in common" goes beyond the sexual life they share, the possibilities of periodic abstention from intercourse are greatly enhanced. The individual couple must find their spiritual strength for the practice of Rhythm in prayer and sacrifice, and as one husband and wife wrote, "The mutual surrender, consent and sacrifice which are required for the proper fulfillment of conjugal love are presupposed and necessary to our minds for the suspension of conjugal love."[29] The couple can help each other integrate the use of Rhythm into their search for perfection, and they can be helped by their confessor to see the time of denial as a time of purity and prayer, of mortification and preparation, so that the time of intercourse can become an expression of mutal love at its highest, and of the charity they bear to each other and to God.*

HEROISM IN MARRIAGE

But what about the problem of difficult medical cases in which Rhythm is inadvisable because of its uncertainty? Pope Pius XII, in his address to Italian midwives, saw the practice of total continence as the only solution. He said: "But it will be objected that such abstinence is impossible, that such heroism cannot be attained." But he added: "It is wronging men and women of our times to deem them incapable of continuous heroism. Today, for many reasons—perhaps with the goad of hard necessity or even sometimes in the service of injustice—heroism is exercised to a degree and to an extent which would have been thought impossible in days gone by. Why, then, should this heroism stop at the borders established by the passions and inclinations of nature?"

The fact that continence in marriage is objectively possible does not, of course, easily solve the dilemma of the woman whose situation makes abstention seem imperative, but whose husband is

* Before leaving the subject of Rhythm, one of its effects should be pointed out. The real or supposed necessity to practice Rhythm has had certain noticeable effects on child-rearing. One of the reasons given by some Catholic women for refusing to breast-feed their babies is that breast-feeding interferes with the normal resumption of the menstrual cycle and thus renders impossible the practice of Rhythm. It has been countered that breast-feeding itself is Nature's way to space offspring. An old folk-tradition says that the nursing mother never conceives, and some mothers of large families today who regularly breast-feed point to the fact that, without any other action on their part, their children are all two years apart, as proof that breast-feeding does prevent an annual baby. However, other women have not had this same experience and have become pregnant while breast-feeding. One could wish that some scientific research on the relationship of breast-feeding to frequency of conception would be undertaken. It is unfortunate that Catholics, most interested as they are in promoting normal married and family life, should have done so little to study seriously such relationships—which are left too frequently to empty talk or idle speculation.

unwilling to refrain from the exercise of his marital privileges. It is one thing to try to follow a heroic path oneself; it is another, when one is married, to try to exact heroism from one's spouse. Can one jeopardize one's marriage? Can one continue to live in the constant state of tension which may very well accompany sexual unfulfillment, when this has serious repercussions on the children of the marriage as well as the parties to the marriage itself? These are questions that cannot be answered facilely. While the majority of women are not placed in such a drastic situation, a sufficient number of women are involved so that their problem cannot be glossed over.

Our age, of course, is not unique in presenting moral dilemmas and situations evoking heroism. Other ages and cultures had their moral problems too. In certain countries of Europe and Latin America where the "double standard" is accepted, recourse by the husband to other women seems to make possible the avoidance of intercourse with his wife and serves as a solution to the problem of future pregnancies. That such a course of action seriously violates the moral law goes without saying. Undoubtedly it is more repugnant to American Catholics than artificial birth control (even though, objectively, both are mortal sins) since it is a violation of our basic notion of marital love. Furthermore, while in certain cultures concubinage did not interfere with the sanctity of the home and the proper upbringing of the children, in our culture such marital infidelity would inevitably break up the home and deprive the children of normal family life. Consequently, an American wife who would put her husband in the position of having to have recourse to another woman is faced with much more serious social consequences than she would be in another culture. However, while birth control may be one cultural temptation and having a mistress a parallel temptation in another culture, to live as a Christian one can succumb to neither. To live the moral law in its entirety, in especially trying circumstances, requires heroism in either culture.

Women who find themselves in what apparently are insoluble dilemmas, caught in the midst of conflicting duties, have to turn to God with ever more fervent prayer. That He will give them enough light and love and strength they must believe. They can and should take counsel, but it is improbable that they can get a simple answer to cut through their problem. God can and does work miracles, it is true; but usually He wills that husband and wife stumble along together seeking Him, helping each other conform to His grace. But what if only one partner continues to seek Him and the other, feeling overburdened by difficulties, gives up the search? Well, then, the one must struggle on, and although wife or husband may not have the strength for two, he or she, imploring desperately God's mercy, can win the grace for two.*

What of the wife who is not overburdened by her fertility, but is in quite the contrary position and has no children at all? Her situation is not at all uncommon. She and her husband may try to remedy it, seeking medical advice and following all the counsel given. Still unable to have children, they may turn to adoption as the answer for them as well as for some child in need of a home. The old-time horror of adoption no longer prevails in our society, and many childless couples have found in adopting children a way to a deeper, richer, more generous life together.

But what about the couples who seem unconcerned by their childlessness? Eva Firkel writes: "There are married couples who are completely wrapped up in each other and yet stay alone throughout their lives. They are sufficient to themselves. To make this love truly human an essential factor is lacking, which is self-forgetfulness . . . For a couple love selfishly if they are so attached to each other that the outside world ceases to exist for them and their love fails to grow into the desire for the child . . .

"Such selfishness will be punished at the latest after the death of one of the spouses. Then the survivor will no longer be able to cope with life alone. But even before, such people will often

* There are many married women who seem to have a mysterious vocation to suffering as surely as any nun. They are asked to bear—not their fair share—but their share with Christ, of the sins of the world. Their vocation seems the clearer when it proceeds not from a masochistic personality but a personality that is attuned to all that is happy and good in life.

find no peace. They are constantly afraid of losing their happiness; even the shortest separation will produce panic. Thus they will become over-anxious . . . For they are unconsciously aware of a guilt. A person who wants only to have and never to give, that is to lose, perverts the meaning of human life, which is not to keep and to hoard but to give and surrender so as to create anew. What is new in a marriage—even though it may itself contain immense powers of spiritual creation—is the child. Now, it is irrelevant whether the child is actually given; the essential point is that it should be desired."[30]

The important thing is that the child should be desired. There are childless wives who are selfish, but there are childless wives who are as creatively maternal as any mother of a large family. Usually their vocation seems clearer to the spectator than it is to them themselves. They may wonder why God allows them to go childless but to the bystander who sees what they are able to accomplish for other people the answer is clear. For, with the freedom they have they are able to perform those acts of charity which are impossible to mothers hampered by the care of children of their own, and to single women whose time is taken up in earning their own living. There are childless wives who are free to do all those acts of thoughtful charity which otherwise might be left undone. A woman who is cheerfully willing to sit for a few hours with an invalid, to visit the poor and forgotten in the nursing homes which are mushrooming all over the country, to give a hand to her relative or friend who has a large family and, consequently, to make available to these children advantages which are beyond those their own mother can give, and to keep alive in her home the tradition of gracious hospitality, proves that even childlessness can be blessed. It is still true in our day that "many are the children of the desolate," and the childless wife shares with the mother their common vocation to creative love.

NOTES

1. Ralph Linton writing in *Women, Society and Sex,* edited by Johnson E. Fairchild (New York: Sheridan House, 1952), p. 72.

2. Margaret Mead, "What is Happening to the American Family?", *New Emphasis on Cultural Factors* (New York: Family Service Association of America, 1948), pp. 2, 3.
3. *Ibid.*, p. 3.
4. *Ibid.*
5. *Ibid.*
6. Denis de Rougemont, *Love in the Western World* (New York: Pantheon, 1956), p. 294.
7. George Lawton writing in *Women, Society and Sex*, p. 98.
8. Florence Hollis, *Women in Marital Conflict* (New York: Family Service Association of America, 1949).
9. Lawton, *op. cit.*, p. 100.
10. Hollis, *op. cit.*, p. 209.
11. Ferdinand Lundberg and Marynia F. Farnham, *Modern Woman: The Lost Sex* (New York: Harper and Brothers, 1947), pp. 283-288.
12. Gertrude M. Lewis, *Educating Children in Grades Four, Five and Six* (Washington, D. C.: Federal Office of Education, 1959), as reported in the *New York Times*, November 9, 1959.
13. Margaret Mead, *Male and Female* (New York: Morrow, 1949), p. 289.
14. David Riesman, Nathan Glazer, and Reuel Denney, *The Lonely Crowd* (Garden City, N. Y.: Doubleday Anchor Books, 1955), p. 174.
15. Mead, *op. cit.*, pp. 290-91.
    Nevertheless, pre-marital pregnancies do occur. It has been estimated that one out of five "first" babies is born before the parents have been married nine months. (As reported by Thomas P. Monahan at the Convention of the American Sociological Society, September 3, 1959.) This gives some idea of the number of pre-marital conceptions that take place, but, of course, we cannot judge accurately how many of these conceptions end in abortion.
    The Kinsey studies as well as other sociological studies of premarital sex behavior estimate that approximately 98% of American men and women indulge in pre-marital petting. (As reported by Winston W. Ehrmann at the Convention of the American Sociological Society, September 4, 1959.)
16. Cf. John O'Brien, *The Vanishing Irish* (New York: McGraw-Hill, 1954).
17. Donal O'Sullivan, S.J., "Theology of Marriage," *Theology Digest*, Vol. IV, No. 3 (Autumn 1956).

18. Quoted by O'Sullivan, *op. cit.*
19. A. Plé, O.P., "The Virtue of Chastity," *Theology Digest,* Vol. V, No. 1 (Winter 1957). See also Dr. Franz X. Arnold, "Theology of Sense and Sex," *Theology Digest,* Vol. II, No. 2 (Spring 1954).
20. Gerald Vann, O.P., *The Water and the Fire* (New York: Sheed and Ward, 1954), p. 123.
21. *Ibid.,* p. 125.
22. *Ibid.*
23. Jessamyn West, "Love," in *Women Today,* edited by Elizabeth Bragdon (New York: Bobbs-Merrill, 1953), p. 95.
24. Marjorie Hillis, *Live Alone and Like It* (New York: Bobbs-Merrill, 1936), p. 95.
25. Joseph H. Fichter, *Social Relations in the Urban Parish* (Chicago: University of Chicago Press, 1955).
26. Joseph Buckley, S.M., *Christian Design for Sex* (Chicago: Fides, 1952).
27. Mr. and Mrs. X, "Responsibility in Catholic Marriage," *Integrity,* Vol. X, No. 1 (October 1955), p. 5.
    The normal difficulty of practicing self-control in marriage is aggravated in the case of those who suffer from emotional disturbances and a sense of personal inadequacy. A man who is successful in no other area of his life, or who has no other satisfaction, finds in sex his only source of pleasure. A woman who has a loveless past, is emotionally immature, and is as a consequence insecure in her husband's love, may have an exaggerated need for its physical manifestation. These are factors that are too often overlooked in assessing the possibility of Rhythm or continence in a marriage.
28. *Ibid.,* p. 8.
29. *Ibid.*
30. Eva Firkel, *Woman in the Modern World* (Chicago: Fides, 1956), p. 105.

6

Working Wives

In a recent conversation between a young man about to be married and his boss, the employer extended the conventional congratulations and the young man made the conventional request for a raise. The answer, always unpredictable, was in this case a question: "What's the matter with the girl you're marrying? Is she lazy?

The story connotes a change in the American attitude toward working wives. At the turn of the century—indeed, as late as 1925—matrimony provided not only a good reason but the recognized occasion for a man to ask for a raise. During the depression years, of course, the employer would normally refuse to help support a wife should a young man be foolish enough to get married.* During World War II the pattern changed so that the young wife was self-supporting while her husband was away in the Army, and by 1950 the wife was expected by public opinion to pull her oar financially—as the young man discovered when he requested a raise.

In a book on the subject of modern woman published in 1952, the authors remark that at marriage a girl can give up her job or not without there being any difference in public reaction.[1]

* During the depression years there was positive hostility toward married women who worked; popular feeling supported the employers' policy of giving the few available jobs to men. Such feminists as Eleanor Roosevelt, alarmed at this development, made renewed efforts at that time to champion the right of a married woman to a career. See Mrs. Roosevelt's book, *It's Up To the Women* (New York: Stokes, 1933).

This may have held true for the country as a whole, but as far as the metropolitan New York area was concerned, by that year the wife was definitely expected to go on working—that is, until she was sure there was a baby on the way. This is the pattern which continues today in urban areas. And the unusual woman who marries the unusual man who agrees with her decision to stay at home during the first year of marriage to learn to be a good wife and possibly to remedy all the deficiencies in her housekeeping techniques before the advent of children, is criticized as lazy or irresponsible. This public disapproval holds true whether or not the husband is in the position to support her quite adequately.

The thinking behind our acceptance of the position that a wife should continue working until she becomes pregnant has never approximated the thinking of the radical feminists that the wife should pay her full share of the household expenses and not be a financial burden on her husband, who should have neither the duty nor the privilege of supporting her and thereby rendering her his domestic slave.* But popular opinion has concurred with the notion that the wife may as well continue working to help pay for the furniture, perhaps help save toward a house of their own, and, in sum, get all the money she can before the arrival of a baby forces her retirement.

That the pattern of the wife's working before motherhood has not completely upset the traditional pattern of the husband's being the financial support and adequate provider for the family is seen in the number of women who thankfully and gracefully retire from their jobs when they know there is a baby on the way. There are, however, women whose goals the pattern of working seems to distort. They are the wives who delay having children far into the indefinite future when "we can afford them." These are the women who first work because they need to, then work

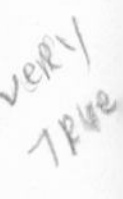

* One woman, who later changed her radical ideas, wrote during her extreme feminist stage: "Children should be a joint responsibility. For a month preceding birth and for a month afterward, the man should care for the woman and child financially. Later they should share equally in the physical and financial care of child or children."[2]

because they are paying off the furniture, then because they are helping to buy a new car, then because they must help meet the monthly mortgage payments on the house, then because . . . and so on, through a future of infinite rationalizations.

At present these wives seem to be the exception.* Statistics bear out what we see every day: there are a great number of young women wheeling baby carriages. Girls who marry in their late teens or early twenties seem to be one with their husbands in agreeing that they should have their children soon. Conflicting evidence leaves it thus far uncertain whether having babies as soon as is biologically possible after marriage foretells a big family. There is some evidence that the "baby boom" does not continue into the mature lives of many couples who at the beginning of their marriage seem to be making a large contribution to it. Statistics seem to support the theory that married couples today have two or three children in close succession at the beginning of their marriage. Then their family is "finished" (to use the popular, inelegant expression) and the wife is free to go to work. "Recent analyses show that one-half of all our married women are only 26.1 years old when the last of almost three children is born. Half of the group are only thirty-two years old when their youngest child enters school."[3]

REVERSING THE PATTERN

These facts are reflected in the present composition of the working force, and the noticeable change that has taken place during this century. For in 1900 only fifteen percent of the working women were married; today over fifty-five percent of women workers are married. Perhaps even more revealing is this comparison: in 1890 the average age of the employed woman was under twenty-five; in 1955 her average age was thirty-eight. Among married women the proportion at work had grown from

* The phrase "at present" is used advisedly, so quickly does the pattern of American life change. We refer here primarily to the pattern of American urban culture; in the different sub-cultures of our vast and diversified country other patterns may prevail.

one in seventeen in 1900 to more than one in five in 1955, with the percentage growing rapidly.[4]

The stereotype of the female officeworker has thus changed. No longer the young, glamorous girl busy making dates on the boss's telephone wire, she is likely to be a smartly dressed, gray-haired matron, or an expectant mother dressed in "business-styled" maternity garb. Fifty years ago the sight of a woman in a "delicate condition" in an office would have shocked the average male; today women work up until a few months or even six weeks of delivery without apparently distressing the most sensitive male employer.* The American office has indeed been transformed since the days of the Gibson Girl. There is a good chance that the boss's secretary will be a grandmother rather than a girl just out of Katharine Gibbs.

Educators who recognize the new pattern in American working life are inclined to be indulgent of it. Although the president of Smith College may have his qualms about it, there are other college administrators who quite calmly accept the fact that many of their students have an engagement ring in their freshman days, are married during sophomore year, and produce a first baby the week after Commencement. Even vocational or professional education is not wasted, they reason, for after a few years of pushing a baby carriage, their alumnae will join the working force. Instead of a career preceding marriage, the career now often follows marriage and motherhood. But one way or another, a career there will be. It is no longer controversial, nor does it loom large in the lives of married women, but there it is. Husbands, families, employers, and society at large seem to have accepted it.

At least the secular world has. The Catholic wife, even if she

* The National Industrial Conference Board reported in the fall of 1959 that one-third of the American labor force is made up of women—*14% more of them than at the peak employment of women in World War II.* Of these, over one-half are married and almost one-fifth of them are in the most likely child-bearing years—the years between twenty and thirty-four. Child-bearing among the younger ones in this group has increased seventy percent since 1940.

subscribes basically to the same value system as her non-Catholic friends, cannot follow this typical pattern—that is, if she is normally fertile—without running counter to some important religious values and precepts of the moral law. Since the problem of birth control was discussed at length in the previous chapter, no more need be said here, except to emphasize again the conflict in which Catholics who try unthinkingly to follow the pattern of contemporary society inevitably involve themselves. The average Catholic woman knows that she cannot plan on finishing childbearing at 26.1 years; she has simply to face the fact that if this is to be the prevailing pattern in the United States she will have to be out of step with the pattern.

And yet she may face what appears to be an impossible dilemma. The less a husband's wage is expected by itself to support a family and the more children a Catholic couple have, the more pressure there is on the Catholic wife to work. The expression "to make ends meet" may conceal, it is true, a multitude of luxuries; still, the more it is assumed that the average family will have two breadwinners, the harder it becomes for the husband to give his family everything which comes under the American definition of a decent standard of living. There are certain ramifications here for Catholics which cannot be ignored. Since Catholics do not subscribe to a secular system of education and since a Catholic system costs additional money, the Catholic family bears a heavy burden. There are mothers who work (or so they say) solely for the purpose of paying their children's tuition in a Catholic high school. And if a family has several children in high school at the same time, the tuition bill is no trifling sum. Especially if there are also young children in the home, the wisdom of encouraging the mother to work to make a Catholic high-school education possible for her teen-agers may be questioned, since it might be argued that by so doing she is sacrificing other important values in the home and family. This—to say the least—is a debatable question, incapable of easy resolution. Implicit in it are the difficulties in which Catholic women are involved in a society geared to change, in which they try valiantly to maintain their traditional values. They find themselves caught, most often unwittingly, in situations in which to preserve one value (in this instance, a Catholic secondary-school education) they may have to jeopardize another (the Catholic tradition of the mother as heart of the family and co-ordinator of all activities in the home.)

IS A MOTHER'S PLACE IN THE HOME?

It might be wise to point out here that the Catholic value system does not provide a simple "yes" or "no" answer to the question of wives' and mothers' working outside the home. A wife and mother who works outside the family without detriment to her core role has no reason for qualms of conscience, nor has anyone the right to make her feel guilty. She may be filling her role in Christian marriage as successfully and as forthrightly as a woman in a more traditional culture whose prerogatives and duties in the home are much more clearly defined and accepted. What is important here, however, are recent tendencies and trends. Should day nurseries be increased? Should housekeeping helps and labor-saving devices be encouraged so that it will be easier for married women to work? Or are these very benefits detrimental to the family in the long run, since they make the mother's exit from the home more likely and thus deprive the children of her *presence*—an intangible for which, apparently, there is no substitute? These are ticklish questions which bother a great many thoughtful people. It is true that the subject of mothers' working—as well as all topics in the realm of changing sex roles—is so emotionally suffused that only the rare person can discuss it with complete dispassion. Nonetheless it would seem that there are certain people who counsel caution in improving conditions for the mother who is forced to work, not because they are unsympathetic to her plight, but because they see steps toward alleviating her difficulties as tacit social encouragement of all mothers to take outside jobs. It is a common social irony that medicinal remedies for a pathological condition in time come to be looked upon as healthful food for the normal.*

Is it only financial pressure that makes a wife work? Here it might be helpful to recall what Dr. Lawrence K. Frank noted, that we know so little actually about the twelve million working wives that we can only hazard a guess as to the inner motivations and objective situations which cause them to take outside jobs. Probably very few people would claim today that financial considerations are the only ones which cause a wife to work. In fact, some working wives are ready to agree with some social critics that their working is not particularly economic at all. When they take into account the expenses connected with their working—household help, nursery school fees, a larger food budget (since they don't have time to hunt for bargains or use the longer-cooking, less costly cuts of meat), their own personal expenses, including a larger wardrobe than is required at home, transportation and lunches—they may agree that the additional income provided for the family at the end of the month is negligible.

Why then do wives and mothers work? One reason social commentators have agreed upon is that loneliness often drives women from the domestic scene. Chesterton and other writers on the multifold role of wife and mother may be right in saying her situation is challenging, but their analysis is incomplete if they omit the very real consideration that it is also a lonely one. Five children under the age of seven may keep a woman moving; they do not, however, provide her with conversation. She is left alone on the domestic front—giving, giving to the children—with no one to share her day-to-day worries and cares; nobody with whom to make "small talk," no one to dispel her anxieties as soon as she puts them into words. The root problem of loneliness in

TRue

* The unintended effects of social reforms are frequently puzzling. If, for example, we make acceptance of the illegitimate child easier, and if out of charity we make socially forgivable the sin of its parents, do we do away with the important social control that deterred young people from premarital relations? Similarly, if we allow the working mother to deduct the cost of household help from her income tax are we in effect penalizing the wife who stays at home?

the nuclear family is often overlooked, and well-meaning people who point out the fact that the mother's daily work requires more intelligence, skill and talent than the file clerk's may be mistaking the real issue. It is precisely because housework is so gruelling and lonely that women want to flee from it.

As David Riesman noted,[5] during the last war the pursuit of sociability attracted many women to factory jobs. The most monotonous-seeming job acquired glamor when it was performed in company with other women, with similar experiences, eager to escape from their loneliness, and happy to have companionship. It is a mistake to treat most women as intellectuals and to feel one has won the day simply by proving that their domestic chores are at least as provocative of thinking as the majority of jobs in commerce and industry. Most women are not intellectuals: they merely want somebody to talk to. And if life in general has moved out of the home, they want to move out after it.

The current development of suburbia may have interesting results in holding back the tide of working wives and mothers. *The Organization Man* gives us a graphic picture of *Kaffeeklatsching* in Park Forest.[6] Are the women in these new suburbs discovering the values of companionship and *gemütlickheit* right on the home front? If the housewife of twenty years ago felt she was neglecting her duty unless she stuck to the grim business of attending to her work and allowed recreation to be reserved for a few clearly defined hours a week, the modern housewife in the new suburbs has no such qualms. Entertaining is no longer formal, and neighbors who feel free to drop in at any time of day to consume endless cups of Instant may be filling a woman's need for adult female companionship. Such socializing in the suburbs not only helps to supply some of the function of women relatives in the old-time extended family in participating in practical tasks—sewing curtains, freezing foods, baby-sitting—but may have a more significant function in providing the woman in the home with a relaxed, companionable setting for her work. (Naturally there is also cattiness and gossip, but most women would rather be party to it and suffer the consequences than be left alone with their thoughts.)

The phenomenon of wives and mothers working must be seen in terms of the whole social context, and thinkers who are worried about the effect working mothers may have on our society must think of their situation in terms of the whole. Neither legislation nor propaganda to the effect that mothers in the home are good for the nation will return women to the home unless the home starts supplying some of the satisfactions which working wives and mothers feel they are getting from their jobs.

Even if domestic conditions could be made ideal and wives and mothers given their just rewards in terms of prestige, social approval, and rewarding companionship in the home, a woman cannot be happy bringing up children and managing a household unless she is psychologically as well as spiritually attuned to self-sacrifice. Well-meaning efforts to make life richer for wives and mothers have been jejeune to the extent that they neglect to take into consideration that for the good of the family a woman cannot have a role identical with her husband's. Not masculine whim (no matter what Simone de Beauvoir might say) but nature made woman the bearer and nurturer of children. Not only personal psychological risk but injury to the welfare of the offspring is done when a woman acts as if her duties as mother can be laid aside when she punches a time-clock. The argument "My husband is not expected to stay home with the children, why should I?" usually reveals a refusal to accept the realities of biology ("Nature didn't make your husband capable of bearing a child!") as well as the realities of this hard world we live in (we cannot ever do everything we want, and every good thing exacts a consequent sacrifice). The professional woman who argues that she goes to work and leaves her preschool children with domestic hired help because "otherwise I might resent my children," may be merely mouthing a popular rationalization of her position. That in certain cases individual mothers would resent their children because they have in reality already rejected them and that therefore it might be appreciably better for the children if their mothers do go to work is undoubtedly true. But what is pathological cannot be presented as normal. The normal woman does not resent her children, although it is perfectly normal for a mother at times to experience healthy exasperation with them. (The fact that she has a normal need of time for herself so that her children do not devour her is a subject considered in the next chapter.) It is rather silly if she is made to feel that her very acceptance of them and her willingness to stay at home to raise them smacks of abnormality. Although all sympathy should be given to the woman who is emotionally immature or a psychological cripple and therefore incapable of a sustained relationship with her offspring, her aberration cannot be raised to the level of an ideal.*

(Here we might mention parenthetically that while the simple fact of a wife's working is not opposed to the Christian value system, the sort of thinking which considers the woman's interests in isolation without referring to the common good of the family most definitely is. According to the Catholic marriage ceremonial, the couple are told: "Sacrifice is usually difficult and irksome. Only love can make it easy; and perfect love can make it a joy. We are willing to give in proportion as we love, and when love is perfect the sacrifice is complete." The woman sacrificing her egotistical desires for the good of her child usually reaps a harvest of joy. For most women with normal maternal feelings such sacrifice is not necessarily heroic. As one mother, formerly a professional woman, said: "I'm not aware of making any great sacrifice to stay home with my baby. Being with him is eminently rewarding, and I wouldn't have it any other way." In motherhood altruism is usually its own reward.)

So far it seems that society has not come up with any adequate substitute for a mother in the home. Arguments that pre-cooked food, community nurseries, professional household help, and so on, would render the mother's working outside the home less

* Ironically, some women who go on working for fear of resenting their children seem oblivious, although they are adept child psychologists themselves, to the personality and the qualifications of the hired houseworker with whom they leave their children for the greater part of the day.

hazardous to the health and comfort of the family still leave untouched the central issue of the child. External helps may make marriage and a career more workable for the childless wife or for the mother of grown—or fairly grown—children, but no replacement has thus far been found for the mother of preschool children. Unless there is a sudden change in the way we evaluate the emotional and psychological needs of the young, it is extremely doubtful that we shall ever succeed in putting them on an efficient, factory-like schedule. Now that we are efficiency-minded we are still faced with the problem of the child whose value is traditionally supra-efficient. The working mother whose situation depends on a day nursery's caring for her child still faces the fact that when he catches a common cold and has to stay in bed, her arrangements are upset. His very dependence precludes efficiency.

It would be wrong to imply that working mothers inevitably ruin their offspring. Contrary to popular opinion, no reliable sociological study has produced sufficient evidence to prove that the fact of the mother's working causes delinquency.* As Tom McConnon's recent memoir, *Angels in Hell's Kitchen,* reminds us, there were always poor women like his mother, "who toiled all day as a chambermaid and worked at home until after midnight to keep her children clean, neat and well-behaved. A heroic woman and a devout one, who prayed every step of the way to and from her job, Mrs. McConnon held her family together by love and by sheer strength of character."[7] Many of these women —and of course it is possible to glamorize them and forget that not all of them were either competent or successful mothers— seem to have proved that a mother can work outside of the home without injuring her children. But such women worked precisely because they were mothers and not to escape from their primary

* Sheldon and Eleanor Glueck, who have done extensive research on delinquency, while they seem to have found a clear causative connection between delinquency and the presence of an over-strict father and a mother who either rejects the child or whose affection is unstable and sporadic, have shown no relationship between the mother's working and delinquent children.

job; their economic plight and consequent wage earning were a clear-cut necessity. The phenomenon of today's working middle-class woman has different aspects and cannot be evaluated so readily.*

WOMEN WHO SHOULD WORK

There are wives who work because they need the money, those who work because they are lonely, those who work because they do not enjoy domesticity and those who may be rejecting their children. What about the women—the married women—who work because they have a particular talent or a special training which allows them to make a contribution to society which is of prime importance? With the present shortage of teachers, registered nurses, and social workers, married women with experience in these fields may well heed social pressure which urges them to return to their work. It could even be argued that the married woman who has a professional competence which society needs is being unduly selfish if she does not make the effort to place her skill and training at the disposal of people other than her family. This is especially true if her children are grown and her household responsibilities take up only a fraction of her time. At this point, even the conservative would probably agree with Edith Stein's thinking that "whenever the circle of a woman's household is too small to permit the full use of her gifts, it is only reasonable

* Phyllis McGinley doubts that any woman can successfully combine marriage and a career. In her wise and witty book, *The Province of the Heart* (New York: Viking Press, 1959), she writes that "when I speak of *careers* I do not refer to *jobs*. There is no doubt at all that a clever and efficient woman—one with the common number of hands—can manage both marriage and a job. All it takes is vitality, brains, luck, superb health, tact, imagination, and a willing heart. But then a job is something which has vacations and sick-leaves. It can be left at any time by giving notice, and can even be picked up again later on. It is a way of earning extra money or using up extra time or energy. It is not a whole way of life. A career, on the contrary, needs the whole woman. It asks all the creative force, the love and pains and fervor, which other women spend on their households." (pp. 175-176) A job, Phyllis McGinley feels, can be subordinated to marriage and motherhood, but a career is a whole way of life and must inevitably, if followed by the married woman, "imperil her home" (to borrow Edith Stein's phrase).

for her to reach beyond it, as long as her work outside does not imperil her home, the communion of parents and children.[8]

Added to the possibility that, especially in the so-called "empty nest" period of her life, a woman may be personally happier if she is working outside the home and as a consequence may make life less difficult for her husband, is the fact that in our culture today there is little prestige attached to volunteer work.[9] The leisured woman, who in a prior age engaged in many volunteer activities which called for her skill, today would find that professionals have taken over her role. The woman who finds herself assisting with fund-raising drives and little else may find her volunteer work considerably less than soul-satisfying. It is no wonder then that she turns to paid work, not really because she is money-hungry but because she wants to do a job that is rewarding in terms of personal satisfaction and social approval, as well as evocative of her highest skills.

That there are some women whose children are grown who should be encouraged to brush up their skills and return to their jobs does not mean that this is every woman's solution. Nor should the fact that a family of adolescents no longer need the physical care of the mother make her forget that she still may have a job, and a very important one, in the home. As a converted radical feminist, whose own experiences in raising a family as well as working outside the home caused her to rediscover the traditional role of the mother, writes: "Every home, it seems to me, needs one person in it who isn't under compulsion to be a certain place at a certain time, and in these days of universal insecurity a middle-aged woman isn't wasting her time if she is maintaining a haven for its underwriters and for the fledglings who are preparing to underwrite or maintain future havens."[10] Perhaps the mother's role as co-ordinator and integrator, as the person who is always "there," looms especially large during the very years of adolescence when so many mothers are most inclined to feel they can safely leave the home without doing their children any harm. Perhaps part-time work at this point in their lives would enable mothers to be at home with their children when they return from school and at the same time ease them into the future situation when they will have to get along without their children just as their children will have to do without them.

Women during the "empty nest" period should be urged more frequently to make the contribution to other wives and mothers for which they are eminently fitted. Isabel B. LaFollette has made a special effort to encourage older woman to share their housekeeping skills. Writing about her Woman's Service Exchange she says: "In our promotion I have constantly aimed at the dignity and value of using the home-making skills where they are so badly needed, and have hoped that having the women coming to the same office and to the same counsellor as those seeking other types of work would give the personal-service job the prestige it deserves."[11]

There are unfortunately few women who will work as a mother's assistant or housekeeping helper. Ideally there should be more women like the outstanding older woman who, while she receives a financial remuneration for her services, works mainly for the satisfaction she receives in assisting busy young mothers with their household jobs. This particular woman evidently thinks of herself with dignity and although she receives many job offers, she goes to work only for those mothers whom she feels have enough children so that they really need her. Her competent presence one day a week in a number of homes in a certain suburb makes it possible for the busy mother to get a day away from her children as well as to get some helpful advice on her household tasks. Provided such "mothers' assistants" are well-balanced people and not busybodies they are invaluable, and one can hope that their numbers will increase.

THE HUSBAND OF THE WORKING WIFE

One important person has been overlooked in this discussion of the working wife, and that is her husband. How do husbands feel about having their wives take outside jobs? Like all the other questions that have been considered, this one has no simple answer. A typical husband's attitude toward a working wife has, it is true, changed over the years. A few decades ago a respectable, "manly" man expected that he would support his wife; society thought him a "lazy bum" if he did not. Unless he was an incapacitated invalid, having his wife go to work was a crushing humiliation. But times have changed, and men with them. A man with a working wife is no longer accused of improvidence or laziness, and he can agree to her working without losing his dignity or self-respect in the eyes of his peers. The young father may want his wife to stay home with the children, but he is no longer penalized by society if she does not.

But not every man behaves like the average man, and there are some men today who cannot have their wives work without suffering some impairment of their ego. A middle-aged woman who takes a job because her husband is not doing well financially may find that her action tends to worsen his already low morale. Only great tact and delicacy on her part will keep alive his self-respect.

While in most marriages, if the relationship between husband and wife is good and they view each other with mutual respect, the wife can go to work without causing a major cataclysm, there are some marriages in which happiness seems to have a more precarious balance and can be upset by the woman's taking a job outside the home. Whatever the source of a husband's inferiority feelings in such cases, they can be re-aroused by the wife's working. There are some women who realize this fact and as a consequence they refrain from taking an outside job even though their presence at home is not necessary. They realize that marriage is their basic vocation and they are willing to make the sacrifice of their professional work to keep a happy home.

On the other hand, there are husbands who recognize that their wives would be more content, once the children are grown, if they returned to their jobs. These husbands are willing to help their wives adjust to a new schedule, and they go out of their way to encourage them to take what may well be a frightening step out of the home back into the business world.

In a marriage where the channels of communication between

the spouses are open, where the husband and wife have been able to share each other's ambitions and dreams, the woman considering work outside the home has a decided advantage. Not only will the husband give her tacit encouragement to use her talents on behalf of the wider society, but by his active approval and interest in her work he will play a major part in her professional success. Such a woman lives in the reality of her marriage even in her hours away from home, and her husband's love is a source of strength for everything she accomplishes.

NOTES

1. Sidonie M. Gruenberg and Hilda Sidney Krech, *The Many Lives of Modern Woman* (New York: Doubleday, 1952).
2. Worth Tuttle Hedden, "People in Skirts," in *Women Today,* edited by Elizabeth Bragdon (New York: Bobbs-Merrill, 1953), p. 50.
3. *Potentialities of Women in the Middle Years,* edited by Gross (Michigan State University, 1956), p. 20.
4. Statistics from *ibid.,* p. 23.
5. David Riesman, Nathan Glazer and Reuel Denny, *The Lonely Crowd* (Garden City, New York: Doubleday Anchor Books, 1955), p. 310.
6. William H. Whyte, Jr., *The Organization Man* (New York: Simon and Schuster, 1956), Part VII.
7. Orville Prescott, "Books of the Times," *The New York Times,* December 2, 1959.
8. John M. Oesterreicher, "Edith Stein on Womanhood," *Integrity,* Vol. VII, No. 12 (September 1953).
9. Riesman et al., *op. cit.,* p. 322.
10. Hedden, *op. cit.,* pp. 61, 62.
11. Isabel B. LaFollette writing in *Potentialities of Women in the Middle Years,* p. 165.

7

The Mother: Nine Pairs of Hands

A PRIEST was remarking that he used to feel embarrassed when he was celebrating a Nuptial Mass. It seemed that throughout the Mass the Church pointed a finger at the bride and went to great pains to admonish her. When he came to the Nuptial Blessing after the *Pater Noster*, he was especially glad that it was in Latin and that the bride possibly did not catch the words. For, he felt, it seemed grossly unfair that it was she of whom everything was expected. "Let her follow the model of holy women: let her be dear to her husband like Rachel; wise like Rebecca; long-lived and faithful like Sara. Let the author of sin work none of his evil deeds within her; let her ever keep the faith and the commandments. Let her be true to one wedlock and shun all sinful embraces; let her strengthen weakness by stern discipline. Let her be grave in demeanor, honorable for her modesty, learned in heavenly doctrine, fruitful in children."

It was, the priest continued, as if the Church felt that everything depended upon the wife. And was this fair? What about her equal rights? And didn't her husband have an obligation to be virtuous, too? That is the way he used to reason, he said; but then one day it occurred to him: the Church was not being arbitrary and unjust toward woman. The Church was just recognizing reality. In marriage the greater part does depend on the wife; she is the one who perhaps most needs the prayers.

Of course, not ecclesiastical legislation, but God, made woman the bearer and nurturer of the young. The man risks neither his life nor his health in fulfilling his role in conception: the wife may risk both in pregnancy and childbirth. True enough, an expectant father who is overly sympathetic may share his wife's morning sickness, but it is the woman who suffers the great inconveniences and discomforts of pregnancy, the pangs of childbirth, and the main burden of infant care. Traditionally, it has been the mother who kept the home stable. Surveys of mixed marriages have pointed up anew the fact that it is the mother's religion which is embraced by the child, her influence which predominates. Promiscuity and alcoholism when they occur in the mother have much more drastic effects on the family than when these same conditions are habits of the father. And while a good mother can safeguard the children from the vices and worldly dissipations of the father, only an unusual man could keep life from being sordid for the children when his wife has gone astray.

On the other hand, during the last decade there has been greater emphasis on the role of the father in the upbringing of the children. Psychiatrists like Dr. Strecker have expressed their worry over the way women in America have ruined their sons; the rejected among the draftees in World War II and the psychoneurotics who revealed themselves on the battlefield were chiefly the results of momism, these psychiatrists claimed. Mom left to herself wreaked havoc on American manhood, and her children need their father to take a more prominent place on the family scene. The young father of our middle class who takes an active part in the care and raising of the children is not only responding to the needs of his wife in servantless America but also is making a conscious effort to fulfill his role in the lives of the children. Father is no longer supposed to be merely the good provider or the stern disciplinarian who steps into the scene occasionally as a wrathful judge. He is supposed to be a companion to his children and to provide his boys with the model of manhood. But the contemporary father does not know exactly how he is supposed to act. His critics would say that while he helps his wife more, she respects him less than her mother (certainly her grandmother) did her spouse, and while he spends more time with the children than his forebears did with theirs they respect him less, too. The defenders of the contemporary father could say that he himself is the victim of his up-bringing and that he should be commended for trying to take the active interest in his children that his father failed to take in him. Since the dicta of child psychology change as the wind blows, the modern father cannot be expected to be less confused than the experts, and if, in spite of the absence of a clear policy, he tries to get to know his children, plays ball with his young sons and takes the whole family on outings, his efforts are all to the good. The defenders of the modern father can claim, further, that he is helping to remedy the effect of exclusive feminine influence on the young, and that boys especially are going to benefit from having him present to them the pattern of the adult male, which the three or four former American generations—at least in the urban areas—could only view from afar.

DRUDGERY OR A LIFE OF EASE?

But with Daddy changing diapers and drying dishes, can Mother relax and feel that her life is much easier than woman's used to be? There are conflicting answers to this question. People who are concerned with measuring the work of the housewife and mother claim that she still puts in a very long work-week, in spite of the frozen foods and prepared mixes which have lessened the time she spends in cooking and baking, and the vacuum cleaners, dishwashers, automatic clothes washers and dryers which expedite her task of keeping house and wearing apparel immaculate. As her explanation of this paradox, one woman pointed out: "We are not yet, in America, using labor-saving devices to decrease labor, but only to increase standards!"[1] And two other women, agreeing that the American housewife is given impossibly high standards, comment that in women's magazines "there is never a glimpse of worn furnishings, or finger marks on the woodwork, or left-overs being served."[2] The American woman is expected to keep her house and children perfect and presentable at all times, and automatic washing machines mean merely that she changes their clothes many times more frequently than did the mother of a few decades ago. The American woman is run ragged keeping up appearances, and the atmosphere of her house is less restful and her pace of living less leisurely than the household presided over by the pioneer woman or the Victorian wife.

On the other hand, other critics point out that the wife at home today keeps herself so busy precisely because she isn't busy enough! More than one compulsive housekeeper has been noted who scrubs the cellar walls and wages a relentless war to keep everything in place—even heading the nails in her husband's tool kit in the same direction!* Of course, the truly compulsive housekeeper would manifest her neurotic compulsion in anything she did, wherever she was. But there are other housewives, not really compulsive personalities, who seem to throw themselves into housekeeping as if they felt they had to justify their existence to themselves and to others. These housewives are usually childless or mothers of only children. Their intense preoccupation with housecleaning becomes their defense against what they may feel is the implied criticism of mothers with large families or wives who have a full-time job in addition to their household tasks. That these women tire themselves unnecessarily and that they spend too much time in housework is often revealed when they finally take outside jobs or a heavy load of volunteer activity, and then discover that their household runs just as efficiently as when they devoted every waking moment to it.

Women today who complain about the drudgery of housework are often really complaining about the lack of creative achievement in modern housekeeping. The old-fashioned housewife who could point with pride to shelves full of preserves, who could outdo her neighbor in producing different kinds of relishes, and

* It is to these under-occupied housewives that two British authors must be referring when they write: "Something must be wrong in a social organization in which men may die a premature death from coronary thrombosis, as a result of overwork and worry, while their wives and widows organize themselves to protest against their own lack of opportunities to work."[3]

who could bless the breakfast table with hot apple pie, may have known more real drudgery, but she also may have known more personal satisfaction and received more social recognition. She could think of herself as an accomplished person, indispensable to her husband who could not duplicate her achievements. The wife today may have little incentive to get up in the morning to make breakfast for her husband when she knows he can add water to the frozen orange juice, boil water for the instant coffee, and pour the cornflakes into a bowl as skillfully as she can.

Observing the pleasure of women who spend much time doing their own baking or cooking their own special dishes for a large family, one realizes that it is often the boredom of today's cooking which is really fatiguing. Although they may not have more strength than other women, they bring to their tasks a zest which seems to multiply their physical energy. It is ironic that today the women who enjoy cooking are the ones who, because of budgetary considerations, have to seek out inexpensive recipes and experiment with herbs and spices, while the women with well-filled pocketbooks who could afford lavish cooking with an unending supply of butter, cream, and wines bore themselves by continually using prepared gourmet foods.

There is another reason, however, that some women find housekeeping an almost insupportable burden. They were never trained as children to perform the simplest household tasks, and their acquisition of the needed skills in adult life is sometimes painful in the extreme. The prospect of preparing a simple meal is a worry, and the thought of serving a luncheon to guests appalling. Perhaps they are daughters of women who were not good housekeepers, or perhaps their mothers never let them into the kitchen. Whatever the cause for their ineptitude at housekeeping, their lack of skill nullifies any possible pleasure they might have had in it.

Currently, however, there is a rather amusing rationalization for the unskilled housewife. How often has it been said that So-and-So is not a good housekeeper "because she's an intellectual"? Women who a generation or two ago would have been thought of as social failures because they lacked the talent to make a home, along with the imagination to cook and decorate well, now have the convenient excuse that they are too intelligent to be good at these things. That lack of skill in housework is no sign at all of the presence of a superior brain is borne out by the fact that some of the best housekeepers are also the most brilliant women. No one is arguing, needless to say, that a woman needs to be an intellectual and excel in abstract thinking to be a good housewife; what one is saying is that intellectual ability and mental cultivation do not correlate negatively with the ability to perform practical household jobs. The talent to write a novel can coexist with the talent for preparing beef stroganoff, and even a woman philosopher can find no excuse in her speculative ability for not getting the dirt out of the corners.

It is not the amount of education but her psychological attitudes and the initial orientation in the home by her mother that places a woman on the road to housekeeping failure or success. One sometimes hears an intellectual, mother of perhaps two children, complain that her household work in a small apartment prevents her from even having time to read and that she and her husband have no opportunity to go out together. While her account of her plight may be accurate, it remains true, nevertheless, that plenty of women with similarly developed intellects and like economic and social conditions manage to be good mothers and adequate housekeepers without having to spend all day cleaning house. They can keep up with their reading and intellectual interests, and manage a night out with their husbands occasionally without breaking their budgets. The difference between them and the woman whose case is cited seems not to be one of intellectual powers or degree of education, but one of motivation, personality, values, and a practical orientation to housework. Granted that there may be many variables involved, there is sufficient evidence that for an intelligent woman with sufficient respect for housekeeping, enough motivation to want to make a good home for her husband and children, and a set of values in which she has confidence, the discipline she has received through a solid education can be a positive aid. As one housewife with graduate training remarked: "I think my education was a positive help to housekeeping. For instance, research work taught me to organize my tasks, and the ability to think problems through is a great aid in running a household."

Returning to the initial question—is the modern housewife overworked—the answer seems to depend on the particular woman and her special circumstances. A woman with a new baby, three other preschool children, a house to keep and a garden to tend may well be busy every waking moment, and her husband, if he takes over on an occasional Saturday to give her a day off, may well wonder how she can stand the terrific pace. With all her labor-saving devices she needs every ounce of energy she can muster. Most of all she might wish she had nine pairs of hands. With one nose in need of wiping, one baby in need of changing, one toddler's head to be released from between chair rungs, one shoe lace in need of tying, a telephone to be answered, and the cereal on the stove needing to be stirred, she may well feel she does not have the manual equipment for her job—especially if at the same time one bottom needs to be slapped. The busy mother of a large family of young children may feel so occupied every moment of the day that she falls into bed at night completely exhausted. She may well have to budget her energy and cut corners in housework by deciding what are the important things to be done and conserving her energy for them.

If she is sensible she will not deny herself a spare half-hour daily to rest or to read while the children take their naps (that is, if she is fortunate enough to have all their schedules synchronizing), nor should she feel guilty if she occasionally leaves a half-tidied house and goes out for an afternoon. As one mother of several toddlers put it: "I think it's more important for my effect on the children that I get a few hours off occasionally than that I work constantly. If I waited until I was completely caught up with my work before I went out, I'd never get there. It seems to me important to keep alive my own personality. I don't think a mother of very young children can go in for very many outside activities, but what you do take an interest in you are concerned about not as an escape from housework and children but because these activities are a part of you."

Especially does social pressure make it difficult for a mother of many children to relax. In spite of the Baby Boom, mothers of large families still feel on the defensive. As one such mother put it, "The only child across the street can go around with holes in his T shirt, and the two children next door can look like orphans, and their mothers get away with it. But I'm always aware that if my children look less than perfect, people will say: 'See what happens when you have a large family: the children are neglected!' " Another mother of a big family who tries very hard to keep a clean, attractive house remarked with chagrin: "When you have a lot of children, other people think you don't care what your house looks like. We have one woman in the neighborhood who annoys me. The day she cleans her house she sends her only son down to my house to play, since she wants to keep *her* house clean!"

Not only are mothers of big families sensitive to public opinion, but usually they are aware that they must make their home reasonably attractive lest their children feel deprived. More than one adult who grew up in a large family has expressed his commitment to the small-family ideal. Intelligent mothers of big families, in order to avoid this reaction on the part of their offspring, feel they have to make an added effort to be successful homemakers. Achieving the goal of efficient housekeeping without sacrificing other values is indeed a tall order.

The modern mother of a young, growing family seems to take a different attitude toward keeping alive her own interests outside of her home and children than did the mother of a generation or two ago. Several young mothers have remarked that they disapproved of the attitude taken by their own mothers that a woman was supposed to be completely devoted to her home and family, and if she had time left over for any outside activities it was a sign that she had neglected some duty. Women today feel that this course of action backfired. They point to their own mothers who are completely at loose ends now that their children are grown, who feel that they are no longer needed, who had developed no other interests apart from the children to share with their husbands and now seem to have little in common with them, and who did not bother to keep up their personal friendships during their active lives and as a consequence suffer from great loneliness in their old age.

Years ago society supported the mother in her feeling that she should have no interests outside her household, but society today definitely expects a woman, especially if she has had a college education, to have some form of leisure-time activity and take at least some small part in community affairs. Whether her outside activity consists in collecting for the March of Dimes or serving on a committee for the P.T.A. does not seem to matter, but unless she is involved in something she is likely to feel guilty. In fact, so great is the pressure in some circles and some communities to take on a list of volunteer activities and to serve on innumerable committees that the mother of a large family may need to muster all her courage to say "No" when she feels that she cannot get further involved in these affairs without slighting her family duties. The mother of a large family who participates in numerous enterprises and has a long list of memberships after her name—unless she is the Superwoman—has to let something go, and it is unfortunate if the "something" vitally concerns her children.* However, this is a question of balance, and the sensible woman who can assess properly her own time and strength can take on one or two activities outside her home (especially choosing those which are in keeping with her own personality and interests or to which she can make some special contribution) without making her husband or children the sacrificial victims.

But what about the mother of a large family who honestly cannot see her way clear to engaging in activities or interests out-

* It seems an inevitable human experience that one generation always over-reacts against the previous generation's practices. The women today whose outside activity is a protest against their mothers' preoccupation with domesticity may well raise children in turn who will have more sympathy for their grandmothers' way of life!

side the home, particularly when the children are small or when there is continual illness in the family? Dr. Harding seems to present a prudent answer to her problem: "It must be admitted that the urgency of never-ending duties is sometimes so inescapable as to force the devoted mother, at least for some years, to make with open eyes the sacrifice of all other cultural interests. Yet even so her own personality development need not cease if she is able to realize an inner value which is served in serving her children. If she does what she does of her own free well, in loyalty to her own love or in the spirit of a deep acceptance of *her* way, she will not, when her children go, be left inert and empty, nor will she be compelled to demand emotional recompense from them."[4]

MATERNAL SLAVE OR DEVOURING MOTHER

There are mothers who keep their children in a sort of emotional slavery enchained to them by the bonds of their maternal sacrifice ("all I have done for you"). How does this happen? In some cases, in the beginning, the positions are reversed: it is the mother who is the strong one enchained by the weakness of her children. "The weak know no mercy. Their weakness makes demands on the strength of the strong until the last gasp, and the strong cannot turn to throw them off . . . But a mother who allows her children to enchain her too long will find the positions reversed—she becomes the weak one. When they grow up and cease to need her, she cannot let them go."[5]

Sometimes the very woman who prides herself on her maternal generosity faces the strongest temptation to enter a needless and dangerous servitude. She is the woman whom Dr. Harding describes as taking "no account of the rest of her personality" but who "forces herself into being the all-loving and all-giving mother of her ideal. By this attitude she forces her children always to be the recipients; they become not only all-receiving, but also all-taking."[6] The children are the victims of their mother's disordered maternal instinct; feeling that she has been cast in a role of heroic proportions, she throws herself into it, and apparently her children let her play it to the hilt. These are the children who, to the bystander, appear to be selfish little beasts, unconcerned about the devotion and goodness of their self-sacrificing mother. But she, not they, is the cause of their selfishness. She has misunderstood the demands of love and has forgotten that we are commanded to love others as we love ourselves. Her attitude toward herself lacks respect (she is the door-mat for her children) and it is no wonder that her love seems to fail to stimulate self-respect in her children and the ability to love their mother with respectful love in return. Speaking of overfond mothers, Eva Firkel writes: "This exclusive maternal love hides not infrequently unfulfilled desires, interior insecurity and aimlessness, a festering fear of life."[7]

There is another type of mother who is also over-identified with her children, but in a different way. Jung calls her the "devouring mother." Unlike the self-sacrificial mother who has encouraged her children "to walk all over her," the devouring mother appears to have the upper-hand. She is the one who feels that her maternity gives her the right to control the lives of her children. Her urge to dominate them is so complete that it militates against any recognition of them as personalities in their own right. The devouring mother does not admit that her children have the native human rights "to live their own lives and die their own deaths . . . to suffer as well as to enjoy."[8] They are her puppets, and by a tug of the string she expects to evoke the proper response in activity and emotion.

There are maternal egotists whose children become a mere projection of themselves. Such mothers show clearly that the experience of maternity *by itself* does not make a woman generous and altruistic. These are the mothers who, in their girlhood, were inclined to be self-centered. With marriage and the birth of children their self-centeredness enlarges, as it were, to take in their husband and children. If formerly they were interested in clothes for themselves, now they are interested in clothes for their children. If formerly they were inclined to seek compliments and displays of affection for themselves, they now seek them for their offspring.

Even women who are normally generous have to resist the temptation which motherhood brings to react as if their children were the only children in the world to be considered, and as if the rights of other human beings had to yield to the demands of their offspring. As one writer remarks: "A developed mother's love is deep and absorbing in nature, and it tends to canalize a general interest in children into an intense love of the mother's own children. For a time, at least, it is so absorbing that it tends to displace a general concern for children in the interest of the mother's own children . . ."[9] The mother can easily become like a bear ready to defend her cubs from every real or supposed attack of a hostile world.

There are other women, however, who never seem to fall into this temptation. The strong affection they feel for their own children does not exclude care for other people's offspring. They are the women of whom it is said that they love all children; whether or not they are their own. These mothers seem to be genuinely and altruistically maternal. They can admire other people's children, they are responsive to the needs of all children, and they seem to be able to use the experience they have acquired with their own children for the good of every child with whom they come in contact. Just as the maternal egotist can be the mother of a large family as well as the mother of two children or an only child, the maternal altruist may have a small family, a large family, or may even be childless.

This needs to be stressed in view of the normal Catholic concern with large families. Apparently, the number of children does not by itself determine the parents' reaction to them. There are only children who are rejected, and there are likewise children in large families who are deprived of love. An only child can be overindulged, but so can a mother overindulge a number of children. Likewise the ability to identify with the problems of other parents does not in the end seem to be determined by the number of children one has. One would normally expect that a mother of a big family would be able to understand better the problems involved in the raising of children. But strangely enough everyone has probably met mothers with a number of children who do not seem to understand or to sympathize with the difficulties parents of big families face today—especially if these other parents are in a different economic or social bracket. It would seem there are some women (extreme introverts and extreme extroverts?) who are psychologically incapable of identifying with the problems of others, of putting themselves into other people's places, and this fact remains true no matter how many times they themselves become mothers.

That people perhaps talk too glibly about motherhood as a deeply maturing experience is discussed by Dr. Esther Harding: "I have known women, mothers of several children, who have never become aware in any profound sense of what is taking place, who never realized in the least degree that an act of creation was being performed through them. Something more is needed beyond fulfilling the biological instinct and adapting to the needs of the child."[10]

That deprivation of affection or overindulgence is not determined ultimately by the number of children one has, and that the mother who is capable of a mature, balanced, respectful yet intense love for one child is usually capable of the same love for several, does not mean that children in a large family are to be treated as if they were only children. Obviously the mother of an only child has to create opportunities to teach him to share which would be a normal part of life in a large family. Obviously, too, children in a big family have a certain security in numbers. The mother leaving them with a sitter may not have to take the same steps to reassure them as would the mother of one child. Pitfalls and problems arise in both situations, and the conscientious mother may have to be especially careful not to over-compensate her child or children for the particular weakness she may feel to be present in her family situation. Thus the mother of many children may wear herself out giving her children attention for fear lest each one suffer from being one of so many; while the mother of an only child may find herself being too strict with him out of fear that he become spoiled or selfish.

The number of children as well as the social and economic situation of a particular family has an important bearing on the child-rearing practices to be adopted. This is a fact of common sense that has too frequently been overlooked. Thus, most parents do not seem to be as aware as his fellow experimental psychologists that Dr. Arnold Gesell's famous studies of normal development in children were made in an upper-middle-class environment with families of few children. His findings do not necessarily apply to children in a different kind of environment, nor can they be considered as the norm for a family of quite different composition. It would be foolish for a mother without servants and with a big family to adapt as her standards the ones followed by the "Gesell" mother with two children and a maid.*

Of course, it is Dr. Spock and not Dr. Gesell who currently is the oracle on child care. He advises mothers to follow their own common sense, and in a television program on raising children he went so far in his efforts to free them from excessive dependence on the expert as to tell them that if they personally believe in spanking, and they happen to pick up a book by a child expert who does not believe in spanking, to throw away the book: that particular expert is not for them. Experts in child care today seem to be the first ones to admit that theories and methods seem to come in cycles. It was noted on the same program that whereas a few years ago parents were cautioned to raise their children completely free from fears, the experts today see this as a dangerous goal; for the child free from all fear is also a child free from conscience. The inculcation of values implies a healthy respect for sanctions, and it is impossible to teach the good without pointing out that there is evil and that evil brings punishment.

* This is especially worth noting since Dr. Gesell was studying not what child behavior should be, but what child behavior is. He made no pretense of writing a Gospel for mothers to follow, and mothers of a large family who find their children behaving differently in some respects from the Gesell norm have no reason to think they have evidence that something is wrong with their children.

The mother who is able to use the thinking of the experts in a balanced, healthy way is the mother who is a balanced, emotionally mature person herself. It would seem that only the immature woman would expect that she could make a perfect job of raising her child; only the immature woman would set such an unattainable ideal for herself. The mature woman who is conscientious will try her best, but she knows that her own personality failings will have their effect on her children; she knows furthermore that, try as she will, she cannot protect them from all feelings of inadequacy or insecurity. She accepts them, and she helps her children to accept them, as the normal, inevitable condition of life. She knows that the over-protected child—the child who is never allowed to experience fear or frustration or unhappiness—will be totally unprepared for what his future will bring. The insecurity he will know when he steps into the real world from the ideal world in which his mother has placed him will probably equal, if not surpass, the insecurity of the child who was prematurely exposed to difficulties too intricate for him to cope with or to sorrows too big for a child's heart to know. Balanced maternal love not only protects but strengthens; it safeguards the child from the weight that would crush him, but it seeks to make him able to face the responsibilities of life and the tests which increase with his years.

The Christian mother who is an integrated person accepts the truths of her faith as part of herself. She accepts original sin as a factor in her own make-up as well as a reality in the life of her child. She avoids a naturalism which would see the child merely as a creature naturally inclined toward the good with no impulses which need to be curbed. The Christian mother knows there is a limit to permissiveness: that the child left to himself will not inevitably choose what is good. However, she is also aware of the necessity of the deeper permissiveness which allows and encourages the child to grow to be what God has destined him to become. For she is aware of the uniqueness of her child, the individuality of her children. She respects each child's own grace, each child's gift. She comes to know as well as her own each child's faults, each child's weaknesses. If she is attracted to one of her children more than the others, if she finds one child especially difficult, another child particularly compatible, without denying her own emotional reaction, she nonetheless seeks to respect and to love each child as he is.

Parents sometimes, in the way in which they compare their children, reveal that they somehow or other expect brothers and sisters all to respond in the same way to the same treatment. Children of the same parents as they are, brothers and sisters are nonetheless quite different; the genes they received from their parents are capable of multitudinous combinations. Unless they are identical twins, siblings start life with a different hereditary base which, physical though it is, influences their behavior, temperament, predominant fault, inclination to particular virtues, etc. The Christian parent remembering that grace builds on nature acknowledges the different natural base of each child and is careful to consider the child's nature in directing his moral and spiritual training. Moreover, recognition of psychological differences among brothers and sisters would keep the parent from becoming unduly upset when one child fails to conform to the pattern of his docile older sisters or brothers. The maverick seems to experience special difficulties in a pious family if he is unmoved by the religious practices which appeal to the others. Then the parents have to seek out his special gift.

The Christian mother has to have confidence in her authority. In an age of family democracy, when it is popular to advocate allowing children to formulate their own rules of behavior, she might consider the words of one psychiatrist, Dr. Abraham Myerson: "It is my belief that at first the parent should be the benevolent absolute ruler of the state, since the infant has no judgment or knowledge. At two or three, perhaps at four, a constitutional monarchy ought to be set up with rules and rights for both sides, but with the power still in the hands of the parent. At puberty the parents become heads of a republic, since in height, strength, beauty and intelligence—in fact, in all save experience—they are rapidly reaching second place. And sooner or later parents and children alike become fellow citizens. Happy is the home where this transition of status takes place gracefully, happy the home where the ever-changing theories of publicity-seeking authorities on child development are excluded in the name of science and sense!"[11] In these homes parents are not afraid to dominate or to punish; they are not afraid to use the authority which is theirs, but at the same time they endeavor to diminish their authority and to allow the children more freedom as they develop and as they show that they have learned how to use their liberty.

The mature woman is self-confident without being self-complacent; the mature Christian mother is confident in her ability to raise her children, drawing on the grace of the Sacrament in which she and her husband live out their union. Her trust in God and the grace of her state as it equips her to bring up her children is enhanced by her humility, her consciousness of her own faults and weaknesses, and especially the sinful wilfulness which may cause her to have a blind spot in the vision in which she sees her children in God. For, the Christian mother ought to be humbly aware that not so much what she does, but what *she is,* is in the last analysis her revelation of God to her children. "When a woman brings a child into the world, she can no longer take the easy road of repressing her emotional and ethical problems . . . The child reacts to the mother's unspoken thought almost as if he had had the thought himself."[12] That is why the Christian mother, realizing her awful responsibility, has renewed impetus to open her soul to the love of God and to allow the light of His love to guide her in her care for her children.

But along with love, the mother seeks to instill in her child humility and hope. These, on the supernatural level, parallel the emotional goods which on the natural level the mother is urged to give to her child. For, supernatural love—charity—is the elevation of that "tender, warm and loving care" which is supposedly the child's birthright. Humility at first sight may not be recognized as the exalted form of self-acceptance which it is, but scrutinized closely it is seen that humility is truth, and it is in guiding him to accept the truth about himself, to recognize himself as he is with all his assets and failings, that the mother helps her child to attain to a healthy self-concept which is the basis for self-confidence. And, finally, the Christian mother, recalling that she and her husband brought children into being for the ultimate purpose of enjoying God forever, seeks to give her child an insight into the nature of hope. She does this, not so much through her words, but through her actions, through the sense of security she gives her child in the God Who has destined him for happiness.

NOTES

1. Evelyn Ardis Whitman, "I'm Tired of Grandma," in *Women Today,* edited by Elizabeth Bragdon (New York: Bobbs-Merrill, 1953), p. 223.
2. Helen Sherman and Marjorie Coe, *The Challenge of Being a Woman* (New York: Harper and Brothers, 1955), p. 10.
3. Alva Myrdal and Viola Klein, *Women's Two Roles* (London: Routledge and Kegan Paul, 1956), p. 187.
4. M. Esther Harding, M.D., *The Way of All Women* (New York: Longmans, Green, 1937), p. 199.
5. *Ibid.,* p. 194.
6. *Ibid.,* p. 195.
7. Eva Firkel, *Woman in the Modern World* (Chicago: Fides, 1956), p. 108.
8. Harding, *op. cit.,* p. 205.
9. Ruth Reed, *The Single Woman* (New York: Macmillan, 1942), p. 130.
10. Harding, *op. cit.,* p. 182.
11. Abraham Myerson, "Woman, the Authorities' Scapegoat," in *Women Today, loc. cit.,* p. 310. In this same article Dr. Myerson wrote: "Many years ago I discovered that there can be no simple formula for raising children. When I was a young psychiatrist, father of one child, I loftily developed a lecture entitled, no less, 'A Decalogue for Parents.' Like a new Moses I enunciated ten commandments based on the successful rearing of son number one. Along came son number two, a noncomformist, who shattered my feelings of certainty. I changed the title of the lecture to 'Ten Hints for Parents.' With this modification of authoritarianism, I got along well enough until the third child was born, a girl; then I gave up the lecture entirely." (pp. 308-309)
12. Harding, *op. cit.,* p. 211.

8

The Widow

SHE was pregnant and her husband had just died, leaving her with several small children. At his wake her grief was well-controlled; all she said in tearless agony was, "To think my children will have to grow up never having known their father."

From time immemorial the widow has been an object of special pity. To defraud widows and orphans has traditionally been considered one of the sins which cry to heaven for vengeance, and when St. James detailed the marks of true religion, he said that it was to visit the widow and the fatherless in their grief. Today her situation seems different. The widow is well provided for. Even if she has young children, she does not face the terrifying economic plight of widows in the past. Life insurance, social security, the widows' pensions of certain states, and mortgage insurance assure her and her children of a roof over their heads and enough money to supply their necessities even if they have to live frugally. Widowhood is no longer synonymous with destitution. But while we welcome the social legislation which has made this improvement in the widow's lot possible, we are in danger of obscuring some of her other acute problems.

The young widow today faces the likelihood that she will have to bring up her children without a father, without any masculine advice and emotional support. As one widow with three school-age children remarked: "Certainly I should like to marry again. I'd like to have a husband's help for my children; but what man in his right mind is going to marry me with three of them already and the possibility of more?"

In the past a widow could reasonably expect to remarry. In many societies, children were not necessarily an economic liability and a man, for economic as well as emotional reasons, clearly needed a wife. The man who married a widow would probably himself be a widower with several children and would enter the marriage as a practical arrangement for living for all concerned. It would also provide companionship, even if it lacked the romantic qualities which characterized the first marriage. But today a young widow with three or four or more children has only a very dim hope that a satisfactory proposal will be forthcoming. From the beginning of her widowhood, she usually knows that she will have to bring up her children alone.

The thought of remarriage, of course, is not likely to occur to a young widow in the first wave of her grief, nor, for that matter, to an elderly widow either. Bereavement is an experience they have to live and suffer through, and in the height of their grief, especially if they have been fortunate enough to have known much happiness in their marriage, the prospect that they will ever know joy again is indeed remote.

Today death is hurried out of the home; it is no longer etiquette to mourn and it is considered poor taste to demonstrate grief. The widow, therefore, may look in vain for an outlet for her sorrow. Naturally, no one wants to force "widow's weeds" upon anyone, but a woman in mourning did serve to warn the bystander of a sorrow to be respected. Today, after the funeral is over and perhaps a month or two has gone by, a widow is supposed to "buck up" and she may consider herself a nuisance to others if she does not. Whatever she feels, she is forced to hide her grief. There is not expected to be any merciful release of tears, and while not everybody may expect her to be able to dance at somone's wedding within a month of her husband's death, too often she is criticized by her acquaintances if she does not immediately resume a regular pattern of recreational activities. The harm such repression of grief can do to her psychologically, and how damaging it can be in postponing the healthy healing of her sorrow can be conjectured. The bereaved of other cultures who were encouraged to display their grief perhaps experienced a quicker restoration of peace than the bereaved today who are expected to suppress their emotions. Too often, undoubtedly, "suppression" means "repression." Wailing and weeping, tearing one's hair, arraying oneself in sackcloth and ashes, obviously do not belong to the patterns of American culture, but the release of sorrow which these actions signified was itself therapeutic, and the need for healing (not the concealing) of grief can easily be forgotten.

Christians in America have also been influenced by the cultural attempt to overlook the reality of death. Certainly there was nothing especially Christian about Queen Victoria's mourning of Albert; Victorian widowhood was ostentatious and seemed to imply a denial of Christian hope. Victoria, who expected an apology from the unfortunate couple who presented her with a great-grandchild on the anniversary of her husband's death even though decades had already passed since that sad event, is surely not the model of the Christian widow. But the present attempt to forget the fact of bereavement as soon as possible is not especially Christian either. Death is a reality to be faced, and those who suffer bereavement have to face it in all its complexity. Certainly, for the Christian, death means the entrance into eternal life. The Christian widow lives in the hope that her beloved is enjoying, or soon will enjoy, the vision of God. But death is also the result of sin, and when it has come into a household, it brings fear and anguish, and pain. It is a travesty of human feeling as well as a denial of fraternal charity to pretend that a woman who, in the sight of God, has become one flesh with her husband, has not suffered a tremendous loss when that union is broken by death.

The affliction of Job, as well as the mourning of Mary and Martha, exemplify the possibility of perfect resignation to God's will coexisting with the deep and agonizing experience of the sorrows of this life. Union with God's will, acceptance of His designs, while they bring peace do not necessarily bring a surcease of pain. In fact, the person who is most capable of love—who has opened her heart most fully to the demands of love—suffers most deeply the acute wounding of love which is death. Saint Elizabeth of Hungary, who loved her husband intensely and reacted with strong emotion to the news of his death, is the model of Christian widowhood, not the woman who can quickly dry her tears after her husband's burial, since she is not, and never has been, capable of great love.

The balance of the Church in the liturgy for the dead is quite remarkable. The "Dies Irae" is balanced by the "In Paradisum" in a way that individuals in the Church sometimes miss. This may in one way be seen in the case of two young women both of whom lost their husbands in sudden deaths. The first widow was criticized by certain members of a Catholic group to which she belonged for not "snapping out" of her sorrow with sufficient rapidity. The second widow was held up as a model by her Catholic acquaintances because she showed such resignation in her bereavement—she even wrote to those who sent her condolences that she did not need them as she rejoiced that her husband had gone to God. The two reactions had interesting and probably predictable sequels. The first widow looked sorrowful for some time, carried on with her duties and looked after her children, but obviously missed her husband. Her grief healed slowly and evidently in a healthy way, and a few years later she was fortunate enough to be able to remarry. The "heroic" widow, after keeping up a display of joy for a half a year, quite suddenly had a complete mental breakdown.

The time of bereavement is the time for the widow to give Our Lord the tribute of her tears. Along with her sorrow at the loss of her husband, with whom some vital part of herself seems to have died, may well be various and conflicting emotions—a certain anger that she could not stop inexorable death, a sense of guilt that she failed her husband repeatedly and now can never make up to him for all her failures.* Just as so many times in her life she failed to give him the pure love she sensed he deserved, now at death she fails to give her husband the tribute of pure grief, undiluted by self-interest.[1] But this is no cause for shame or added guilt. Rather this is the time for simple acceptance of her misery, her weakness. Her tears, unworthy though they may be, can be offered as a humble love-offering to God for the soul of the beloved.

It may help the widow to realize that faith assures her of reunion with her husband, and the dogma of the resurrection of the body—that body which formed one flesh with her own—may suddenly take on a new and deep meaning. Or it may not. God sends His consolation to different people in different ways, and no one need worry if she fails to find comfort in a mystery of faith that others have found extremely consoling. Rather, she should try to keep her spirit in peace, for this is a time when her soul needs a rest as much as her body and her emotions, which have been over-taxed by what may have been a long and grueling experience of illness and death. A single word of prayer, a simple glance at the crucifix, may be all that she can manage and all that God expects from her.

But in her sorrow there are plans to be made, practical tasks to to be done. In a way the widow is greatly helped if she has children young enough so that their physical care keeps her anchored safely in accepting the duty of the moment, which is a sort of sacrament of the moment. But the elderly widow may feel that with the death of her husband, duty has ended. There are no chores that need doing—or to put it more exactly, it makes no difference to anyone whether or not they are done. The widow who has always been an excellent cook suddenly discovers that she is content to open a can for herself, or simply have a cup of

* In certain cases grief is complicated with other emotions. A woman whose husband is killed shortly after they have had a quarrel may feel an added measure of guilt. A woman whose mentally-ill husband commits suicide may be under emotional pressure from his family who blame her for his death. On the other hand, the widow of an alcoholic may experience a feeling of relief at his death, and then feel guilty because of this reaction.

tea; there is no point in doing more, and it will take a deliberate effort on her part to invite guests in and cook for them, or to seek out an invalid and bring him something she has cooked. Yet such acts of charity can be as therapeutic for the bereaved giver as they are welcome to the recipient.

The widow may think that the best thing to do is to go away from everything that has been familiar to her. Her first act may be to put her house on the market. As Marion Langer remarks in a book which could be most helpful to widows[2], in doing this she is trying to get rid of her pain by trying to get rid of every object connected with it, every object that reminds her of her husband. She is fortunate if her good sense or the prudent advice of friends intervenes, and she decides to go slowly, to wait for time to restore her perspective before she makes radical plans or major changes in her way of life. Since she is so uncertain what to do, and may feel herself torn in so many directions, it would be wise for her to wait until her body and nerves are rested and her mind is clear before going ahead to take a job or to enroll in a course in preparation for one.

The fact that there are many job opportunities for the older woman in our society is an advantage for widows who no longer have to scrape by on a pittance and fill their empty days with soul-shriveling gossip as was the fate of too many widows in times gone by. The widow who is free to go out to work or to involve herself more intensely in apostolic and charitable activities will find that in serving others she eventually achieves a rapport with her grief. Time does not make her forget her husband, but his absence becomes more bearable. There is a sense in which all love unifies; where love is, God is, we say; can we not also think that where charity, love of others, is exercised one is united more closely to God and to the dead beloved?

The younger widow has the advantage of greater resiliency to help her recover sooner from her grief, but at the same time on account of her youth it is more difficult for her to accept a "spiritual" answer to her problem, or to find a solution in unselfish service of others without a thought of a very personal, particular human love. If she has no children, she can resume the social life of a single woman and seek to marry again, and since she has a certain experience with men her chances of making a second marriage are considerably better than the chances of a single woman her age meeting a desirable mate. Further, she has her husband's friends and connections as an entrée into the company of men. However, if the young widow is left with several small children, not only may she not have the freedom to participate in social life, but she may doubt, as we mentioned before, that any man would care to take on her burdens.

For young widows for whom remarriage seems unlikely, the preservation of chastity can present a real problem. This is a situation that is rarely considered, and the widows who do not know how to seek counsel from their pastor or confessor may find themselves grappling with temptations and a sense of frustration which can be extremely disturbing. A widow who during her married life experienced no temptations against her marriage vow may feel ashamed that her widowhood seems to leave her a prey to her sexual needs and sensual desires. Failing to find help, some widows have gradually drifted into extra-marital relationships, which needless to say, provide no permanent solution for their need for love and companionship, even if they may provide temporary sexual relief. More than one widow in her loneliness has entered into a hasty (and later regretted) marriage with a man incapable of the responsibilities of marital life.

There is a great need for spiritual writing for widows, which would consider the peculiar problems of their state in our times. One widow told me of her distress in finding it stated in a certain spiritual book, written some centuries ago, that it is unchaste for a woman to remember the happiness of her physical union with her husband. She was understandably disturbed, but did not know where to look for clarification. Although widows who are fortunate enough to have found good spiritual directors have been helped to mortify their desires, women who are too diffident to approach a priest with such problems usually look in vain for such assistance. It seems that this is one particular area of lay spirituality that is quite untouched; especially important does it seem today when actuaries predict that the average married woman can expect to spend about sixteen years of her life in widowhood. If she is going to make these years bear spiritual life, she will need special consideration of her problems.

Widowhood makes one aware of the importance of keeping alive contacts with other women and cultivating deep and lasting friendships. As one widow remarked: "It is only my friends that make life bearable. When I get fed up with the children and am at my wit's end, stopping to see my friend or chatting with her on the phone is a big help." Such close friendship can guard against loneliness and a hasty, ill-considered remarriage or extra-marital alliance. For a widow with children, close contact with families having children of similar ages can be a source of encouragement and practical assistance. A widow who can turn for advice and help with her sons to a brother or other male relative who is willing to play a fatherly role in their life is especially fortunate. To have to bring up her children without a father is indeed a tremendous task; the sensible widow is therefore ready and grateful to accept the services of a father substitute.

It is rather surprising that although devotion to Our Lady has flourished under many forms and according to the needs of her many clients, devotion to her under the aspect of her life as a widow seems to have been overlooked. And yet Mary who was really married to Joseph (even though their marriage was virginal) did spend many years as a widow if we are to believe tradition. She knew what it was to have her husband taken by death and she knew the loneliness of the "empty nest." Immaculate virgin as she was, she did not, of course, suffer from some of the trials which participation in sexual life make inevitable for the ordinary widow, but she did know loneliness, she did know sorrow, she did know the need to readjust.

We know little about the details of Mary's earthly life and certainly little about the way she spent her widowhood. We surmise, however, that after Our Lord's Ascension she concerned herself with the needs of the infant Church and that she spent much time in prayer. From Mary, then, the tradition of charity and prayer as the occupation of widows has descended in the Church. And from Mary, and through Mary, the widow today can learn what it means to gather up all the riches that she has accumulated during her married life, the riches of love for husband, of love for children, and offer them to God that her love will become a sacrifice for the good of the whole Church.

NOTES

1. Cf. Karl Stern, M.D., "Psychiatric and Social Work with Old People," *Integrity,* Vol. VIII, No. 4 (January 1954). Dr. Stern writes:

"In every case of death we have guilt feelings toward those for whom we mourn. The point is that in old people all this is apt to remain on a deeply unconscious level and to be 'lived,' as it were, on the somatic level. From a psychoanalytical point of view this displacement is probably a defense mechanism; to 'act' one's grief 'out,' with the accompanying feeling of guilt, would endanger the personality too much.

"Two other features which we observed in the grief reactions of old people can probably be explained on the same basis. Whenever we lose a person who has been close to us we are apt to embellish his personality in our phantasy. We do not like to talk about his faults. *De Mortuis nil nisi bene.* In old people at times this assumes at times a bizarre degree. One of our clients who had often come running for help when her husband was in a state of drunken violence, not only developed a blind spot for all this after his death but spoke of him as one speaks of saints. These same mourners often show suddenly an irrational hostility against a living person in the immediate surrounding. We explain this as a displacement of the hostility they once harbored against the deceased person. This, too, is a defense against the threat of ambivalence (contradictory nature of emotions) which the aged mourning person is unable to tolerate. His feelings, which have always been divided, become now divided in the most literal sense of the word: all the hostility which was at one time directed against the person now dead is beamed towards an innocent survivor, and all the love, in an undiluted form, lavished on the deceased."

2. Marion Langer, *Learning to Live as a Widow* (New York: Mess-

ner, 1957) This book by a clinical psychologist contains an excellent analysis of the experience of bereavement and the emotional reactions of widows. Another book on widowhood, Marjorie Hillis Roulston's *You Can Start All Over* (New York: Harper, 1951), although it is much more superficial, still has a certain value for its practical tips to widows on readjustment.

9

Divorce and the Divorcée

No one would claim that divorce is a peculiarly American problem, but no knowledgeable American would deny that divorce is a problem particularly in America. It is estimated that at present over one-half of the divorces granted annually in the world are granted in the United States. Currently there are about four hundred thousand divorces every year in the United States, and an additional one hundred and sixty thousand separations. While a great many more childless marriages end in divorce than marriages where there are children, it is still true that over one-half million children annually are intimately concerned in the divorces and separations that occur in the United States.

Divorce, needless to say, has reached the proportions of a major social problem. Civil officials, social welfare workers, marriage counsellors, and clergymen view the situation with great alarm and attempt to stem the tide of divorce, while social scientists analyze our society to find its root causes.

Why is divorce so prevalent in this country? Ralph Linton, an anthropologist, gives what at first sight may seem a rather startling answer. "The great enemies of enduring marriage in our society are not the loss of faith or deteriorating moral standards, but the typewriter, the delicatessen and the laundry that does mending and sews on buttons."[1] In other words, people do not *need* to stay married. The partners in our culture do not have to make a go of marriage because they are not economically dependent on each other. This is not a condition that prevails in other cultures, particularly in less industrialized, less sophisticated areas, where the roles of husband and wife in marriage are clear-cut, where the woman cannot provide for herself or for her children economically without the husband, and where the husband cannot eat or have clean clothes unless his wife is there to take care of him.* Margaret Mead, in seeming agreement with Linton, noted that all the traditional goods and values associated with marriage can now be obtained in America outside the marriage relationship. Sex, food, money can be found elsewhere. "Assured companionship and parenthood thus become the two socially desirable values that cannot be obtained outside marriage."[3] Even these, of course, do not need lasting marriage, and can be continued by remarriage.

Margaret Mead, in analyzing the contemporary American marriage, further remarked: "The most serious aspect of the divorce rate is not so much the number of divorces as the expectation of divorce. A generation ago a great many people had never seen a divorced woman. And if you have never seen a divorced woman, it is awfully hard to think of yourself as being one. . . . It seems to me, as an anthropologist, that the most serious thing that is happening in the United States, the most significantly important, is that people enter marriage now with the idea that it is terminable. Of course, that does not apply to the part of our population that is within the fold of a religious community. It does not apply to our Catholic young people. It does not apply to some of our Protestant young people, especially in rural regions . . . but on the radio, in films, in the magazines, and in our urban secular communities, the idea that marriage is terminable has even permeated the proposal: 'Let's try it, and if we don't like it . . .' This expectation permeates every quarrel. It is a background for having

* The very real contrast in marriage patterns in the United States with patterns prevailing in other cultures was brought home to me while doing research on this subject in Puerto Rico.[2] Lower-class Puerto Ricans who were interviewed and asked if they were happy with their partner invariably evaluated his or her worth in practical terms: "She cooks for me, she prepares my clothes;" "he buys the food; he protects me and the children."

children, because 'maybe they will hold us together.' We have now set up the family, therefore, as a terminable situation."[4]

The above quotation reflects Dr. Mead's observations in 1947; since then conditions have worsened considerably. It is not rare to find a Protestant minister, especially in the metropolitan areas, who is divorced and remarried, and although it would be an exceptional Catholic who would enter marriage with the *expectation* of divorce, divorce statistics among Catholics in America do not justify a rosy picture.

The current youthful age at the time of marriage further increases the possibility of divorce. Dr. Judson Landis in a sociological study found divorce rates six times higher in marriages where both spouses were under twenty-one when they married than in marriages in which both were thirty-one or over at the time of marriage.[5] Evidently then there are no grounds for thinking that the current divorce rate will decrease in the years to come.

HAVE CATHOLICS ADJUSTED TO DIVORCE?

What is the reaction of Catholics to this situation? Have we come to take the dissolution of marriage for granted? Obviously the numbing of the collective conscience has had inevitable results for the Catholic as well as for other Americans. The sacrament of matrimony does not change, neither does the lifetime duration of the marriage alter. Yet, the modern Christian marriage is lived out in a culture where divorce is acceptable, and where the social pressure which in former ages bolstered the permanency of an otherwise shaky marriage has completely collapsed. All this is almost too apparent to mention. Yet the sob stories in favor of divorce, which to the Catholic should be so much alien corn, nevertheless have subconscious effects. "Of course, *we'd* never consider getting a divorce." But the devout Catholic who says this finds himself approving his divorced sister's remarriage. "She's lonely and anyway who's going to support her and the baby? She can't manage on her alimony."

It is not easy to pit faith against the facts of life in the modern world. Moreover, while the natural, sociological reasons against divorce and remarriage are many, the Catholic loses ground if he tries to prove that *every* remarriage is miserable, or that *all* children of divorces become mentally disturbed or delinquent. The effects of immorality are not that simple. The Catholic opposition to divorce is rooted not in shifting pragmatic sands, but on the firm ground of faith. The Christian dispensation involves a whole change of life; Moses allowed divorce to the Jews on account of their hardness of heart, but Christ came not merely to soften hearts but to redeem them, and to make human love participate in His own love. Divorce is no longer something to be argued about merely on the natural level, for married love has been transformed and marriage itself exalted.

But, how are we to make all this understandable to our contemporaries? And how do we show disapproval of divorce yet understanding and charity toward those attempting remarriage after divorce? The social ostracism by the faithful which in ages of faith and in a Catholic country had salutary effects on the wayward member of the Church seems in our era to have little effect. For, even if his Catholic friends do not recognize his remarriage, society will. Yet how can the faithful Catholic continue social contact without seeming to manifest approval? This question, of course, is only a facet of the whole issue of Catholic behavior in a secular age. While faith and principle never change, applications do. Customs such as social ostracism can become anachronistic and need re-examination in every era.

Certainly charity would demand continued interest in the unfortunate friend who has become involved in a divorce and remarriage. There are cases—and they are not rare—of Catholics who have had the courage to break off an illicit relationship and return to the Church through the friendship of a fellow Catholic. Understanding and compassion for the spiritual anguish and emotional conflict of the person involved in a "bad" marriage need not blind the Catholic friend to the objective reality of the situation; on the contrary, they should stimulate him to encourage the divorced Catholic to continue to pray and to attend Mass and to see to the religious education of his children.

THE PERILS OF "STICKING IT OUT"

The Church, in allowing couples to separate and even to get a legal divorce to protect their civil rights (not, needless to say, that such a divorce breaks the marriage bond or leaves the couple free to marry again), has in practice shown its disagreement with some apologists who have urged that the worst sort of home is better for children than the home broken by divorce. For the Church recognizes that there are some conditions which are so intolerable that they rule out continued living together. The Church does not insist that the child be kept in a home where he is constantly exposed to obscenities, or where the couple expose before him their mutual infidelities. In such a case, living with one parent in comparative peace may be better than living with both in a nightmare of horror.

But each case must be judged individually. The increase in the number of priests with special training in marriage counselling as well as the increase in the number of professional people who bring to their practice of social work or psychotherapy a Christian orientation would seem to justify optimism. If there are more Catholics today considering divorce, there are also it would seem more Catholics than there were a generation ago who are aware that they must make positive efforts to make a go of their marriage, that "sticking together" is not enough. The spectacle of young people who are unhappy and seriously disturbed because they are the products of loveless marriages and a tense family life has never been a cheerful one. Often their parents prided themselves on having "stuck together" even if it meant that they never exchanged a word for twenty years. It is encouraging, then, to note that married couples today are aware that they must prevent such disasters. The wider use of Cana and pre-Cana conferences and more effective marriage counselling is their answer to divorce as well as to unhappy marriage.

What of the woman involved in an unhappy marriage? Certainly she should make every effort to improve the situation and to re-establish a good relationship with her husband. Often it is the breakdown of communication between the spouses that is the root of the difficulty. When husband and wife can no longer share with each other their thoughts and feelings a marriage is seriously endangered. Some people, of course, have great difficulty in expressing themselves, in revealing themselves to others; childhood experiences account in large measure for the secretive, fearful attitude that certain persons bring to any human relationship. They find it difficult to trust another, so they behave as though they must always keep themselves to themselves, and they hesitate to venture forth into the unknown land which intimate communication with another human being means. But the fact that there is a marriage at all indicates that the couple have, at some time or another, successfully communicated with each other. It would be misleading, of course, to give the impression that communication necessarily involves fluency with words or the ability to put one's thoughts into spoken language. There are couples who have excellent communication but who are sparse with words. They can reveal their thoughts and feelings to each other in a look or gesture; of them sometimes it can be said even that they "speak in silences."

But what can be done in the case of the couple who are "tongue-tied" emotionally as well as literally? True communication between them becomes more difficult, more infrequent. Husband and wife each tend to shut the other out. The man no longer tells his wife of his work or his worries; she in turn shuts her thoughts up within herself. They have, as it were, kept their inmost selves from the life they hold in common. They go through the motions, but that is all. What matters most to each, they no longer share. They know they are becoming virtual strangers; yet love often persists. Can they re-learn a common language?

If the channel for communication can somehow or other be re-opened it is possible for the couple to solve their own problems without outside assistance. Sometimes it seems, however, that the block which keeps them from communicating is immovable unless there is help from someone else. More than one wise wife, in seeking assistance from her parish priest or from a professional marriage counsellor or family social worker, has discovered that she has been able to save her marriage even though her partner has refused to go himself for counselling. Normally it is ideal that both spouses seek help, for usually the case is not clear-cut; the responsibility for marital unhappiness does not rest completely on one partner's shoulders and husband and wife both need to make certain modifications in their way of thinking and acting if the marriage is to succeed. But it has happened sometimes that, through the outside assistance she obtained, a wife has been enabled to see the situation in a realistic way unclouded by excessive emotion and has gone on to salvage a marriage which seemed hopeless. She has been able to keep a home intact for her children even when the husband's personality disturbance or character disorder was such that he could not be expected to change radically.

There are other wives who, after repeated and whole-souled efforts to remedy an unhappy marriage, have been advised by their counsellor or priest advisor to seek a permanent separation. Such a decision, drastic as it is, can only be made after prolonged prayerful consideration. In some cases, however, even though separation might be the best solution for protecting the children of the marriage, it is not possible. The woman with four or five small children might not find the idea of living apart from her husband financially feasible. If her husband's behavior cannot be expected to improve, if he is crippled by an emotional disorder which apparently renders him incapable of assuming adult responsibility,* she seems to be in an impossible dilemma. Hers may not be a common situation, but it is by no means unique in our day. There are women who are persevering in marriages where daily they shoulder a seemingly unbearable burden. They are fortunate if their reliance on God's grace and their abandonment to His Providence is matched by a willingness to accept whatever human help is available to make their marriage workable.

* It is significant that the women attending the Second Annual Congress on Better Living, held in Washington in the fall of 1959, agreed that emotional immaturity of the spouses was the greatest single cause of family dissension.

There are certainly women who with grounds for divorce and advice to seek one waited patiently for an erring husband to mend his ways and in the end experienced the joy of reconciliation. But the woman who has gone ahead and gotten a divorce and the woman whose husband has sued her for divorce are obviously pursued by a multitude of difficulties, both from within and without. The divorcée has to meet the criticism of the world in general, which, even though it now accepts divorce, still enjoys gossiping about divorced people. If the divorcée is a Catholic, she will probably encounter severe criticism from her co-religionists. Since there are some Catholics who have yet to realize that a person can be divorced and still be in good standing in the Church, the divorcée has to be prepared to endure some harsh judgments. Even if she is completely blameless and clearly the innocent party in the case, there may be some raised eyebrows when she goes up to Communion.

People in general are inclined to regard the divorcée as a "loose woman." Even though she may be as chaste and as virtuous as the Christian wife whose marriage has succeeded and who continues to live in faithful wedlock with her husband, the divorcée is viewed with a certain suspicion. Admittedly she has a great need to be on her guard, for temptations to unchastity are many. As one divorcée wrote: "While the world points at the divorcée with a certain scorn, it also beckons enticingly . . . Not only is she considered fairer game than her single sister, but she is easier game in that she finds it hard to control impulses and passions that once had a natural outlet in marriage. Besides she is blinded by her craving for affection. No longer can she hide behind a wide-eyed look of real or pretended innocence. Though not a virgin, she must live as one. Her marriage vow adds adultery to unchastity."[6]

While, like the widow, she must mortify passions that formerly had an outlet in marriage, unlike the widow she cannot hope for remarriage. For, in God's sight, she is still a wife, bound by vow to be faithful to one husband. Even if his adultery has given her the right to refuse common life with him, and even though the

Church has allowed her a permanent separation, she is still his wife and her body can belong to him and no other.*

Gertrud von le Fort writes: "Even the rejected wife retains her nuptial character and is, in her banishment, immeasurably significant. As wife she nevertheless continues to stand in the eternal order of woman's life as the other half of man. It is then that the sacrament of matrimony, as the highest form of the mystery of charity and its actual consecration, stands forth in its inflexible sublimity and in the fullness of its sacred character, precisely at the moment when the marriage is most endangered. The divorced woman remains a wife and the other part of the man because she is so before God."[7]

The divorcée is still fed spiritually through the sacrament of matrimony; she is still joined by it to her husband, and even when he is remarried or has disappeared, the graces of their wedlock remain a reality. It is inconceivable, then, that the heavy cross she bears in her loneliness and innumerable trials will not avail for his salvation. That the faithful Christian wife will continue to pray for the husband from whom she has a legal divorce goes without saying; that, however, she may not be able to bear to keep him in her thoughts is possible. A divorcée who was trying valiantly to lead an intense spiritual life confessed that while she offered her sufferings for her husband she was not able to think of him while she prayed. The last few years of their living together had been so full of horror and his physical violence had been such that she still suffered nightmares of remembrance; consequently, to preserve her peace of mind she avoided conscious prayer for him. Whether or not her solution was the best one, anyone would agree that it was an understandable one to choose.

Wife as the divorcée remains, she likewise continues to be mother of the children of her husband and herself. She therefore

* The permanence of the marriage vow, the dignity which the Church accords to it, and the sacred character of the relationship which it engenders are attested to by the fact that while, under certain circumstances, divorcées are admitted into secular institutes, they are only permitted to make their vow of chastity perpetual when it is morally certain that reconciliation with their husbands cannot take place.

continues to have the obligation to keep alive in the children affection for their father and to nurture in them reverence and respect for him. That this is no easy task is obvious, especially if they too had suffered from his cruelty, especially if they blame him for his sin against their mother and consequently against themselves. Like the widow, the divorcée knows the grave responsibility of bringing children up without a father. So many of the decisions on behalf of the children that she would feel are the father's to share, the divorcée must shoulder alone. While the day-to-day situation of the widow and the divorcée may have much in common in regard to their children, there are important differences. The widow may have to fill the place of her husband in the lives of her children; she may regret feelingly that they have to grow up never having known him personally; but, if she has happy memories of him, she can make her husband a reality for her children. His love will continue to hover over them, and the children can be raised in the security of knowing that their father cared tremendously for them. But the divorcée will rarely have pleasant memories to give her children; she will find it next to impossible to evoke, in most cases, the image of a father who had a loving care for them. As a result, she will have to bring her children up without this emotional support. On the other hand, perhaps they will see their father from time to time; perhaps, even, they will have regular visits with him. In these instances, the mother needs to be especially wise, loving, and generous to keep the children from feeling they must choose sides and cannot love both parents simultaneously.

That the divorced Catholic woman needs special help to live a spiritual life is evident. If she is blessed with an understanding, prudent, holy pastor or confessor, her difficulties will be lessened considerably. One could hope that efforts to group divorcées together for mutual support in leading a Christian life will prosper. There is an organization of Divorcées Anonymous, but the drawbacks for the Catholic in joining a group who consider remarriage permissible are too clear to need further mention. Certainly one can hope that as organizations such as the Christian Family Movement grow in extent and depth in this country, they will be able to turn their attention to the problems of divorced Catholics as well as to the problems of widows. While it would be patently unwise to include widows and divorcées in the same group as married couples, it would seem practical in a parish or community to have small groups of widows and divorcées (possibly loosely federated to the CFM?) who could meet together, have Gospel inquiries, and perhaps use social inquiries especially adapted to their situation. Indeed, many of the topics of the CFM inquiries (for example, the influence of television on children, the interracial problem, contact with neighbors) concern all married women, even if they are separated from their husbands by death or court decree. Perhaps in the future groups of such women can be formed to help one another personally to lead a more fervent Christian life, at the same time as they help one another to exert an apostolic influence in their family, parish, and community.

NOTES

1. Ralph Linton in *Women, Society and Sex,* edited by Johnson E. Fairchild (New York: Sheridan House, 1952), p. 82.
2. Dorothy Dohen, *Background of Consensual Union in Puerto Rico,* unpublished Master's thesis (Fordham University, 1959).
3. Margaret Mead, *Male and Female* (New York: Morrow, 1949), p. 329.
4. Margaret Mead, "What Is Happening to the American Family?" *New Emphasis on Cultural Factors* (New York: Family Service Association of America, 1948), p. 3.
5. As quoted by Eleanor Stoker Boll, "Should Parents or Cupid Arrange Marriages?" *The New York Times Magazine,* December 13, 1959.
6. Anonymous, "Spirituality for the Divorced," *Integrity,* Vol. IX, No. 7 (April 1955), p. 12.
7. Gertrud von le Fort, *The Eternal Woman* (Milwaukee: Bruce, 1955).

10

Single Women: Problems

As was indicated in the first chapter, the single woman is told many different things about herself and is given much conflicting advice. She is told that being single is a sign of selfishness, but she is also told that it is a sign that she is more discriminating than her married sisters. She is given to believe that to live without sex is impossible, but she is also led to think that her chastity puts her a cut above married people and gives her an edge on salvation. She is made to understand that she is doomed to frustration, but then she is told that there is nothing abnormal about her path in life.

Of course, these different opinions are not rendered by the same people. Various writers, preachers and counsellors look at the single woman from individual vantage points and present her with solutions according to their own scale of values and, possibly, according to their own prejudices. Some writers make the life of the single woman seem very gay, full of charm and opportunity, unhampered by burdens or drawbacks, and quite desirable. Not only freedom to fulfill her own potentialities, but also opportunities for service to the common good far transcending those offered the married are open to her, is the line of another writer on the single life.

Not only conflicting value systems divide authors and commentators on the single life (one would quite properly suspect that a believer in free love would view singleness differently from a believer in pre- and extra-marital chastity), but also evident personal attitudes, experiences and prejudices divide those who owe allegiance to the same values. Thus, one priest implies that a woman should thank God she is single while another priest infers that singleness is a state from which she should pray to be delivered. One feels that the discrepancy in the advice given by various priests is not the result of any difference in theology (although there is reason to think that it may arise from a stressing of different aspects of the same theology), but a result of a difference in psychology.

Writers and counsellors when discoursing on the single woman generally see her from the "problem" point of view. What they say or write is not intended so much to be an objective treatment of the situation of the single woman and her relationship to society as an attempt to answer the subjective perplexities and problems of the individual single woman. No one is interested in building up a theory of single woman; everyone is interested in helping single women in practice. This seems to be the case even when the writers or speakers declaim about the single life in lofty and glowing terms; at the risk of seeming cynical, one ventures to say that they are not talking of the ideal single woman because they think she can be ideal, but because they feel that presenting an ideal will give the single woman a spiritual and emotional uplift, will bolster her morale, and give her some support in the face of discouragement and possible despair.

This "problem" orientation of whatever is said or written about the single woman is difficult to avoid. Marriage, the religious life, or the *dedicated* single life in the world (which is the subject of a subsequent chapter) all have their problems, of course, but they all have their ideals. And it is because of the ideal that they are chosen. The ideal is at once the objective reason and the subjective aim of each of these vocations, and consequently discussion of these vocations can be centered around the ideal. But the single life lacks its won ideal, its own *mystique,* its own end.* Singleness is viewed either as the condition of those who have not as yet chosen or entered into a definite vocation, and thus is the normal state of the young, of those poised on the threshold of life; or it is the condition of those already mature, who for some reason or other have not chosen a definite vocation or who have been prevented from following their choice by either interior or exterior obstacles. There is always something tentative about singleness, and that is why single people so often seem both to themselves and to others as bather-spectators who forever stand on the beach, along the water's edge, and who never enter the ocean of life. Their apparent "vocationless" state is sometimes a puzzle to them, even when it is not a burden. It often is both.

Most writers on the single woman do not consider young girls who are, so to speak, "temporarily single," and focus attention on those women who have completed their educational preparation and think and feel that they should already have been settled in life. The age at which a "young girl" becomes a "single woman" is getting rapidly younger. Even though a greater proportion of girls go to college than went a generation ago and prolonged education would seem to imply delay in entering adult life, the lowering of the age for marriage is a mark of the post-war period. Girls want marriage, "the sooner the better," as Margaret Mead said on a recent television show. A median age of slightly past twenty for girls entering marriage for the first time means that the age at which a girl becomes an old maid or a "single woman" is considerably lower than when the median age for marriage was higher by several years. Girls today may feel that they have to join the procession of St. Catherine well before the traditional age of twenty-five.

Older people—whether they are parents, teachers, or spiritual advisers—have to see a single girl's evaluation of her situation against this prevailing pattern of early marriages. Otherwise they

* Needless to say, the single person shares the ideal and the end of every Christian. But the single life itself lacks its own ideal and end and is not a state with its characteristic marks as is marriage or the religious life.

are inclined to be amused rather than sympathetic as she bewails the fact of being unmarried at twenty-three or twenty-four. During the 1930's an unmarried woman had no reason to get the jitters until she reached her upper twenties,* and the characteristic feelings of loneliness and depression did not hit the single woman until she was into her thirties. But now the subjective realization that she probably is not going to get married comes to her considerably earlier. This, of course, can have its advantages, since she can be helped, and can help herself, to adjust to the situation—or make plans to change it—before she becomes as settled as the self-accepted-as-single woman of a generation ago.

THE REASONS FOR SINGLENESS

There are other differences between the single woman today and her counterpart in the 1930's. At that time there were cases of girls who postponed marriage because their financial help was needed by their families. The older single woman who today says that she lost her chances of marriage during the depression when she felt it was her duty to help support her younger brothers and sisters may not simply be rationalizing her position. In a time when financial resources were tight, scholarship opportunities few, and a major depression overshadowed everyone's personal life, the single woman who sacrificed to educate her younger brothers was not rare. But she was a phenomenon of depression years and is not typical today. That is why when well-meaning older people will give as a reason for a woman's not having married the fact that she is supporting younger children in the family or educating her brother for the priesthood, they sound definitely dated. Their words are scant consolation to single women who see no resemblance between what they are saying and the reality of their own situation. Perhaps even in the depression, women did not remain single to give support to the family or educate younger siblings—maybe that was not the real reason at all; but at least it was an

* It is interesting to note that in *Live Alone and Like It* (published 1936)[1] a woman is cautioned not even to think of an affair until she is thirty—that evidently being the age at which she can safely give up hope of marriage!

acceptable rationalization of their position for themselves and for society at large, and it may have afforded the single woman some status as well as some inner comfort. But today it does neither.

Another rationalization which should be permanently buried is the one that single women are single because they are caring for their sick and aged parents. Usually this rationalization disregards cause and effect and the time element. Single women are not single because they are caring for their parents; they are caring for their parents because they are single. Perhaps years ago, or in certain cultures, it was decided in advance by the parents that the six children should marry "with the exception of Mary who will stay with us in our old age," but in contemporary society it is not so. Mary stays with her parents in their old age because she is the only one who is not married and the others are too busy with their families to take care of the parents.

The feminists, who loudly proclaimed a woman's right to a career and her freedom to remain unmarried, for a long time gave a convenient rationalization to unmarried women. They were "career girls." And indeed some of them were. They had freely chosen a career and did not want to get married. But as many social observers have remarked, since women have the right to a career, they have lost their desperate desire for one. Further, the dilemma "marriage or a career" has not existed in acute form for at least twenty or twenty-five years; that is, ever since woman discovered that she could have both and society approved of her decision.* With more of the women in the working force married than single, the fact that a single woman is gainfully employed is no longer a rationalization of her position. A mere job is not a very desirable cake, especially when other women—married women—can both have their cake and eat it.

Where does all this leave the single woman? Without very much

* It is true that for Catholic women the dilemma of marriage vs. career has not been solved so neatly since they cannot resort to birth control. However, there is reason to doubt that there are many Catholic women who forego marriage because they want to pursue a career that they could not square with it. Even if there were, the point would still be true that for society as a whole the fact of a career is no longer a justification for a woman's remaining unmarried.

justification in the eyes of society for her singleness. The glamor girl, the heroine of the movie, TV play, and the short story, gets her man. She is a failure if she does not. The single woman today is on the defensive. She does not seem an enviable figure in anyone's eyes, sometimes least of all her own.* What is she to do?

I remember with amusement hearing about a friend who attended a lecture on single women given by a Catholic married man. His thesis was (rather oddly, since the Church has always upheld a woman's right to an existence independent of man) that a single woman had to attach herself to a family; of herself she had no right to exist. At the conclusion of his talk, the friend, a single woman, went up to him and with great spirit declared: "If you think I'm going to drop dead you're all wrong."

Single women need that spirit. A single woman who wants to marry should not retreat into the depths of self-pity and depression, but have the courage to examine her situation and to take whatever steps she judges necessary. First of all she should find out why she is single—not that finding out will necessarily remedy the situation and get her a husband, but finding out may help her to remedy whatever may be preventing her from leading a rich, useful, happy life as well as from getting married.

There may be objective reasons in her locality that make getting married difficult. Obviously one such reason is the imbalance of the sexes; cities swarming with female office workers, like New York and Washington, are not usually swarming with men. It is unfortunate that urban areas which offer immediate job employment for single women do not usually afford them much opportunity for their long-range plan of marriage. However, before a woman chucks her job on the Eastern seaboard and heads for Alaska and other points West noted for the sparsity of females, it would be well for her to look into herself and find out if there is anything other than keen competition keeping her from a husband.

* Maybe even in 1936 the single woman did not seem to be in an attractive position. Marjorie Hillis advised her that the first and most important thing she had to do was to get "a mental picture of yourself as a gay and independent person, and spunk enough to get the picture across to the other persons."[2]

Highly intelligent and gifted women may have a harder time finding a suitable mate than girls whose talents are more nearly average. Certain types of jobs and professions have a low marriage rate. Thus, teachers and social workers are the proverbial spinsters, and nurses are swept to the altar before they have gotten used to wearing their caps. While this may be true of these professions taken as a whole, there are often reasons other than her job that keep the individual teacher or social worker from marrying. Then, too, a woman is certainly more attractive if she is happy as a teacher than she would be if she were miserable as a nurse. Vocational advisers—and girls themselves—would be short-sighted if they advocated certain jobs only because they are better matrimonial avenues,* regardless of the aptitude of the individuals for the jobs.

THE UNLOVED AND LONELY

This is not to say, however, that girls should not or need not work at getting married. There is a quietist school of thought that advises: "If it is God's will for you to marry, your husband will find you even if you are hidden up in the attic." Obviously this is nonsense. St. Paul was struck blind and fell from a horse before he found out he was supposed to be a Christian and an apostle, but no one would hold this up as the normal way to discover one's vocation. A religious superior does not drag a girl off to the convent, and neither should a husband be expected to find her to carry her off to his house. Things may have been easier in other days, but ever since our society did away with arranged marriages men and women must look for their spouses. And even though in the United States it still is up to the man to propose, the girl at

* A social worker was told by an adviser that she had better get out of social work if she wanted to get married. She replied that she was happy doing social work, that she believed it to be God's will for her, and certainly was not going to leave it for something which did not suit her personality: that was no way to get a husband. She was right, at least for herself. For within a short time she married and is now the mother of several children.

least has to put herself within hearing distance. (In actual fact, she usually has to lead him up to the proposal and she has often put the words into his mouth.)

Some girls do not marry because they do not have an opportunity to meet men. However, the common assertion that if a girl wants to get married, she will get married, is one with which many single women hotly disagree. They argue that they themselves *did* and *do* want to get married but that they never had the opportunity, never met the right man, and so on. Maybe so. Yet in support of the theory that, at least in marriage, wishing that is really willing will make it so, are the words of one writer: ". . . as we observe young women, we see that those who marry are generally those who have one idea—not two ideas. They have one idea and that is marriage."[3]

There are some young women who say they want to get married but never seem to follow through on their words. They always have to work the night that some mutual friend wants to introduce them to an eligible man; they are offered a job in the same line of work that they have been doing in an office where there are more men, but they give some excuse for not taking it; they meet a man on vacation but do not encourage him to see them on their return home. Their actions belie their words. Do they or do they not want to get married? Consciously, they do; underneath, they are afraid. They may be afraid of men, afraid of marriage, afraid of being rejected. Often the girl who acts over-eager with men has the same fear as those women who withdraw from opportunities to meet them; the girl who scares men away may be as frightened as her shrinking-violet sister.

There are probably many causes which keep women from marriage. A perceptive writer has this to say of some of them: ". . . very similar causes underlie either maladjustment in marriage or unmarriedness.* Unmarried men and women or unhappily mar-

* There are girls of whom it is said that they "don't know how to flirt" or that "they are too shy to get a man," who are well suited to domesticity, are fundamentally sound personalities, and who if they had lived in an age of arranged marriages would have been very successful wives and homemakers. However, they do not seem to work out well in an era of romantic

ried men and women do not feel confident that they are lovable."[4] She goes on to write: "Normally the girl moves through adolescence . . . pleased and delighted with herself as a woman . . . but many girls . . . feel unsure of their worthiness, express doubt regarding their ability to choose a desirable mate. Actually they have grave doubts of being attractive to any man."[5] That one's self-concept and the feeling that one is attractive and capable of arousing the love of a man has a great deal to do with the possibilities of getting married is borne out by the fact that often objectively plain and uncharming girls marry while women who are objectively much more attractive remain single.

What causes these doubts? Why does a girl feel that she cannot attract a man? Why does she think no one could love her?

It would be risky to try to give a decisive answer to these questions. The answer varies with the case. There are some girls who are the proverbial "ugly ducklings" in their families, who have always suffered from comparison with brighter, gayer, prettier sisters. Their disturbance may not be too deep and they may be able to profit a good deal from the counsel of a professional adviser, or even from the encouragement of a trusted friend.

But then there are girls whose psychic wounds are deep. Children of seriously disturbed parents, one or both of whom have rejected them, they grow up without feeling that anyone loves them. They themselves become incapable of attracting anyone's love and, even if they attract the attention of a man, they are incapable of sustaining a relationship. They suffer from an inability either to give or to receive love. Usually, since their personality disturbance is great as well as deep-rooted, they need to be referred for psychotherapy and will not be able to profit from any well-meaning amateur "pep talk." Concerning people who do not marry because they are incapable of love, Father Häring writes sympathetically. He says our judgment of them should be mild. "Perhaps they are incapable of loving because they have never or rarely

love. But this does not belie the fact that there are other cases where the root-cause of a woman's not getting married would be the same as the root-cause of maladjustment in marriage.

received true, selfless love. Perhaps they fit under the [Gospel] category of those 'whom men have made incapable of marriage.' "[6]

There are single women who seem to be very confident personalities, who sometimes have been highly successful in their careers or professions, and who would never be suspected—least of all by themselves—of suffering from feelings of inferiority or of incapacity to attract love. These are the women who often win great public respect and admiration, and of whom people say, "Isn't it amazing she didn't ever marry!"

Yet at bottom these single women may suffer from the same problem as less adequate, less attractive unmarried girls. Dr. Harding writes: "A deeply buried sense of inferiority and unfulfillment usually haunts the woman who has been preoccupied with her profession and has not given her love to any human being. She seeks to compensate for her feeling of inadequacy in love with achievements in the world hoping that the recognition she will receive will take the place of the love she has missed . . . This compulsive devotion gives her work drive, but also tinges it with a partisan quality which is bound to arouse opposition and distrust, increasing in turn the barrier between the woman and any possible love experience."[7] If, instead of repressing her sexual instinct and desire to love the woman treats this lack of fulfillment as a conscious problem, she will reap the benefit of her struggle, even though she still remains unfulfilled in her love life.

There are families where parental over-protection has kept daughters from marriage. This is especially the case today, when modern conditions of dating and courtship make it imperative that parents allow daughters to get into the fray, to use an inelegant but nevertheless realistic phrase. Parents who during adolescence overprotect their daughters, view every teen-age dance as a possible hazard, and anxiously scrutinize every boy who steps into the living room, may permanently damage their daughters' ability to relate well to men and eventually to marry. This is especially the case if the girl, while resenting the parents' attitude, lacks the courage to declare her independence.

For the single woman there is often a long drawn out and

unresolved conflict between her desire for independence and her desire for security. If her parents have made her feel that their love for her (and hence her security in retaining their love) depends on her acquiescence to their wishes, she may be hampered from growing into an adult, independent personality. We have heard much in the past years about momism, especially as it relates to sons, but it should not be overlooked that the same phenomenon has had its effect on daughters. Girls who have never been allowed to leave the parental hearth, who are, as it were, emotionally cloistered, are prevented from getting married as surely as if their fathers erected protective concrete walls which no man could scale. Sometimes parents do not realize that they themselves are the chief cause of their daughter's singleness; they say how much they regret their child's being unmarried while at the same time they will not loosen the unbreakable emotional ties that keep her home with them.

Among other single women who are emotionally handicapped one often finds a common cause: they are the children of unhappy marriages. Especially are daughters made to pay for a woman's mistake in choosing the wrong husband. There are mothers who never cease telling their daughters about the horrors of matrimony, who openly denounce their fathers to them. But even if the hostility between the parents is not put into words, the children suffer from an unhappy marriage. There are women who make their children pay for their own disappointment in marriage. Eva Firkel comments that ". . . the children of such mothers will be given a distorted view of the natural processes. But since their own nature will develop and demand its rights, they will be subject to incomprehensible tensions, which result from longing desires and physical maturity on the one hand and a gloomy picture of sexual relationships on the other. From these, serious inner conflicts will arise in the child which may lead to a permanently twisted mentality."[8] Needless to say, the essence of the tragedy for such a child is not that she does not marry but that she becomes incapable of love. She needs skilled help to enable her to function as well as possible under her handicap even if she cannot be permanently cured.

The adviser to the single woman has to determine in each case whether to leave her with the rationalization for her single state or to help her to determine the real reason why she is not married. There is the principle that one does not take away a crutch from a cripple if he is not cured and therefore capable of walking. In dealing with human beings we tread on sacred ground. The inept, unskilled counsellor may do more harm than good, and there are some persons who are left better off as they are. Especially for rank amateurs dealing with disturbed single women the decision to do nothing except pray for them may not be the sign of cowardice or laziness but the surest mark of prudent charity.

What of the single woman herself? What if she discovers the "real" reason for her singleness? Naturally if she discovers it in time and comes to accept it, she can then make every effort to try to get married. For her consolation let it be noted that there have been women whose various emotional handicaps kept them from marrying who, either through outside therapy or by their own efforts, have overcome them and have entered into very successful, happy marriages.

But what if a woman discovers this too late? Even if there do not seem to be immediate prospects of marriage she can still hope. There are women who marry in their late thirties or forties and marry happily. These marriages, sometimes to widowers or to men whom the woman may have known for years but who in youth did not seem so desirable,* may not be very common but neither are they rare phenomena. But even if she does not marry, knowledge of herself and acceptance of the situation which has prevented her from marrying will be an asset in helping her make a happy adjustment to single life. It can never be forgotten that "God writes

* The song with the lines, "After I have looked around the world for a mate then I might decide that you will do," is truer than one might think. There are girls who remain too romantic for too long a time. They are fortunate if their romanticism is cured in time for them still to marry the common-garden-variety of man whom they spurned under the influence of their youthful dreams.

straight with crooked lines—even sins." And it might be added, even neuroses. Pope Pius XII, who expressed his sympathy for the plight of those women who in our times "remain perforce unmarried,"[9] hastened to point out their providential role in the modern world, a role which will be discussed later on in this book.*

THE PROBLEM OF CHASTITY

"To live today in our great cities without loss of faith and purity requires no less heroism than was needed in the days of bloody persecution."[11] Without dramatizing her situation the single woman will sometimes find herself in circumstances which underline the truth of these words of Pope Pius XII. The problem of chastity for single women is a serious one. There may be a few Catholic single women for whom it never becomes a problem at all—at least, never a conscious problem. Repression of their sexual instinct, or, perhaps a rather angelic nature protected by grace, keeps them from ever having to grapple with temptations against chastity. But for the majority of single women today this is not so.

Even the young girl whose sexual instinct may not yet have been aroused moves in an atmosphere where sex is paramount and where she may be tempted to "experiment" even though she feels no strong physical urge to do so. (The Kinsey studies support most writers on sex differences in agreeing that, unlike the male's, the female's sex instinct grows stronger as she grows older; it is usually much stronger in a woman of thirty than in a girl of eighteen.) How much harder is the situation for the single woman whose sexual instinct is stronger, when pressures from within combine with the social pressures from without to encourage her to let down the barriers and engage in an extra-marital affair.

* Some pamphleteers give the impression that single life is something desirable in itself. Here, however, is a comment by Father Faherty from his excellent compilation of the writings of the last several popes on women. He is referring to the attitude of Pope Pius XII to single women. "He did not put up the single state outside the religious life as something at which to aim. He seemed to consider the numerical increase of single women the result, mainly, of the calamitous circumstances of modern times."[10]

It becomes increasingly clearer that the single woman today cannot and will not preserve her chastity unless she sees it as a positive value to be cherished and defended. Or she will not preserve it in a condition of psychological balance. It should be remarked that often even when external chastity is preserved, it is at the cost of distortions which will be discussed later on. The days of negative virtue are pretty much over. The single woman may have trouble getting a proposal, but she has no difficulty getting a proposition. The secretary of a conservative business concern can have an affair with her boss quite openly without losing her respectability. That is why Léon Bloy's castigation of the bourgeois woman on account of her negative virtue (in opposition to the saint and the prostitute both of whom he felt were capable of making a positive response to reality) is definitely dated. For it is more often true that the "good" girl remains good not through narrow convention, not because she has no opportunity to be bad, but because she fights to preserve her chastity in a society which pays her no special tribute for doing so.

The Catholic single woman may find herself practically alone in thinking chastity an absolute value and in maintaining that sexual relations outside marriage are never permissible. This is not to say that the Catholic woman is the only one with moral values. (Unfortunately Catholics are often smug in feeling that they are the only ones with high standards of morality.) It is to say, however, that her moral values are different. There are people of great integrity in the world today, who have a respect for the rights of others, who treasure human dignity, and place a high value on marriage and faithful love, but who would still feel that there is a place for sex outside of marriage. They certainly are not promiscuous—and Catholics do them an injustice if they think they are—but they would maintain that under certain circumstances it is not only permissible but indeed praiseworthy for a woman to give herself to a man outside marriage. They see sex as a precious thing only to be used with a man one loves, but as long as intercourse harms no third party (the possibility of a child resulting being removed by the use of contraceptives) they see nothing immoral about the act. Sexual relations between lovers whose marriage is unavoidably postponed for an indefinite period, or between a single woman and a married man whose wife is hopelessly insane, are thus justified in their eyes.

The Catholic who, of course, cannot agree with this position, meets it increasingly. She may find herself having difficulty answering it, for it is not the sort of thinking that yields itself to the old-fashioned apologetic argument. One cannot prove that every act of illicit love wreaks havoc on humanity, anymore than that loss of physical virginity thereby renders a woman hopelessly depraved or promiscuous. To answer this argument, and to prevent herself from being persuaded by it, the Catholic woman has to realize that not utilitarianism nor even the possibilities of human, temporal happiness are the crux of her moral stand, but belief in a God who transcends human judgment, as He transcends human vision. The law of perfect chastity outside marriage is a difficult law indeed. It is hard for a woman made for a man to have to accept the possibility of living her whole life long without any sexual union. But accept this law she must, and, as a Christian, she can rejoice in accepting the love of Christ and the grace of God that go with it.

Underneath some of the thinking which would urge single women to indulge their sexual needs is the premise that sex can be as casual for a woman as it is for a man. Some of the early feminists believed this, and in *Modern Woman: The Lost Sex*[12] the authors give in detail the ironic life history of Mary Wollstonecraft (author of *A Vindication of the Rights of Women,* one of the first feminist treatises) who maintained that there was no reason that sex for a woman could not be the same as it is for a man. Mary saw no reason that alliances based on sex had to be permanent. The climax of her tragic story came when she found herself pregnant and desperately trying to convince her lover to marry her. The feminist viewpoint had backfired!

The authors of *Modern Woman: The Lost Sex* point out that the sex life of men and women cannot be the same. "Sexual intercourse, psychologically, can never be an experiment for a woman in any true sense. It is either the real thing or it is nothing. The same holds true for a man, but when he achieves orgasm the sexual end for which nature has ordained him has been achieved. He has discharged his seed. Nature demands nothing more of him. He can instantly die so far as the future of life is concerned.

"Nature demands much more of a woman, and something different. She is designed to receive the seed. True, with contraceptives she may evade the end for which nature has designed her. But she cannot evade the end psychologically."[13] Pregnancy, childbirth and lactation are the normal completion of the act of intercourse for her. The single woman who thinks that sex can be a passing moment for her, as it can be for a man, is acting against her own nature, and, as Lundberg and Farnham put it from their pragmatic viewpoint: "In proportion as she inwardly rejects the idea of receiving the seed—that is, of being impregnated—she fails to attain full sensual pleasure from the sexual act."[14]

The single woman who fails to find sexual relief or happiness in casual relationships may well need to consider that sex cannot be for her what it is for a man. And however we, as Americans, may scoff at cultures which frankly admit a double standard and pride ourselves on our single standard, we must question whether a single standard of immorality does not hurt a woman much more than a double standard. The old double standard (as much as we as Christians condemn sex outside of marriage for men too) at least protected the family and protected a woman from herself. For casual intercourse, opposed as it is to her nature, can never satisfy her.*

Single women associate with men inevitably, notably on their jobs. Sooner or later, the single woman may meet a married man to whom she is physically attracted, who may or may not reciprocate the attraction. What is she to do? Obviously, she cannot

* *Modern Woman: The Lost Sex* gives an excellent exposition of the different biological and psychological make-up of males and females, and an interpretation of the double standard which puts it in proper social perspective. However, certain opinions of the authors (notably that celibacy voluntarily chosen is always the result of sexual aberration) are repugnant to a Catholic.

always run away. She has to accept the fact that in today's world she will be in contact with men, and she has to come to terms with herself and with her relationship to them. Naturally, she has to be prudent: one does not fan up a fire and then complain because one gets burned. Yet at the same time, she cannot be overly concerned about possible (often extremely remote) dangers to her chastity. Single women who regard every man as a potential seducer and take the attitude—even in the most harmless situation—that they are in danger of being raped show that they are suffering from a serious disturbance.

THE WORLD OF TWO SEXES

A mentally healthy single woman can enjoy companionship and conversation with men without any of these neurotic fears. A normal woman realizes that men and women are complementary to one another in other aspects of life besides the directly physical and sexual. A woman who associates only with other women develops her personality only partially and tends to become rather one-sided. That is why contact with men is good for her. Male cousins, in-laws, business associates, the husbands of friends, can all unwittingly help her to keep her balance and to preserve her femininity without exaggerated distortion.

There are some women who think only in terms of marriage and seldom talk to any man unless there is "a future in it," unless he is eligible. They are narrowing their own outlooks and limiting their own personality development, and it is possible that when an eligible man does come along they will not be ready for him because they do not know how to converse and act with a man. Single women who have the opportunity to do professional work with male associates on a common project, to joke with men in the office in easy, innocent comradeship, to participate with men in a study group or volunteer organization can testify that they have benefitted a great deal emotionally and intellectually through contact with the other half of the human race. Married women can do a great service to their single friends in including them in mixed gatherings. The married need not act as match-makers (though they can do that, too, if they wish) but they should try to admit the single woman into the world of two sexes, even when "there's no future in it." Single women who have enjoyed recreation and good conversation with couples, being good friends with both husbands and wives, have had an element of richness added to their lives. Of course, the single woman has to adopt a sensible attitude. She cannot intrude herself into their lives; she has to be satisfied with the areas she can have in common with them, and has to be emotionally balanced (and shall one add, pure of mind?) so that she does not let herself desire anything that is "off limits."

A well-balanced, Christian single woman does not deny the goodness of sex; she recognizes that, without marriage, she must live without a very important part of life. She knows that nothing is to be gained by belittling the fact that men and women are made to complete themselves in marital intercourse and that marriage is the normal destiny of a human being. However, she realizes that it is possible to live without sex. She becomes a "frustrated old maid" only if she tries to deny her feminine nature and its needs and to turn her sexual instinct against herself. To achieve this balanced attitude may be difficult but it is not impossible. A healthy sublimation of sex can be attained.

Not desiring to revert to a former stage of her emotional development and feeling keenly her incompleteness without a husband to make her whole, to take her truly out of herself in the ecstasy of marital union, the single woman, if she perseveres in beseeching prayer and dependent trust in God's grace, can count on the Holy Spirit to effect that transcendence of human sexual love which on a natural level seems impossible to her.

That there will be struggles which while she is enduring them seem endless, that her loneliness can be humanly unbearable, that her body rises up in humiliating rebellion does not change the reality of God's love for her. That she has not the psychological satisfaction of being the "bride of Christ" as does the nun, does not negate the goodness of her life lived out moment by moment in doing the will of God as she sees it. Frankly accepting her nature, not rejecting her femininity by desiring to be either a man or an angel, she can grow in graceful womanliness, and find in her apparent "vocationless" state (whether it is temporary or permanent) gradual fulfillment of the real vocation of all Christions: the perfect love of God which is sanctity.

NOTES

1. Marjorie Hillis, *Live Alone and Like It* (New York: Bobbs-Merrill, 1936), p. 95.
2. *Ibid.*, p. 19.
3. Gertrude P. Driscoll writing in *Women, Society and Sex,* edited by Johnson E. Fairchild (New York: Sheridan House, 1952), p. 57.
4. *Ibid.*, p. 53.
5. *Ibid.*, p. 59.
6. Bernhard Häring, C.Ss.R., "Love and Celibacy," *Theology Digest,* Vol. VII, No. I (Winter 1959).
7. M. Esther Harding, M.D., *The Way of All Women* (New York: Longmans Green, 1937), pp. 254, 255.
8. Eva Firkel, *Woman in the Modern World* (Chicago: Fides, 1956), p. 109.
9. *Woman's Duties in Social and Political Life,* Address given October 21, 1945.
10. William B. Faherty, *The Destiny of Modern Woman* (Westminster, Md.: Newman Press, 1950), p. 130.
11. Pius XII, *Papal Directives for the Woman of Today* (Washington: N.C.C.W., 1947), p. 6.
12. Ferdinand Lundberg and Marynia F. Farnham, M.D., *Modern Woman: The Lost Sex* (New York: Harper, 1947), Chapter VII.
13. *Ibid.*, p. 278.
14. *Ibid.*

2. [illegible]

6. [illegible]

7. [illegible] Westminster [illegible]

8. [illegible]

11

Single Women: Friends, Work, and Leisure

ONE of the most intense sufferings of single women is loneliness. G. B. Stern, the English novelist, in the story of her conversion expresses this feeling well when she says that it is the gnawing awareness of "not being first with anybody."

It is natural that a woman desire to have one particular person whom she puts above all others in her life, who needs her as she needs him. As someone has remarked, "Even if one is locked in marriage to a seemingly merciless husband whose drinking habits rock the peace and security of each member of the family, there is, nonetheless, a unifying thread—a tie between need and growing fulfillment. But for the single woman it is different. There is no one to whom she is of primary importance—for better or for worse. No one who phones her each day, to whom she is intimately bound; no babies who are hers to feed and dress and comfort, no one to wait for—be he around the corner or three thousand miles away; no daily routine which humdrum as it may seem, finds meaning in the common sharing of a goal . . ."[1]

The single woman has to accept the fact that she is not a first with anybody. (True, she may still be first with a mother or father while they are alive, but if she is sensible she realizes that they will probably die before her and she must be ready to have the tie broken, and, even more important, she recognizes that their presence cannot make up to her for the lack of a husband and child.) But because she is not "first with anybody," the single woman is, in one way, freer to have a larger circle of persons to share her devotion and love. The place of friendship in the life of the single woman therefore inevitably looms large.

FRIENDSHIP

The development of rich, mature friendships is something for which she should hope and pray. While giving her love, sympathy, service, and interest to her friends, the single woman should beware lest she corrupt the idea of friendship and try to force her friends to give her the concentrated attention she would have the right to expect only from a husband who had pledged to share his whole life with her. A woman would put an impossible burden on her friends if she expected them to fill for her the same emotional role as a husband and children. In an era when sexual aberrations are so common that they have become the expected—or, suspected—thing, an unhealthy relationship between two women no longer shocks society. But more common than such abnormal relationships, and more of a hazard to the average woman, is the situation in which two or more single girls cling desperately together for protection against the realities of the world. Friendship becomes a block in the way of mature personality development; they hesitate to look for a new job, to join a different organization, or to move to a new city because they do not want to leave their friends. At an earlier age, these were the girls who huddled together in a group at the teen-age dances. A decade or so later they are still (probably unwittingly) preventing one another from growing up or reaching out to a new vocation, as surely as years ago they prevented one another from dancing. Their friendship, needless to say, does not afford them real protection: rather they are in the ironic position of people in a heavy sea who cannot swim, acting as if clinging to one another will prevent them from drowning.

But healthy friendship is an excellent thing. One recalls Cicero's words concerning friendship: "Of which no greater gift is given to man by the immortal gods." And if friendship had such great value for a pagan, how much more of a blessing is it for a Christion? For, as Christians, we love our friends in the friendship of Christ Who is also our friend.* There are persons unfortunately who appear to be too proud for friendship, but usually their haughtiness hides a fear of being rejected and hurt. They are not so much afraid that they will be imposed upon, as afraid they will not be needed. Their pretense of indifference to friendship masks a fearful—rather than a hard or unloving—heart. For single women, this pose of independence is especially dangerous; for it can keep them from enjoying happy human relationships as surely as it may have kept them from marriage.

The single woman, frankly admitting she needs her friends, puts herself in the position where she can be needed by her friends. Provided that she sees friendship as a means of true *liberation*—freedom for each of the friends to grow as she personally should grow; freedom always for the friends to enlarge their circle; freedom to develop together in mature understanding and love—she need never be afraid of it.

Obviously it takes two to make a friendship just as it takes two to make a quarrel, and obviously, too, it takes two to keep a friendship. But in any human relationship, one cannot measure the extent of one's giving. Women must be aware of a pettiness that can take the edge of joy off a friendship. ("She didn't remember my birthday so I won't remember hers." "She always expects me to phone her and she never phones me." And so on.) While, as Cicero remarked, it is the essence of true friendship that it should be immortal, nevertheless, one has to work at keeping one's friends. A true friendship can persist even when one goes off to a cloister and the other stays in the world, or one gets married and the other remains single, provided both friends are will-

* It is rather a strange thing, but there are many Christians who think of fraternal charity as something we give to the poor with our coin, but not as the love we give our friends.

ing to make the necessary adjustments. The single woman who expects her friend who marries to be able to spend as much time with her as she did formerly is herself the cause of the destruction of the friendship. In friendship, as in everything human, there is inevitable change, for one cannot grow unless one changes. So, while both growth and change can be painful they are usually to be welcomed. A friendship to be preserved over the years, through all the changes and vicissitudes of the friends' lives, must be adjusted and readjusted. If both friends realize this, their friendship can deepen as it progresses.

There are words from a poem of Hilaire Belloc's that seem especially apt here.

> From quiet homes and first beginnings
> Out to the undiscovered ends
> There's nothing worth the wear of winning
> Save laughter and the love of friends.

"Laughter and the love of friends" are two tremendous helps in living a full and holy single life and should not be underestimated; their presence in our lives indicates that we are living life well. For there cannot be laughter—true laughter, as opposed to bitter wit—unless there are humility and a lack of self-pity. And there cannot be the love of friends unless we are loving and, as a consequence, have made ourselves lovable.

THE BIGGEST SLICE OF HER TIME

Another great part of a rich, emotionally healthy single life is, of course, daily work. The single woman, especially as she grows older, will come to regard it as the most important element of her daily life, taking the major portion of her energy as well as her time. In her twenties a girl may feel that her work is just something to bring in the money and that she can make her greatest contribution to society outside office hours, but as she gets older and perhaps cannot keep up the busy pace of leisure-time, volunteer and apostolic activities, she will see that her work must be the chief focus of her endeavor.

What about work? Objectively, there are some jobs that are more important than others, jobs which, in other words, make a greater contribution to the common good. Thus, a social worker is doing more important work than a milliner; a nurse, than a girl behind the candy counter. But hats and chocolate, while they are not indispensable, do have their part in the whole—it is good that there are people who both make and sell hats and fudge. Too often people narrow the concept of "useful work" to those jobs that directly serve the highest or the most desperate needs of man. I once had an argument with a man who could not see that working in a chewing gum factory serves a useful purpose. He got the point when asked if he chewed gum. He could also have been reminded that gum chewing is helpful to pregnant women suffering from heartburn and dyspeptic old people.

One can serve society without performing the most important function in society. For the common good it is necessary that a multiplicity of tasks be performed. We may long for a simpler, less specialized age, but meanwhile we live in an age of specialism and it is usually our lot to have as our particular job only one task. It may be small comfort to know that this task does serve the whole when what we do is only perhaps a minor part of serving even one of the many needs of men. The problem of the objective requirement of work and the subjective satisfactions thereof is something beyond the scope of this book. However, the complexity of the situation should be pointed out since there are far too many single women who labor under an inferiority feeling because they are not nurses or social workers—or members of the one or two other occupations which they have been led to believe serve the common good.

But granted that a woman comes to realize that there are a multiplicity of worthwhile jobs corresponding to the many and complex needs of individuals and society, what is she to do if she does not find her own job sufficiently satisfying? There are many single women who, as the years go by, say: "I know what you say about my job's being useful is true, but I want to do something more. I want to have the satisfaction of being directly of service." This desire of single women becomes more serious as time passes, and certainly these subjective reactions to jobs should be considered. It is all very well, in the few years before her marriage or during the "empty nest" period, for a woman to spend thirty-five hours a week typing out insurance forms or ushering people into an advertising agency, but if she does not marry and her work has major importance in her life, it is both understandable and praiseworthy that she should want it to evoke her greatest capacity and effort in the best service of society.

In this connection, there are three factors vocational guidance counsellors and the persons whom they advise must take into consideration: individual aptitudes and talents, personal desires, and the needs of society. Certainly it would be rather ridiculous to encourage a girl—especially after she has been out working a few years and it appears that she will remain single—to develop a skill for which there is no demand. But at the same time the immediate job openings should not be the decisive factor in determining for what work a woman should be trained. Those women who completed college just before the war years who felt a desire to teach young children may very well be tempted to blame their advisers for steering them away from elementary school teaching and leaving them unsatisfied (and society unprepared for the Baby Boom).

WHERE SHOULD A WOMAN WORK?

Women are generally happier when they are engaged in work which is directly of service to people. Single women who are thinking of seeking more agreeable work, or of acquiring more education in order to enter another profession, generally are looking for the personal contact they do not get in other areas of their lives. A bookkeeper who becomes a baby nurse, a secretary who takes courses at night to prepare herself for personnel work, the typist who goes to college at night to become a teacher, and the assistant buyer in a department store who goes on to get graduate training to enter social work, see their new careers as a means of greater service as well as greater personal fulfillment. They are to be encouraged to strike out on new paths. The problems they face —financial and otherwise—make the acquiring of a new occupation difficult, and, regrettably, well-meaning families and friends, motivated by concern for their material security, often discourage them from leaving a job or type of work which they have come heartily to dislike. The woman who can gather her inner resources together and make the change in spite of all opposition has admirable courage.

Most women feel more satisfaction in their work when they see it as a direct service to others. Usually they feel more involved personally in care of a sick child than in worry over a sick society. Thus, they prefer social work to sociology, nursing to laboratory research. But there are some women who by intellect and temperament are geared to serve "the sick society." They have the devotion and persistence for research work, and it would be foolhardy to steer them away from that occupation under the mistaken notion that they should be doing more "feminine" work. Choosing solitary scholarship rather than work with people, they should not be made to feel like mavericks who do not fit into the social scene.* As Edith Stein noted, there are no occupations which are rigidly masculine or feminine. "But wherever soul, intuition, empathy and adaptability are demanded, where the whole person matters: that he be nursed, formed, helped, understood, portrayed—there is the great area for truly womanly work. That is, in education, every type of social work, those sciences which have man and his activities for their object, those arts which

* Unfortunately, women who would rather work by themselves—as research librarians, or biochemists, for instance—are often made to seem selfish. As Ruth Reed remarks sensibly about the vocation of the solitary woman scholar: "Degrees of selfishness appear to be measured by sociability or volume of acquaintances and social contacts . . . And yet even the simplest observation tends to show that an interest in meeting people is by no means evidence of an unselfish interest in them."[2] There is no need to do violence to those who have ability to work alone in a museum or laboratory, by turning them into salesgirls or social workers.

depict him, business and government, national and municipal affairs, particularly where personal contact and care are needed."[3] In other words, everywhere.

There are some single women, however, who seem condemned to work at occupations which they do not find satisfying, and which—for very valid reasons—they cannot leave. Economic facts do not disappear by our denying them and we have to admit that in our present industrial set-up some women seem doomed to perform tasks which, because of their mechanized nature, go against feminine (and indeed human) bents. It is being argued that the introduction of automation will do away with many of the horribly mechanized jobs in offices and factories which were a kind of slavery for the people who filled them. If automation has this effect we certainly should rejoice. But meanwhile, what about women who do not like their jobs, who find them frustrating and boring? One compensation for most women, of course, is the companionship of fellow-workers in office and factory which helps them endure the monotony of the work itself. Congenial companionship is a major job satisfaction for women. Obviously another compensation for unsatisfying work is what can be done with the money they receive in return for doing it. Women who are glad to be self-supporting, who use their money to decorate their apartments, to travel, to take their nieces and nephews out, and to finance their charitable activity, have a compensation for the hours of boredom spent at a "job."*

When Pope Pius XII talked about the providential role of the single woman in our day he was undoubtedly referring to the work in society that she has freedom to perform, which the married woman with children—if she is to fulfill her basic task well—has not. Teachers who have gone to work in underdeveloped countries, secretaries who are employed in government service in United

* Nancy C. Morse, who conducted a survey of the job satisfaction of groups of white-collar workers, eighty-four percent of whom were women, had this to say: "There are employees . . . with relatively routine work who are very satisfied . . . It is not so much that they actually like the kind of work they are doing, but that *they don't notice it particularly*" (Emphasis mine). They like other aspects of the organization and this positive attitude carries over to the job."[4]

States Embassies all over the world, professional women who have volunteered for a few years to aid the bishop of a mission diocese (as journalists, educators, doctors, and so on) exemplify this freedom of the single woman to go where she is needed for the good of the Church or of society. Because she is "not first with anybody" she has the freedom and the opportunity to make the needs of the "least of Christ's brethren" her own. Thus she is able to fulfill the role of spiritual motherhood which the Pope claimed for her.

SPIRITUAL MOTHERHOOD

The trouble with the single state is that it does not provide a woman with a channel for her love. One can say to the single woman, "Love God and serve your neighbor and you'll be happy." But there one directly hits her problem. *How* is she to love God? *How* is she to serve her neighbor? Marriage and the religious life provide for a woman a framework for her love and service, but the single life lacks this framework. Opportunities for charity are not so naturally incorporated into her life as they are into the lives of the wife and the nun; they depend much more on her initiative and imagination. She has to seek and to find ways of channeling her love. When single women are accused of being selfish it is not so much because as individuals they lack the generosity of married women, but because the circumstances of their lives are not prodding them on to *give*. The unselfish single woman has to make a deliberate effort to find means of giving. She has to prepare herself to accept the role of spiritual motherhood.

What is "spiritual motherhood?" It is a phrase which has been tossed around considerably. It seems to make a suitable ending for any Communion breakfast talk or sodality speech to a group of unattached women. That a woman is supposed to be a mother, either in the physical or spiritual sense, is repeated to Catholic women an endless number of times. Spiritual motherhood is held up as an ideal for the single woman, for the childless married woman, or for the woman whose children are grown and gone from her.

Unfortunately, the notion of spiritual motherhood can be misused as a rationalization for the behavior of those single women who, preserving their external chastity, do so at the cost of the distortions referred to previously. Such a single woman claims the fruits of spiritual motherhood too easily by trying to live vicariously the life of her married sister or friend, by wrongly seeking emotional satisfaction in smothering with love a favored nephew, or by making herself a gloating martyr for her unfortunate friends and associates. Her life may not deteriorate into a perpetual binge of self-pity—at least, not ostensibly. But some self-styled "spiritual mother" can rationalize as a species of lofty sublimation what is really a harrowing misuse of other people's lives to compensate for her personal frustration in being deprived of husband and children.

Needless to say, when the Pope was talking about "spiritual motherhood" he was not advocating such neurotic use of the single state. Rather he was trying to galvanize into action in serving the genuine and real needs of mankind the single women who have the opportunity, energy and time for this task. The role he held up to them was a healthy role, indeed. But because it can be easily misunderstood and distorted it deserves more clarification than it has up until now received.

While knowledge does not necessarily make for virture, and clarification of the role of spiritual motherhood will not prevent distortion or abuse of that role, proper understanding should make more possible a healthy fulfillment of its demands. In the first place, the works that come under the heading of "spiritual motherhood" are comparable to natural motherhood only by way of analogy. Of course, the woman who adopts a child fulfills the role of natural mother *in toto,* but hers is the only work which is exactly comparable to the task of physical motherhood. The teacher, nurse, social worker, college house-mother, attendant in a playground, mother's helper, occupational or physical therapist, attendant in the home for the aged (to mention only a few of the professional roles that would seem to be directly associated with spiritual motherhood), volunteer in a foundling hospital, nurses' aide, Grey Lady, Big Sister, scout leader (to mention only a few of the amateur roles which would seem to fit under the same heading)—are engaged in work that is different from a mother's in many ways. Obviously they are not and are not supposed to be (except in very exceptional instances) "all things" to their charges as is a natural mother who is concerned with all the needs of her child. Their role is usually limited to one specific function and it does not call for the same degree of emotional involvement as does the role of the natural mother. In fact, such emotional involvement would be detrimental to the faithful and efficient performance of their role. The teacher, nurse or social worker who would take to heart everything that happened to her charges would soon make a fiasco of her work. Professional or amateur, the spiritual mother is engaged in a particular task for which she has the competence and has to assume a "hands-off" attitude in other areas in the lives of the children or adults she is serving.

Lack of realization of this difference in roles makes for misunderstandings especially in the case of amateur or volunteer "spiritual mothers." (Professional persons are usually forewarned against undue emotional involvement and realize the limitation of their function—a limitation which they have to insist upon sometimes when people with whom they work want them to broaden their role and make it involve other areas of their lives.) Ruth Reed remarks very sensibly, "The children need a mother at home; they need a teacher at school."[5] The roles are fundamentally different.* One does not expect from a teacher what one expects from a mother, and the teacher would be vastly misled if she expected from her teaching the same emotional satisfaction she would have a right to expect from motherhood.

The fact that "spiritual motherhood" is motherhood only by way of analogy has been overlooked by those well-meaning persons who have urged single women to help out the mothers of large families and thus exercise their own spiritual motherhood. Such a single

* This fundamental difference in roles accounts often for the seemingly ironic situation that a woman who is an excellent nursery school teacher does not necessarily make a good mother. Able to fulfill the first role well, in which her function and her emotional involvement are limited, she may not be able to rise successfully to the more extensive as well as intensive demands of the role of mother.

woman volunteer, whether she is baby sitter for a few hours, or for a few weeks when the mother is incapacitated by illness, performs a limited function. Of this the family is well aware, if only unconsciously, when they get annoyed at her for being a "meddling old maid" if she oversteps her assigned function. However, they themselves may confuse her role, and they show they do so when they resent the fact that she does not find their children immediately lovable or overwhelmingly attractive in the way that they do themselves.

There is no emotional "bang" in spiritual motherhood. This is a fact that both the single woman and the family she may try to help should realize. This is not to say that helping out with children does not bring a great many natural compensations: the woman who gets to know a particular family of children well will have an element of joy and satisfaction added to her life. But it is satisfaction she works to achieve: it is not the satisfaction that is natural to the mother of a child who is flesh of her flesh.

That the emotional satisfaction which comes with the works of service which constitute spiritual motherhood is not facilely attained must be stressed because there are entirely too many single women who, having turned to serving others as a means of achieving personal fulfillment, soon quit their charitable and volunteer work when a feeling of contentment and achievement is not immediately forthcoming. The sublimation of the natural maternal instinct is not done in a day, nor is it done merely by effort of will. As one writer remarks: "A great deal of nonsense is talked about sublimation, which is presented as a quick cure that will take away all our troubles . . . Real sublimation is a very different process [from deliberately setting art or work or religion or service of humanity in place of sex desires and physical maternity] and a very slow one. It means that we seek other interests or dedicate our lives to some great cause, and in time, *by a completely unconscious process,* the energy that would have gone into reproduction is turned into other channels."[6] Pope Pius XII, when he remarked that "with a sorrowful heart" the single woman gives herself to good works, was recognizing the fact that she has cause for regret in not getting married. This is something that likewise should be recognized by those well-meaning persons (whether they are married themselves or in religious life) who do not understand the difficulties and frustrations of single women, and who are inclined to grow impatient with them because they do not realize their need for sympathy. Expecting a single woman who has wanted marriage very much to "snap out of it" and to get over her feeling of frustration without a struggle is as patently unrealistic as it is heartless. These single women can be helped to learn to love and to give themselves in loving service only if other Christians understand and sympathize with their situation.

Certainly the care of the old in our time represents another major social need. Single women who turn their attention to this problem either by giving their services to any of the organized works for the aged or by assisting elderly relatives and friends can well find a channel for their energy and devotion. Especially since work with the old is not so appealing as work with children, the need for volunteers in homes for the aged is more pressing, and therefore worthy of the attention of any single woman with time and energy to spare.

Single women who have the care of an aged parent have special and difficult problems. If the parent is sick or infirm they will sometimes find a reversal of the roles which prevailed in their own childhood. They will find themselves having to assume major responsibility, perhaps in making decisions as well as in supporting the family, and often in providing physical care. While in certain aspects their role has similarities to the role of a mother, it has important differences. Obviously it is good for neither themselves nor their parent if without cause they allow him or her to assume a completely dependent role. Needless to say, if a woman is charged with the responsibility of taking care of her father or mother, she must work to do it graciously and with a generous spirit. But she must at the same time strive to keep her emotional balance. Over-solicitude and pointless self-sacrifice are not only bad for the single woman herself but for the parent as well. It is exceedingly unhealthy for her to strive to compensate for a frustration by trying to cast the parent in the role of husband or child. Nor should she allow the care of the parent to occupy her whole life—even if unavoidably it must occupy the chief part of her time. Conscious development of her own inner resources can be an excellent safeguard against the unconscious development of neurotic satisfaction in the parent as compensation for her unmet needs.

Spiritual motherhood resembles physical motherhood in that both demand from a woman her compassion, devotion, self-sacrifice, and delicacy in sensing and responding to the needs of others. A single woman can feel that she is healthily developing these qualities in her work of serving others—whether they be relatives or strangers, whether her care for them be on a professional or voluntary basis—if she keeps in mind the cautions mentioned above and works to achieve a spirit of detachment in her life.

A spiritual and emotional necessity for the single woman is the development of detachment. If she is to prepare herself well for friendship as well as for spiritual motherhood, she needs to focus her life properly. The secret of love as well as the secret of detachment is found in the words of Saint Augustine: "Thou hast made us for Thyself, O Lord, and our hearts are restless until they rest in Thee." With the goal given her by her faith, union with God, and the means given her through her membership in the Church, Mass, and Sacraments, the single woman is prepared spiritually to fulfill the purpose of her existence. With more opportunity for prayer and more freedom to attend daily Mass and Retreats than married people, she is, in one sense at least, a spiritually privileged Christian. Her prayer, which arises to God from the depths of her needs, which starts from the basis that she "is alone and poor," can gradually develop into a hymn of praise and thanksgiving for all His goodness to her and to all mankind. Expanding her prayer as she expands her love, she will find in it a proper expression of her spiritual motherhood. For her prayer, growing in depth with her charity, can become the selfless expression of her compassion for the needs of all humanity. Begging God for them, she learns to embrace in her heart all people for whom Christ died. Her spirit can take her where physically she is unable to be, and limited though she is by time and opportunity and the necessity of earning her own living, her love can travel to the ends of the earth. In daring confidence she can seek to penetrate further every day into the mystery of God's love, and, leaving prayer for action, she is then prepared to love wisely and well all the children of God because she knows what it means to love Him with her whole heart and soul.

THE WASTE OF LEISURE

One major aspect of a single woman's leisure time has already been discussed in dealing with the works of service with which she is free to fill it. So many single women, however, approach the subject of leisure with little imagination. While the failure is not peculiar to them—for lack of imagination is characteristic of the leisure time of a great many Americans—the waste of leisure time in the lives of single women seems to be a greater tragedy.

Sometimes it seems that there is a special dearth of imagination in the approach to leisure on the part of *Catholic* single women. This may be an unfortunate result of their education, both at home and at school. The proverb says that the good is the enemy of the best, but it is equally true that the best is the enemy of the good. One sees single women who try their best to be good Christians, who spend much time praying, but who seem less imaginative in their approach to the needs of the spirit than materialists. Even less sometimes; for, the materialists often are materialists in name only, and in reality are humanists.

But there are Catholic women for whom a whole level of life is missing. They realize of course that men have physical and material needs; they realize too that men have supernatural needs. But the whole area of spiritual *natural* needs goes without recognition. In what is really quite an anti-Christian spirit—for Christianity recognizes that the world God made is good and that the works of men are good too—they fail to see the goodness and the beauty of the world around them and they fail to appreciate the goodness of the beauty that man has created. Art, music, literature are all tasteless to them. In a spirit that is antithetical to true Christianity, such persons show themselves more clearly to be heirs of Jansenism than of the Church which has always safeguarded true humanism.

Certainly women should be encouraged to cultivate "the best" in prayer and good works; but they need "the good" as well. To savor beauty or to enjoy a work of art is an end in itself, and it can also be a means to prepare the spirit for contact with God. Any woman who has learned to enjoy the loveliness of life—who has learned to enjoy song and poetry, the skillfully woven pattern in a rug, the gleam of shining wood, or the smell of freshly baked pie she takes from the oven—is enviable.

To savor, as well as to know and to create, is a power given to every human being. But what if a woman has not developed her ability to savor or to enjoy, which is the power to appreciate and to reverence reality? This, it would seem, is a power that comes to birth early in life; for the small child is led to appreciate and to enjoy probably even before he can express his wonder in words. While this is so, it is not true that one cannot cultivate the gift of enjoyment in maturity. It is a gift that the single woman can give herself if she makes the effort to do so. The first symphony she tries to listen to, the first piece of sculpture she tries to understand, the first mountain she looks upon, she may not find intriguing. She may not enjoy them. But her effort to do so will sooner or later be rewarded, and a new dimension added to her life.

A great sociologist, W. I. Thomas, postulated the *desire for new experience* as one of the four basic wishes of all human beings. It is cause for serious self-concern when we find that that desire has dried up in our lives. There are some single women who apparently always dislike trying anything new (and they are not necessarily older women; some women are mentally rigid in their twenties) and there are others who, even if they have a desire for new experiences, let fear keep them from realizing it. There are some single women who have never successfully resolved the typical adolescent conflict mentioned in the previous chapter between the need for security and the need for independence. Afraid of losing what they have, they are prevented from reaching out to something new. Fearful of losing the love their parents bear them, they will not declare their independence and thus move on to new experiences or new loves. Yet they cannot give up the yearning to be independent or to have new experiences on their own, and thus they suffer a kind of perpetual torture. They are afraid to leave the security of their parents' home for an attractive job offer in another city; they are afraid to leave the security of the tried-and-true vacation resorts no matter how attractive is the lure of a foreign land. They are in continual, unresolved conflict.

Such women are not necessarily only victims of their inner conflicts. Sometimes external pressure keeps them away from new experience. A parent who insists that it is too dangerous for them to travel alone (even though they are a mature thirty), or who manages to feel a heart attack coming on whenever they mention taking a job in a distant city, may prevent them from striking out for independence. Such a parent, who for the first twenty-five years of the daughter's life keeps her at home, ostensibly through solicitude for the girl's health and well-being, and for the remaining years hinders her attempts at independence through demand for consideration for the *parent's* health and well-being, forges seemingly unbreakable chains. Even if the daughter comes to recognize the parent's behavior for what it is she may not be able to free herself unless she receives encouragement and support from a therapist. In the case of Catholic women it has been pointed out that the daughter's feelings of guilt if she tries to break away may be compounded by the incorrect notion that has been fostered in some Catholic circles that children, even when they are adults, as long as they live under the same roof are bound to obey their parents. (Someone has remarked that Catholic single women seem much more likely to stay at home with their parents than their Protestant counterparts. How much this is the result of religious training in reverence for parents, and how much it is the result of the social and cultural situation prevailing in Catholic families—who are more likely to be recent immigrants or second-generation Americans, and therefore more conscious of kinship ties—is hard to judge. Certainly the opposite position of encouraging every single woman to leave home, whatever the circumstances, seems now to be being adopted by some Catholic counsellors. Here perhaps we see one undesirable extreme breeding another.)

Single women can cultivate in themselves the ability to enjoy new experiences. They may sometimes have to force themselves through situations they do not particularly like, but the result in the long run will be rewarding. Making an effort to overcome their mental rigidity means not yielding to nostalgia for what is old or safe. The tourists who make the isle of Capri suffer by comparison with the swimming pools of their native Hollywood or the visitors to the Grand Canyon who worry that the nearby motel is not equipped with television are not necessarily single women. But some single women, unfortunately for themselves, bring this same attitude toward Capri or the Grand Canyon to everything new they come across. If they will make this initial "breakthrough" of taking new things for what they are themselves, if they will make the effort of seeing each new person they meet for what he is himself, their horizons will be broadened tremendously.

"The world is so full of a number of things/I'm sure we should all be as happy as kings," are the words of one of Robert Louis Stevenson's children's rhymes. Perhaps they are too glib, even for children, immature beings who have not yet discovered Vergil's opposite truth that "there are tears in things," and even in the things that give us joy. But certainly for the Christian there is the balance of the two philosophies. There are tears and tragedy in the happiest things of earth, but there is also hope of redemption and of paradise in the saddest and most tragic things.

The single woman, if she is to grow into a mature person, has to let herself experience both the happiness and the tragedy. And to do that she has to leave herself open to life. She cannot be afraid.

NOTES

1. Anonymous, "Comments," *Integrity,* Vol. VIII, No. 12 (September 1954), p. 41.

2. Ruth Reed, *The Single Woman* (New York: Macmillan, 1942), p. 177.
3. John M. Oesterreicher, "Edith Stein on Womanhood," *Integrity*, Vol. VII, No. 12 (September 1953), p. 27.
4. Nancy C. Morse, *Satisfactions in the White-Collar Job* (Ann Arbor: Survey Research Center, University of Michigan, 1953).
5. Reed, *op. cit.*, p. 98.
6. Frances Meredith, *Single Women* (London: Sands, 1945), p. 32.

12

Dedicated Virginity

IF MARRIAGE reveals something of the immanence of God—of God among us—it is virginity which shows us something of His transcendence. Because of the Incarnation, because Christ became man and dwelt among us, the Christian married couple are able to bring forth children who are to be other sons of God. The married are a constant reminder to themselves and to others that God has stooped to man; in every child the Christian sees a sign of the Incarnation and the presence of the Infant Christ.

In the great mystery which is marriage is symbolized the union of Christ with His Church. But in the great mystery which is virginity is symbolized another reality. Marriage discloses that God in His infinite condescension became one of us; consecrated virginity reveals that God is infinitely above us.

Sacred virginity pays homage to the right of God to exact from a human being total dedication, total service. From a simply human point of view virginity makes no sense. Religion interpreted in anthropomorphic terms has little—if any—place for virginity. True, an anthropomorphic religion might see purpose in abstaining from marriage in order to be free to give oneself to the needs of mankind. But Christian virginity is not simply abstention; neither is it merely a condition for more effective social welfare work. Rather for the Christian consecrated virginity is a supernatural reality. It assumes the right of God to the total love of His creature. It takes for granted that it is within His prerogative to ask a human being to give up all that belongs to the ordinary course of earthly existence and belong entirely to Him, to symbolize for all men that the Divine transcends the human. The consecrated virgin is already living in the reality which marriage signifies (the eternal, unbreakable union of Christ and His Church, of God and humanity), because her consecration introduces her into the realm of the supra-temporal, the supra-mortal, into the sacredness of God Himself.

"The Christian virgin is a human person who has consented to God's action separating her from the world, disconnecting her from its profane context, and constituting her in the midst of a profane world as a symbol of God's intimacy, as a sacrament of God's unworldliness."[1]

But Christian virginity, while it shows forth and proclaims the transcendence of God, can exist only in an incarnational religion. For Christian virginity, consecrated virginity, involves the free and full consent of a human being. While it remains true that "you have not chosen me, but I have chosen you," this choice involves the assent of the human person. Because God became man, because Christ came to woo humanity, the consecrated virgin is not an unwilling bride, but a bride who freely gives herself, consenting to all that marriage with the Divine involves. If in the Old Testament men were chosen, were transported to the realm of the sacred almost in spite of themselves (like Saul who found the oil running down his beard before he realized he was to be the new king), to the children of the New Dispensation God gave the gift of freedom. Mary, the Virgin of Nazareth, was first asked for her consent to the Incarnation.

True, God could have chosen her without asking her consent, but do we not see here His infinite respect for human dignity, a divine delicacy in seeking human love? And because Our Lady's gift of her person was a free gift it could be offered as well as requested. And human beings who after Our Lady offer their virginity to God do so in the knowledge of the freedom of their gift.

Freely-offered virginity is only possible in the light of the Incarnation. Otherwise to ask to be His bride would be a terrible affront to God. Like a trembling Esther in mortal fear because she has come into the presence of the king without being invited, the ardent soul could see in her desire for total giving of self to God only the movement of presumption, a dreadful disregard of His majesty.

But Christ is man as well as God. He who is God is also Lover and Friend. And because Our Lord came to earth to invite all men to the eternal marriage feast it is only fitting that on earth there should be some human beings who in body as well as soul already live in the reality of this wedding. Since He has issued a call to the wedding feast, the soul who hungers for love of Him has the right to present herself at His gates. She is, as it were, one of the more eager guests who cannot wait for the feast to begin. She pushes her way in, brushing all obstacles aside, so anxious is she to take her place there. Yet, though angels and men alike may wonder at her boldness, because the Host has invited her, there is nothing they can say . . .

MISUNDERSTANDINGS ABOUT VIRGINITY

Consecrated virginity has always been rather mystifying, as Our Lord warned it would be. Especially in our era it is open to much misunderstanding. And since this misunderstanding exists not only among those who find complete and permanent abstention from sexual life impossible as well as incomprehensible, but also among practical Catholics, it seems necessary at the beginning of a discussion on consecrated virginity as it is lived today both in the convent and in the world, to clear up some of the area of confusion. That the mystery of Christian virginity is, Our Lord said, only revealed by the Holy Spirit and does not, therefore, disclose itself through human explanation, does not free us from the task of cutting through the unnecessary mystification of virginity.

First of all, consecrated virginity does not imply that marriage is more or less sinful. Individual theologians in the past—and occasional preachers and writers today—in an excess of fear of the perils of the flesh may have given that impression, but that has never been the teaching of the Church.

Neither does consecrated virginity imply that preservation of physical integrity *in itself* is superior to married love. Because popular pamphleteers, like the one quoted in our first chapter, unwittingly or not give the impression that the mere fact of virginity, of being unmarried and not having participated in sexual life, is somehow or other superior to being married,* it is well to point out in some detail that it is the *consecration* of virginity that alone gives it its value. As St. Augustine said: "In itself virginity is without any special dignity: it is not superior to marriage, quite the contrary, for the love of the married is stable while the virgin's love is ever seeking its object." It is consecration which fixes the heart on God, and it is consecration—not the fact of being unmarried—that is the essence of dedicated virginity and makes it superior to marriage.

Consecration to God is the special mark of the virtue of virginity. It is consecration which differentiates it from the chastity of the ordinary single person. Father Hermand explaining this point writes: "If we speak of the chastity proper to the celibate state of virgin girls whose intention is not, however, to consecrate their virginity to God, the virtue concerned is not different from that common to married people, widows or bachelors. . . . The same virtue of chastity enables married people to control their sexual relations so that no illicit pleasure enters in and enables unmarried women and widows to abstain completely from all sexual activity. It is probable that the latter have to face difficulties certainly unknown to married people. All the same no specifically distinct virtue is required.

"Consecrated virginity is principally the concern of the soul, of love; renunciation forever. . . . This commitment is sealed, made irrevocable, by the vow in honor of God. And it is this which distinguishes the consecrated virgin from all those men and women who perpetually preserve their virginity, but for inferior motives. In reality consecrated virginity is as far removed from bachelor-

* In the encyclical *Sacra Virginitas,* Pope Pius XII wrote: "Those therefore who do not marry because of exaggerated self interest, or because . . . they shun the burdens of marriage, or because like the Pharisees they proudly flaunt their physical integrity . . . none of these can claim for themselves the honor of Christian virginity."

hood as it is from marriage. The consecrated virgin is someone apart, we feel, not so much because she renounces human love forever by her vow, but because the vow places her in the kingdom of divine realities."[2]

The consecrated virgin then belongs to a different order of reality from the unmarried woman. Needless to say, this does not mean that the latter cannot be her equal or even her superior in holiness and charity. Nonetheless the character of the virginity of the person consecrated to God is quite different from mere "singleness."

With the increased emphasis today on secular institutes and dedication of one's virginity to God while remaining in the world, it is more then ever necessary that there should be a clear understanding of what the vocation to perpetual, dedicated virginity entails. Some of the literature on this vocation in the world almost gives the impression that the single woman who is having difficulty finding a mate should "make a virtue of necessity" and take a vow of perpetual chastity. Lacking is the stress that such a vow is indicative of a particular vocation. It is not something to be embraced simply because one feels since one is single that one might as well have the merits of perpetual chastity as well as its burdens. Neither can one agree with the writer who, noting the problem of divorced persons who cannot marry again, suggested that a solution for them might be found in a secular institute. While this may be the vocation of some divorced Catholics, holding up the life of dedicated perpetual chastity as a solution to a personal problem is putting the stress in the wrong place.

The consecration of virginity or the vow of perpetual chastity is indicative of a particular vocation. While it is true of course that it entails the obligation to keep perfect and perpetual chastity, it means a positive commitment to God, the expression of a willingness to belong totally and forever to Him. It would be as disastrous for a single woman to make such a vow for the purely negative reason that she is obliged to chastity anyway as it is usually for a woman to marry a man for the completely negative reason that there is nobody better around. Continuing to live in the world, as she is, a woman who has made such a negative commitment to virginity will experience all the very real drawbacks of a virginal life without being able to achieve that transcendence of her sexual nature, that complete centering of her affectivity in God, that the graces of a genuine vocation make possible.

For virginity does have its drawbacks. This is a fact that should not scandalize the devout Catholic, but should give him renewed respect and sympathy for the woman who chooses this vocation, as well as make him aware of his duty in charity to pray for those who have vowed to belong exclusively to God for the sake of the whole Church. For perpetual virginity is not a natural state to live in. As Father Paul-Marie de la Croix, O.C.D. writes in a book for religious sisters, "Virginity is usually the preparation of a girl for the right development of the woman that she is to be; therefore virginity brings a perfect balance of body and mind only for a short time. If woman's needs and faculties do not find their fulfillment in marriage and motherhood, this wealth, waiting to spend itself in love and service, becomes an idle treasure, a burden which seems every day heavier to carry. Passing years bring out unnoticed traits of character. Frustrated femininity undeveloped my human love easily makes women embittered or introspective. Irritability, a dictatorial manner, independence, narrow-mindedness, lack of adaptability show themselves, as well sometimes as various none too healthy oddities."[3]

These are the trials of virginity; and pitfalls such as these can only be safely traversed by a total cleaving to God, a whole-souled abandonment to the expansive action of His love. However, this rather appalling list of the disabilities of virginity viewed in itself should not lower anyone's estimation of the very exalted vocation of virginity consecrated to God, but it should emphasize the fact that virginity cannot be embraced hastily or without adequate preparation. This is especially true of such a dedication to God in the world, where the woman will have none of the supports of convent life, of rule, habit or cloister.

The difficulties of religious life, as well as the difficulties of dedicated virginity in the world, are increased if there is no adequate formation given to the young girl to prepare her for the realization—which will deepen as she grows older—of all that she has sacrificed in giving up marriage and motherhood. A Mother General notes: "Physiologically woman is made for her function as wife and mother . . . Her whole organism is ordered to the propagation of life. Woman is specialized in this role. Organically and mentally her life is centered round the cyclic modifications of the ovary. *Tota mulier in utero* said the ancients. In the same sense Father Neilly said, 'All womankind is a cradle.'

"But in the case of a virgin consecrated to God, the cradle remains empty. She avoids the natural and normal destiny of woman, and this cannot be done without a certain danger. Care must be taken and some effort made to preserve nervous and mental balance which might be imperiled when the state of life or the person's own will are in conflict with the fulfillment of natural functions. Forewarned a woman is more easily able to be cautious, realizing that quality of life is more valuable than life itself she can consecrate to Our Lord this balance which has been bought so dearly and preserved with such difficulty."[4]

The woman who has chosen a virginal life must realize that she has made a triple renunciation: of the pleasure of sexual union, of the human love and emotional well-being and support that having a husband brings, and of the joy and fulfillment of having children. That this triple renunciation involves danger has already been pointed out; but it might be well to note further that this danger is acute particularly because virginity involves the transcendence of the culmination of the normal human development of the person in her relationship to other human beings. This normal human development can be sketched briefly from infancy to maturity. First, there is the period when all the emotions and desires of the newborn infant are centered in self; next comes the time when the interest of the baby in the outside world develops as he comes to realize that his mother is not just what-feeds-him but is someone who loves him and whom he in turn can love; then he lives through a period in childhood when his interest is in the same sex; next comes adolescence when he is likely to develop a "crush" on an older person whom he admires; finally, there comes the natural culmination of affective interest with attraction to the opposite sex and consequent marriage.

When virginity is chosen, the final step in this development is transcended. Unless the virgin is guided, then, to live her life on its highest level—to strive to realize fully all that her vocation as "bride of Christ" entails—there is danger that she will revert to a former stage of development, and start to seek compensation for the very things which she had freely relinquished.

PSYCHOLOGICAL AND SPIRITUAL PROBLEMS

In the convent such emotional compensations would make themselves manifest in different ways from what would occur among women leading a life of dedicated virginity in the world; nevertheless, psychologically as well as spiritually, the problem is identical. Instead of developing a "crush" on the mother superior or falling into the trap of what is known to religious as a "particular friendship," the woman who has chosen to remain a virgin in the world, when she fails to live on the level to which she is called by her vow, can seek compensation for her lonely heart in an overdependence on her parents; or in an excessive concern for them (if it is they, and not she, who are in the ostensibly dependent position); or in an emotional attachment to her spiritual director, which can be especially insidious since it can so easily get by under the guise of a "holy friendship"; or in a search for crumbs of affection from her woman friends (with resulting sensitivity if they should slight her, along with a propensity for imagining such slights). Or she can busy herself with a hundred and one works of charity and so-called apostolic activity which she takes on as an escape—consciously or not—from the very life she has chosen. Of course, the religious can do the same thing, and especially since in her case—unlike that of the dedicated woman in the world—she lives her active life under obedience, there is the danger that she can use her manifold activities as a blind to hide from herself the true meaning of her dedicated virginity.

For virginity demands a lonely confrontation with God. And this confrontation demands emotional maturity. Using material things as a compensation for one's essential sacrifice is no less a stumbling block than emotional regression to the mature seeking of the Beloved by the woman who has given her life to Him. These material things can be favorite foods, furnishings, books, television, leisure-time pursuits, etc. If the religious is living in a community which is not especially fervent she shares the aloneness of the dedicated laywoman who, by herself, must withstand the temptation to enjoy the same compensations as do her single friends. The religious, moreover, may be urged in the direction of compensating for her virginal life by the body of Catholic public opinion—and that includes priests as well as faithful. The fund-raising appeal, "Nothing is too good for our good Sisters," may be motivated by the most sincere, disinterested charity but it too often reveals an attitude of complete misunderstanding of the religious life. The words, "Why shouldn't the nuns have these things? After all they have given up so much," show the speaker has missed the point of consecrated virginity.

For it makes no sense to give up the greatest temporal, human goods—a husband and one's own children—and then after one has paid this tremendous price for one's freedom (for what is consecrated virginity in the words of Saint Paul except complete freedom to serve the Lord?) to imprison oneself anew in a jail of material goods.

To look upon the conditions of the religious life as hardships which must be mitigated by any legitimate means is to forget that the virgin freely chooses to follow her vocation. Sympathy is misplaced and true charity denied when the faithful, instead of supporting the nun in her determination to give herself totally to God in the freedom of love, act as if she is someone condemned to hard labor whose condition of life must be mitigated at all costs!

(Needless to say, it would be a complete misunderstanding to infer that we are recommending that one withhold from religious nourishing food, adequate housing, and whatever else they need of material things in order to follow their vocation and do their apostolic work. A material thing is good if it helps one to *live* one's religious calling, not if it is a compensation *for* one's calling.)

Another danger the virgin faces as a result of her triple renunciation occurs when her heart is not centered in God alone but is yearning to return to a former stage of affective development. Then the virgin can tend to apply herself too tensely to preserving her chastity. Instead of concentrating on expanding her love for God, she can let her interest be narrowed and engage in a perpetual warfare over the things she has sacrificed. She becomes excessively prudish, sees in every baby an occasion of sin, and in every man a personal affront to her chastity.

NUNS IN AMERICAN CULTURE

There are some difficulties of a consecrated virginal life which arise from the nature of virginity itself. But there are other difficulties of dedicated virginity which are peculiar to our age.

It is an obvious fact that a girl who becomes a nun in the United States is a product of American culture. Evident too is the fact that she has been exposed to the same influences in American society as any other woman. She brings into the convent with her the effects of whatever tensions in the social structure she has internalized. What may be overlooked, since the nun in choosing her vocation has chosen a supra-temporal role, is the fact that she—no matter how sheltered her pre-convent life and no matter how immune she seems from "worldly" influences—has been inevitably influenced in her development to womanly maturity by all the conflicts to which women are exposed on the American scene. It might seem ridiculous to claim that any dilemma over "marriage and/or a career" has anything to do with a nun,* but deeper consideration of the matter will reveal that the ambivalence of American women toward their roles, as well as the ambivalence of society toward American women, has its effect on the position and the life of a nun.

* The Sister who attempts to juggle her role as a religious with simultaneous roles as student and teacher knows a dilemma analogous to the laywoman's marriage and career problem.

So far, it seems safe to say that there is no doubt about the status of the nun—at least, in those sections of the country with a great proportion of Catholics. The nun usually receives marks of respect that are no longer accorded to other women. The pregnant woman and the mother with young children may have to stand in the New York subways, but the Sister is invariably given a seat. That the traditional respect shown to nuns is continued in America should not cause us to forget that the religious vocation, as it exists in a changing sociey, is itself influenced by contemporary developments. This is apparent to anyone watching a nun, in a centuries-old habit, maneuvering an automobile in modern traffic. The spectator should be forgiven for wishing sometimes that, along with the adaptation to contemporary conditions which permits a religious to drive, would have come a modification in the headdress—so patently designed for the practice of custody of the eyes—which would permit better side vision.*

However, modern life has influenced the religious vocation in deeper, less visible ways. The nun, like all other American women, finds that the scope of her activities has been broadened. And this is true even if one considers only the two major works of active orders: nursing and teaching. The jobs involved in education and hospital work today are at once more numerous, more complex, and more specialized than they were a generation or two ago; certainly they are vastly different from what they were at the time most active congregations were founded. Because of the emphasis on technical proficiency and the development of specialized functions, even a nun involved in education or in hospital work—the two areas where women have traditionally been able to exercise personal service and compassion, where their spiritual motherhood comes most readily into play—is likely to find herself a victim of modern impersonalization. Thus the Sister Bursar in a college

* Of course, some communities have made such adaptations in their habits. The Synod of Rome held in February 1960 directed that, to facilitate their driving automobiles, the headdresses of religious women should be modified, while their habits should be changed to permit greater freedom of movement. Before this, Pius XII had repeatedly urged the adaptation of religious habits to contemporary needs.

toiling over her books all day, or the Sister Laboratory Assistant in a large hospital, while she can reassure herself that her work is still a work of mercy, that she is still serving her neighbor for Christ's sake, may have no contact whatsoever with the people for whom she is giving her life. This is a difficulty scarcely known to the religious woman of former eras.

It is natural that a Sister, as bride of Christ, should want to help other people to know and love Him more. The practice of the spiritual works of mercy is, for her, normally intertwined with the practice of the corporal works of mercy. In an age of technical simplicity this union of the two was quite possible. The nursing sister a century ago frequently gave spiritual preparation to a patient in danger of death. Today this union is possible—a nun can still combine the practice of both corporal and spiritual works in her life—but it becomes increasingly difficult. In the case of a Sister in a large modern hospital, for example, the practice of contemporary medicine and hospital care is so involved that she can exhaust herself simply over the physical health of the patients. Especially is the likelihood that care of the sick body will include care of the sick soul lessened for the Sister who is concerned with administrative and supervisory functions. Then the obligation to make and keep her hospital professionally the equivalent of any other hospital is so much in the forefront of her mind that she often has neither the time nor the energy nor the opportunity to attend to the spiritual welfare of her patients. Certainly she can offer all her work and worry for that intention, but this does not overcome the human frustration of knowing that her days are spent externally in a way no different from those of any other conscientious hospital worker. She is caught up in a situation not of her making. Here, of course, one touches on the great problem of the existence of Catholic educational, medical and social welfare institutions in a contemporary, scientific, highly-organized society. This is a problem difficult to discuss, let alone to solve.

The tension experienced by the individual religious between the traditional demands of the religious life and professional work under contemporary conditions is one of the major difficulties of convent life today.

Is a nun's active work of value in itself or is it subordinate to her aim of self-perfection? The desert fathers who spent their days weaving mats to be taken apart at nightfall did not see their task as an end in itself; the value of their work consisted only in the fact that it was a human aid to their contemplation. They kept their hands busy as an ascetic exercise to promote the freedom of their spirit. That the attitude of the modern religious engaged in active works is quite different is obvious. But how different is it and how different should it be? These are questions that are certainly outside the scope of this book. The difference in the two attitudes—termed the lay and the monastic by Father Congar[5]—is a difference revolving around whether or not one regards the work at hand as an end in itself, with all the rights and requirements of an end. Certainly it is clear that no member of an active religious congregation today sees her studying or teaching or social work as mere mat-weaving geared only to her personal sanctification. But does, for instance, the nun graduate-student see scholarly work as something with its own right to existence, with its own demands and prerogatives, or simply another chore which she accepts with the alacrity of religious obedience in order that the educational institutions her congregation runs will have the necessary number of Ph.D.'s for accreditation?

ADAPTATION OR COMPROMISE

Thus talk of adaptation in religious life today goes far beyond externals of dress and behavior to the roots of attitudes, ideas, and ideals. What adaptations are necessary in active congregations in view of the changing conditions of the modern apostolate and what adaptations are imperative in contemplative convents in the face of contemporary realities can only be decided by religious themselves—and by religious who have grasped the spirit of their order and the life it seeks to promote through wholehearted and faithful adherence to its rule over a period of years. As has been noted by authors wiser than the present one, only fervent communities can adapt themselves.[6] In communities where the spirit is mediocre adaptation will inevitably be compromise, and change invoked in deference to apostolic needs can in reality be introduction of a worldly spirit. Only fervent, prudent religious can judge what things in their life are irrelevant, what practices have completely outlived their usefulness and should be discarded, what are the essentials which are permanent and should continue unchanged, and what are the accidentals which should be preserved but given a new form. Certainly one could not suspect Saint Thérèse of Lisieux of being motivated by the spirit of worldly compromise when, on her deathbed, she confessed that the greatest hardship of her religious life had been shivering from the cold and respectfully suggested that in the future attention be given to the needs of individual constitutions and the rigors of particular climates when the matter of heating convents was being considered. But perhaps the matter of television being necessary for the recreation of religious is not so clear-cut, and one can wonder if the girl who left the convent because the Sisters in her centuries-old community did not wash their underwear every night really had grounds for her call for adaptation and really would make the best candidate for a new religious community or a modern secular institute.

Doubtless the question of adaptation of a religious rule to contemporary needs can be a difficult one for Sisters, and can place a heavy burden of suffering on the individual, a burden which is usually proportionate to her own fervor and to her awareness of the needs existing in the world. Thus, a mother superior planning a new convent suffers anguish that her constitution, in laying down living requirements, demands that there should be a room separate from the kitchen reserved just for dish-washing, "and think of the people all over the world who are homeless and starving." A possible necessity in one age has become an expensive luxury in another.

Especially in the matter of living arrangements and the practice of poverty it is to be expected that Sisters are influenced by the society in which they live. In a society like the United States which is predominantly middle-class, it seems only normal that Sisters would follow a middle-class standard of living. Doing so they usually conform to their surroundings. But their middle-class standard presents a problem when they are teaching in neighborhoods where the people are predominantly poor. The fact that many Sisters are forbidden by their rule to visit the homes of their pupils only adds to the barrier that their own standard of living places between them and the children. Intimate, first-hand acquaintance with the conditions under which their families live might give the Sisters an understanding and sympathy with their struggle for survival hard to obtain when they do not experience poverty themselves. The Sister who expressed her dismay that the children of one minority group in New York come to school dirty may have had her attitude changed if she had been able to visit their homes and found that seven families, each living in one room, shared one bath among them.

Poverty, of course, as one of the evangelical counsels, does not exist just for show—nor even for its apostolic value in giving good example. It is true nevertheless that the mother of a large family who sometimes is almost in despair keeping up with the demands of the parochial school might be encouraged if she felt that Sister had some inkling of her financial plight. Is it farfetched to ask that religious by their practice of effective, as well as affective, poverty show to the world the possibility of living detached from material goods? This invaluable function of religious seems more urgent in proportion as married couples are faced very often with the necessity of going against the materialistic standards of the age if they are to keep from birth control and sin. Needless to say, one is not campaigning for deprivation for religious. Yet "there is no true poverty where there is no hardship,"[7] and it would seem to be normal that there should be some visible expression of poverty in the lives of those pledged to the Christ "Who had nowhere on which to lay His head."

That among Catholics throughout the world there seems to be the urge to make the practice of poverty effective simply by being poor and sharing the condition of the poor is evidenced by the development of new religious congregations like the Little Sisters of Jesus of Charles de Foucauld, and by the springing up of secular institutes whose members seek to lead a life of consecrated virginity in the midst of all the tribulations of the world. These developments in the adaptation of the vocation to total dedication are still novel on the American scene. The fact that the Little Sisters of Jesus, while they have grown rapidly in numbers in European countries, have not attracted many American vocations even though they have been established here for a few years poses a problem. Is it, as some critics have said, that American girls are not generous, that they are not attracted to the prospect of a heroic life? The full Carmels, the waiting list for the Trappistines, the rapid growth of Maryknoll, argue otherwise. It could be suggested that a life of extreme poverty—of living totally immersed in the poor—seems unreal to young American girls who see very little destitution in America even though they may know vaguely that great poverty exists throughout the world. This attitude corresponds to the idea of so many young people that "we never had it so good" and fits into the pattern of the growing conservatism of American youth. If there is a lack of radicalism in general in American life one should not be surprised to find it missing in Catholics.

And yet one other explanation can be offered: whether or not one agrees that the young American girl is conservative, she is conventional. She expects a nun to look like a nun, and while there are girls who are Catholic beatniks (like their male counterparts who grow beards and refuse to take baths in the name of Christianity) their rejection of the conventions of their culture usually accompanies a disturbed personality which renders them unfit for religious life. The normal girl who feels no need to reject her culture usually—especially when she is young—feels embarrassed at any departure from its conventions. If then American Catholics expect a nun to look like a nun one should not be too surprised if religious in modern dress or modified habits are less appealing to girls than their counterparts in thirteenth century attire! Such are the paradoxes of adaptation.

This is not to say, however, that there has been no interest in America in new forms of religious life. Interest in the life and the spirituality of Charles de Foucauld suggests that eventually religious following his rule will flourish here, and that the spirit of simple, universal friendship which he advocated, and especially its practice among the poorest, most abandoned people, will catch on and possibly cut through the excessive institutionalization of charity in which some religious feel trapped.

VOW OF CHASTITY IN LAY LIFE

The interest in a completely dedicated life in the world seems to have grown along with interest in the lay apostolate, and since the lay apostolate is newer in the United States than it is in most European countries it is not surprising that we trail behind them in the establishment of secular institutes. Persons who desire to belong completely to God, to remain unmarried in the consecration of perfect and perpetual chastity, while at the same time leading a completely lay life, have the encouragement of Pope Pius XII, who, in approving secular institutes, gave his blessing to a new form of dedicated life whose members would not only exercise an apostolate "in the world" but "of the world."

The same Pope, in the encyclical *Sacra Virginitas,* noted that the privilege of a vow of perfect chastity extends to other lay people besides those in secular institutes. "And while this perfect chastity is the subject of one of the three vows which constitute the religious state, and is also required by the Latin Church of clerics in major orders and demanded from members of Secular Institutes, it also flourishes among many who are *lay people in the full sense:** men and women who are not constituted in a public state of perfection and yet by private promise or vow completely abstain from marriage and sexual pleasures, in order to serve their neighbor more freely and to be united with God more easily and more closely."

The fact that the Holy Father encouraged the complete dedication of perfect chastity in lay life should not surprise us if we re-

* Italics mine.

member the consecrated virgins and widows of the early Church, who were certainly lay people—religious orders did not come into existence until about the fourth century. The Church has always guarded and treasured the private vow of perfect and perpetual chastity; it is the only private vow which is reserved to the Holy See for dispensation. In this ecclesiastical legislation is reflected the social significance of even a private vow of chastity; it necessarily is of concern to the whole Church. For the dedicated virgin, even though her dedication is completely private and she retains her status as a lay person, is still bride of Christ belonging to Him for the sake of His Church.

A thorough discussion of secular institutes,[8] their number and variety, their history, their organization, or their place in the modern apostolate of the Church, is not possible here. The focus will be instead on the subjective experience of the individual who lives out her dedication in the modern world, whether as a member of a secular institute or simply as a virgin with a private vow. However, it can be noted in passing that at present in the development of secular institutes there seem to be two trends: one tends to emphasize the following of the three evangelical counsels, the essentials of the religious life, while adapting them to lay conditions, and to view the members as "secular religious," or religious living in the world; the other tends to emphasize the completely "lay" character of the members along with their total dedication. At the risk of oversimplifying, one can say that secular institutes which follow the first tendency seem to have grown up under the wing of an already existing religious order and seem to attract members who are thinking in terms of a religious life but for some reason cannot or do not want to enter the convent. The second tendency seems to exist among those secular institutes which arose (almost organically) from the development of Catholic Action and the lay apostolate, and whose members usually have never felt themselves called to religious life but who nonetheless want to place themselves completely at the service of the Church. These two tendencies of course have inevitable psychological implications for the members of the respective institutes. If one thinks of oneself as a religious in lay garb one's attitude is going to be quite different from that of a woman who thinks of herself as a lay person, albeit one with a special obligation to Our Lord. The apostolic constitution *Provida Mater Ecclesia* approving secular institutes speaks of an apostolate "in and of the world." Naturally the stress can be laid on either of those propositions, and the organization of the particular institute as well as the attitude of its members will vary accordingly.

For members of secular institutes who engage in public communal work or projects which preclude keeping the members' identity secret, the living of the life of dedicated virginity has one of the helps the Church accords nuns. At least their status is known; it is clear they do not intend to marry. The habit of a Sister is not only her personal bridal robe, but a symbol to everybody that she belongs only to Christ. People treat her accordingly, and she has public support for her chastity. Women who are known publicly to be members of a secular institute whose members do not marry, while they do not have the psychological help of the habit with its connotation to the world "Do not touch," experience something of the same protection and support of public dedication.

But what of the members of a secular institute who keep their membership secret, in order to safeguard the completely *lay* character of their life and apostolate, or those who keep perfect chastity in the world as a totally private relationship between themselves and God? It is obvious that they have additional difficulties. Ostensibly single women like other single women they accept this position in a spirit of identity and love. They certainly experience in common with other single women the temptations, frustrations and conflicts of the world in which they live. What these realities are have been discussed in the chapter on single women, and it is not necessary to detail them again. But added to the difficulties every unmarried woman experiences—whether she is "dedicated" or not—are certain other problems peculiar to a woman following a private vocation of virginity.

Unlike her single sister, who may or may not be looking for a husband, but is at least free to be, the woman with a vow has to refrain from the most innocent flirtation. She is not a nun, and she certainly does not expect to be treated as one. But how is she to behave?

The following quotation—if we can see beyond its rather foreign flavor—may provide the answer. It was addressed to a member of a secular institute in Italy. "The behavior of a secular religious must avoid two extremes, one proper to past feminine education, the other proper to the present: scrupulous awkwardness in meeting persons of the other sex, and the comrade's familiarity which defies danger. In your manner of speaking, looking, walking, dressing, you must show loyalty and purity which command trust and respect. On the other hand you must not be so rigid as to put astronomical distances between you and others. Therefore do not behave like an imp or like a nun."[9]

Unfortunately, women (whether as a result of biology or culture!) can so easily get themselves bogged down in details, can so readily fritter away valuable energy in worrying endlessly about unimportant things. A woman living completely for Our Lord in the world would show that she lacks emotional maturity and that she has failed to grasp the essence of her vocation if she acts as if the preservation of her chastity depends on her absorption in her external behavior. Whether one's sleeves are too long or too short, whether one should or should not use make-up, how freely one can laugh, and whether one can have a cocktail alone with a man—these are little things. Perhaps it will be argued that they are important little things, but concentrating on them directly is fruitless and might raise more problems than it will solve.

"What the modest woman wears is modest" Pius XII is quoted as saying, and this quotation applies here not only because modesty is the protection for chastity, but because the Pope's words bring out the important truth that external behavior expresses the interior disposition. "What the prudent woman does is prudent," is a complementary paraphrase, and presuming that the woman vowed to virginity has the indispensable foundation of common sense, she will become the prudent virgin much more surely and serenely in proportion as she opens her heart to the love of God, and not in proportion to the hours she spends scrutinizing her behavior for the preservation of her chastity. For it can never be repeated too often that it is love which is the meaning of virginity. When chastity, instead of charity, becomes the focus of the virgin's life, not only does she become emotionally maladjusted but her spiritual growth suffers as well.*

Virginity in the world is a hidden, humble vocation. In it there is no place for role-playing. One can be amused at the young girl who queried "How does one look *dedicated?*" but one would be rather appalled at anyone purposely striving for a "dedicated look" (whatever it may be!). For the crux of the virginal vocation is simply belonging completely to Our Lord, of *being* in love with Him. Role-playing smacks of play-acting, and between the woman who has accepted her vocation from Christ and Himself there is room for none of this. As in any marriage He has accepted her "for better or for worse"; He has accepted her and taken her just as she is. All she can do is to accept herself. Knowing that He loves her *as she is,* she will find less need to hide herself in a role, either in front of Him or before the rest of the world.

The temptation to role-playing is the more real since a woman who is vowed to perfect chastity in the world has so few other helps. Deprived as she is of the support of community life, of many of the psychological helps and spiritual aids of the nun, she can become terribly frightened when she realizes how insecure—spiritually and perhaps materially—her life really is. Then, instead of facing the fact that she must approach God in her awful aloneness, she may instead try to hide behind her role.

Of course, even if she attempts to do this it will not help her for long, for a vocation cannot be preserved if it is built on sand.*

* "And loveless chastity gives birth to a nasty brood: extreme sensitivity about oneself along with a hardened insensibility to the needs of others; meanness and morbidity; narrowness which cannot rise above self; the demand for sacrifice from others when at the same time one refuses to give a single heartbeat for one's neighbor." John Baptist Pesce, C.P., "Chastity's Consecration," *Cross and Crown,* March 1959.

* A single woman had experienced acutely the sense of being at loose ends and finally made a vow of perpetual chastity. She expressed her elation at having found her role in life and said that now her problem was solved and

Perhaps for that reason one can expand the thought, merely suggested before, about the necessity for deliberation and careful choice of a life of dedication to God in the world. As Pope Pius XII stressed in *Sacra Virginitas,* virginity is not to be recommended to young people who cannot hope to "follow sturdily and happily to its end." Priests, he admonished, should prudently examine the fitness of the candidates, "obtaining as often as is proper the help of experts." Especially would careful direction seem necessary for anyone choosing to vow virginity to God in lay life. This life in the world would seem to require not only a great deal of generosity, already acquired mortification, a degree of spiritual maturity which has shown itself in a stable cleaving to God, but a balance that is "psychological as well as spiritual. And that balance is the proof of the reality of a true vocation rather than any intensity of feeling or emotional piety, as these may often hide unresolved sublimations and complexes."[10]

If a young woman, a neophyte in the vocation to virginity in the world, falls in love with the first attractive, eligible man she meets and immediately makes the decision to marry him, one is inclined to judge that her choice of vocation was wrong in the first place and her advisers perhaps at fault for not realizing that it had been motivated by the above-mentioned "unresolved sublimations and complexes" more than by any positive call. The head of one secular institute prudently sent one of their candidates to a professional school where she would meet many men before her final commitment, since she felt it was important to determine whether a candidate to a dedicated life "in the world" could withstand the independent contact and collaboration with men to which she would be exposed in their particular apostolate.

However, it would be wrong to imply that there can be no true vocation where there are *any* mixed or (unconscious) undesirable motives. To say that would be ridiculous. Even if—as often does happen—as one's motivation is purified one discovers that in the

she could never be unhappy again. A year afterwards she asked to be released from her vow since she had come to realize that the vow had made no perceptible change in her life and that she had chosen it for the wrong reasons in the first place.

past one's motives were anything but pure, there is no reason to feel one must make the logical conclusion that no genuine vocation exists. In spite of what T.S. Eliot may say, one "can do the right thing for the wrong reasons" and still have been loyal to God.

Self-doubts and vocational doubts seem inevitably to occur in the lives of all but the most extroverted personalities and are one of the most grievous trials of dedicated virginity in the world. Even while she herself is in the awful anguish of self-doubting, the nun can see in the external reality of her convent the objective reason —the *real* reason which she wills with her whole soul even though her emotions react contrarily—for her being there. The dedicated woman in the world has no such help. The victim, as she may be, of external pressures as well as of interior troubles, she can do little except to wait for God Himself to come to her relief.

Although the vocation to perfect chastity must be carefully scrutinized, it can come from the most diverse conditions. Especially in our age of rootlessness—an age of surprises—we can expect that God's grace working everywhere would attract to religious life or to total dedication in the world, persons who in a former age might not have seemed likely candidates for dedicated virginity. (Referred to here are not persons who are emotionally maladjusted but those whose past life, training, or personal inclinations would not seem to be such as to lead them to embrace the vocation.) In commenting on the different forms an invitation to consecrated virginity might take, the Redemptorist, Father Häring, remarks that: "Even an unanswered or disappointed earthly love can be the occasion of the joy-giving recognition that it is indeed good to belong wholly to the Lord.[11] Although disappointment in love should not be the *cause* of entrance into a convent, there is no reason why it cannot be the occasion for discovering one's real vocation.

Most young American girls today—with the ever-lowered age for the beginning of dating—will, before entering the convent or choosing dedication in the world, almost always have had some experience with boys and have been given some insight into the beauty and desirability of being a happy, well-loved wife. This is not necessarily an undesirable thing; and this remains true no matter how sincerely one regrets the dangers dating entails for the chastity of youth. But the experience of an earthly love is not itself bad. For, as Father Häring goes on to say, "an earthly love can be a great grace to help us to understand what a strong and warm love Our Lord expects from a celibate person, since even this earthly love grips our hearts so deeply. A spark of love which by its nature would lead to conjugal love can with the grace of God be a profound introduction to the mystery of celibacy. Therefore a heart that is capable of human love seems even more requisite for this vocation than for marriage."

And if the spark of love which would lead to conjugal love can be an introduction to consecration to God, it is not surprising that there are some women drawn to religious life or dedication in the world who have already experienced conjugal love. There is the example of a widow who, after a happy married life, entered a contemplative convent. Asked on the day she received the habit if she had found the adjustment hard, she answered, no, that her whole life had prepared her for this. "A good wife and mother never does her own will anyway."

In these times when there are more widows, whose health remains vigorous after their children are grown and settled in their own lives, it probably can be expected that there will be an increase of those who will leave their empty homes for the convent. Probably also there will be an increase in those women, who like the widows in the early Church, will devote their time to prayer and good works while remaining at home. The secular institute may provide the framework for these widows to undertake their new life of consecration to God.

Most secular institutes are willing to consider widows as potential members, and there are two secular institutes in the process of formation which are intended exclusively for widows. The associations of St. Frances of Rome and of Regina Viduarum seek to provide a framework for widows desiring to lead a life consecrated to God while remaining in the world and discharging their family obligations. The members vow perpetual chastity and seek to devote themselves to prayer and works of charity.

ARE POVERTY AND OBEDIENCE PRACTICAL FOR LAY PEOPLE?

The paucity of the means of living a dedicated life in the world has already been remarked upon. To the difficulties of keeping the vow of chastity are added the inability, usually, to follow the counsels of poverty and obedience in the same way as does the religious. Yet poverty and obedience have always been seen by spiritual writers as safeguards for a life of perfect chastity. True, members of secular institutes practice obedience to a superior and follow poverty according to their constitution, but their practice of both must necessarily be limited.* Their lay life entails initiative and independence unknown to the nun. They have to exercise their own judgment, and usually the professional and familial areas of their life are quite outside the overseeing of their superior.

The woman who is living a dedicated life unattached to a secular institute usually will not have the helps of vows of poverty and obedience at all. A vow of obedience made to her spiritual director is usually highly impractical and not to be encouraged, and since there is no vehicle for the practice of the vow of poverty where there is not a rule, to attempt to take on this vow is unrealistic. As a French laywoman who has written a perceptive book, *Contemplative Life in the World,* says, "The question of the vows of poverty and obedience arises quite often for those who live in the world, for their souls thirst for the absolute which these vows represent. But the vows seem to go counter to the goal sought after, which is freedom of spirit, and give rise only to worry and scruples."[12] She goes on to remark that "the vow of obedience to a director is generally a grave imprudence for laymen. In fact, it

* According to the Apostolic Constitution *Provida Mater Ecclesia,* while, in secular institutes, chastity must always be the subject of a vow, poverty and obedience need not be. In the Union Caritas Christi, for example, members take a vow of chastity, but a promise of poverty and obedience. According to a spokesman for this institute, the promise of obedience means that the member will try to discover and follow Our Lord's will in all aspects of her life. While she is expected to take counsel with her *sponsor* (a kind of superior), the decisions she makes are her own, what the sponsor says being looked upon simply as *counsel,* not *command.* However, on extremely important matters affecting the faith or vocation of the member (for example, collaboration with the Communists or adoption of a child), a command may be given by the superior and obedience exacted.

can be as bad for the director as for the penitent, since it perverts the order of things."

In the absence of vows of poverty and obedience what is to be done? "The spirit of poverty is necessary, but it must find expression in a different way than in the religious life. For the layman given to Christ, poverty is expressed in the general tonality of his life, and even more in the genuine discomfort and fatigue that result from the fact that he has given away what could have prevented them, or that he does not try to make a lot of money, or that he has chosen for God's sake a profession that guarantees an increase only in hardships and exhaustion."[13]

Without a vow of poverty, one can still be poor. And the woman dedicated to God in the world has as an added cross a sense of insecurity unknown to a religious who, while she has no personal possessions, shares the goods of the community. The thought of a lonely, destitute old age is a rather harrowing one for the laywoman vowed to God especially as she approaches middle life and gets over the romantic unrealism which may have marked her dedication in her youth. But facing this thought and accepting possible destitution is part of the dedicated laywoman's willing practice of poverty.

God Who gives the grace for any vocation He wills anyone to follow, as the result of her unceasing prayer, will give the dedicated laywoman the grace to seek after that spiritual interior poverty to which exterior poverty should be directed. She will come to realize that this spiritual poverty has ramifications which formerly she could not even imagine. It is the love of this spiritual poverty which a member of the Franciscan secular institute of the Missionaries of Christ the King describes in the following passage. "To love poverty is to smile at ourselves when in a conversation we are the least elegant, the least gracious, the least instructed, the least intelligent; when in the family we are at the last place, and so also at the office or at school, when we know we are not welcome and cannot leave our position; when it seems that we are cut off from everyone, isolated, forgotten, and as though dead to persons most dear to us and to enterprises or activities closest to our heart.

"To love poverty is to thank God really from the depths of our soul when He takes health away from us, or energy, or even memory and intelligence, allowing us only to be aware that it is vanishing."[14]

This utter poverty is a mystery. And using a different approach, Léon Bloy also tried to penetrate it. In his novel, *The Woman Who Was Poor,* his theme is the woman who attains to the heights of material and spiritual poverty. One may be repelled by his fierce romanticism, but there is a deep truth in his words when he writes: "She even learned to understand—and that is little short of the sublime—that woman only *exists,* in the truest sense, if she is without food, without shelter, without friends, without husband, without children; that only thus can she compel her Saviour to come down." Bloy's heroine expresses her happiness: "One does not enter into Paradise tomorrow or the next day, or in ten years' time—but *'this day',* if one is poor and crucified."[15]

That is the hundredfold of poverty to be received even in this life. And the woman who follows a virginal consecration in the world has left herself open to this poverty. Will she be able to live it? Will she reach her ideal? It would seem that the answer is "yes," if, recognizing how poor she is within, she relies completely on the riches of God. And it is not impossible that God, seeing how she has nothing, seeing how deprived she is of external help, will give her in a direct, mysterious way what she needs. Her poverty "compels her Saviour to come down." And is it exaggerated for her to hope that through His gifts the Holy Spirit will give her directly those spiritual goods which the religious receives through other channels?

Even though she has nothing herself, the dedicated woman has much to give to others, for part of the "bargain" she has made with Christ consists in receiving His wealth for His people. Especially in this age the apostolic function of virginity should not be forgotten.

There has been considerable discussion concerning the contribution that dedicated women in the world can make to family life. This is usually evaluated in terms of direct service to individual families, as well as efforts toward the changing of those economic and social conditions that make family life difficult. Overlooked perhaps has been dedicated virginity's first contribution to marriage: that is, the very fact of perpetual virginity argues for the possibility of chastity in all walks of life. It is not farfetched to think that one of the possible designs of Providence in the encouragement that has been given to dedicated virginity in lay life at this time is the support that it will give to married people in an era when a chaste married life has become extremely difficult. The virgin's purity helps to uphold the whole structure of marriage; her heroism in transcending the desires of the flesh is at the same time a reaffirmation of the dignity of those married couples who bear well the burden their holy use of sex has laid upon them, as well as an encouragement to those couples who, for some grave reason, must practice a continence in marriage that they find extremely trying. The virgin's purity is at once an offering for, and a help to, those divorced persons who are forbidden by God's law to think of remarriage and as a consequence must persevere in what may be a truly heroic chastity. Obviously, then, the dedication of the virgin is not for selfish spiritual advantage. Her prayers, her sufferings, her mortifications, are for the benefit of the whole Mystical Body.

The apostolic influence of a life of dedicated virginity, its very real—though not always apparent—fruit for human society in general, should not hide the primary function of the virgin (whether she be a member of an "active" community, an enclosed convent or a secular institute, whether her life appears tremendously active or almost exclusively one of prayer) and that is, to contemplate God for the whole Church. In humility and awe—not counting on her own merits but on her incorporation into Christ—she becomes on behalf of all humanity a being of praise, a witness to the Absolute, a bride of the transcendent God.

NOTES

1. Rev. Peter Canon, "Consecrated Virginity," *Integrity,* October 1955, Vol. X, No. 1, p. 35.

2. *Chastity,* edited by A. Plé, O.P. (Westminster, Maryland: Newman Press, 1955), p. 111.
3. *Ibid.,* p. 130.
4. *Ibid.,* p. 175.
5. Yves M.J. Congar, O.P., *Lay People in the Church* (Westminster, Maryland: Newman Press, 1957). This book is invaluable for the explanation it gives of lay and monastic attitudes toward work.
6. Cf. a discussion on religious adaptation in *Religious Sisters,* edited by A. Plé, O.P. (Westminster, Maryland: Newman Press, 1950).
7. *Ibid.* See the excellent discussion of poverty.
8. The interested reader can write to the Rev. Joseph Haley, C.S.C., of Notre Dame, Indiana, who has taken a pioneering interest in the establishment of secular institutes in the United States and who has sponsored several conferences on the dedicated life in the world.
9. Piccarda, *The Veil of the Heart* (Paterson, N. J.; St. Anthony Guild Press, 1959), p. 56.
10. *Chastity,* p. 131.
11. Bernhard Häring, C.Ss.R., "Love and Celibacy," *Theology Digest,* Winter 1959, Vol. VII, No. 1.
12. A.M. Goichon, *Contemplative Life in the World* (St. Louis; B. Herder, 1959), pp. 104-6.
13. *Ibid.,* pp. 107-8.
14. Piccarda, *op. cit.,* p. 88.
15. Léon Bloy, *The Woman Who Was Poor* (New York: Sheed and Ward, 1947), pp. 354, 355.

13

The Education of Women

THE day before final exams in their Senior year in college, one girl slammed a book shut with a pleased expression on her face and commented: "Well, that's the last book I ever expect to read in my life." The other girls looked at her puzzled and then asked what she meant. She went on to explain: "After all, I'll never need to read a book again." So terminated one girl's college education.

Anecdotes like this make the idea of intellectual training for a woman seem more than slightly ridiculous and play into the hands of caustic critics of scatter-brain females. The girl in question had done well enough in college, but her remark was prophetic and not simply uttered in the emotional exhaustion of exams; she has never read another book.

This happened over ten years ago and it is possible that today, when colleges are more selective about the students they accept, girls like this no longer go to college. But probably they still do, since certain families, especially if they move in an environment in which college education is the norm or if they have a drive for upward social mobility, send their daughters to college even if they have no interest in higher education. And these girls, by following the crowd, taking the courses they have to take, doing the minimum studying they have to do, somehow or other scrape by and get a diploma, without ever falling in love with learning, without ever knowing the joy of thinking, or the pleasure of contemplating the intellectual and cultural riches of the past. College education has not enkindled their curiosity; the most damning thing that can be said about it is that it has produced in them no sense of *wonder.*

Perhaps it is demanding too much to ask a college to have this effect on its students. A sense of wonder is imparted to a child, almost, one could say, from its mother's womb. And while intellectual curiosity can be awakened in a person during the college years, normally it has existed long before that time. An exceptional teacher or an unusual situation can sometimes bring it to birth in a seventeen- or eighteen-year-old who, for some reason or other, has hitherto given little evidence of loving knowledge. But usually in such a case intellectual curiosity was merely dormant, not altogether absent.

One therefore tends to be tolerant in evaluating colleges. The whole subject of education is so full of difficulties, and the particular subject of education for women is so complicated that what is said here must of necessity be highly tentative. Women who have criticised the education they received almost always hesitate to make suggestions as to how it could have been improved. Most mature women, as most mature men, admit that when they were in school they did not bring to their education the subjective dispositions that would have rendered it more effective. "If I had to do it over again, I would have studied more," is the repeated refrain. But then some women go on to blame the schools for not having stimulated them to study or criticize the courses that were offered. Women who attended Catholic schools sometimes criticize the Sisters for the unreality of their education. They say it did not prepare them for life, and, interestingly enough, they say this whether they are themselves married or single.

A CASE HISTORY

Here is one woman's criticism of her sixteen years of Catholic education. In reading it one must realize that it is one type of experience and neither unique or universal. Catholic education has improved considerably in recent years and some of the specific criticisms are no longer valid. However, because this case history details the type of education received by a number of women whose adult situation is the concern of this book, it remains relevant, even though certain of the defects have since been remedied. Further, it provides a convenient focus for a discussion of what the ideal education for women should be.

This woman, as a child, went to the local parochial school which had an excellent reputation and, at that time, very adequate facilities. The community in which the school was located was predominantly a Catholic one. There were no Jews; there were a number of Protestant churches and, of course, many Protestants. The children attending the Catholic school did not, however, have much to do with the Protestant children. The parochial school was the center for their recreation as well as their education; there were Catholic scout troops, teams, and dramatic societies. Even though Catholics were in the majority, there was a carry-over into the parochial school of a defensive minority-mentality, and once when the children from the parochial school got into trouble for throwing stones at a Protestant church, the priest in assembly told them they should not have done it, "even though we know the Protestant church is not the true church."

This parochial school gave excellent training in the fundamental skills. This particular child was well-drilled in the multiplication tables, mastered spelling, and learned how to diagram sentences so that grammar would never be a mystery to her and the syntax of foreign languages something she could tackle with confidence. The catechism was well taught, though preparation for first confession and communion was not without its emotional hazards, and the child went through an agonizing period of scrupulosity. The pastor, who she later discovered was far ahead of his time, had a great interest in the liturgy, and daily voluntary attendance at the dialogue Mass in the upper grades of the elementary school was an experience for which she was fervently grateful.

In the eighth grade, boys and girls were put in separate classrooms. Their curriculum, however, remained the same, and as far as this woman remembers nothing was ever said in the girls' classroom that could not have been said in the boys'. Supposedly the theory was that the sexes should be separated at the time of adolescence. Without expecting the school to take over the sex instruction which is the parents' prerogative, one may speculate on the effect on adolescent girls of the school's overlooking the important physiological changes of that period; this lack of acceptance—by default on the teachers' part—of normal feminine functions was later exemplified in biology class in the girls' high school. Human reproduction was not considered and childbirth was never mentioned even by casual reference at any time during the four years. While this girl never heard a Sister make a remark similar to the one Father Fichter quotes,[1] that if girls knew what the pangs of childbirth were like the convent would be full of vocations, she certainly heard no glorification of marriage or motherhood.

In fact the only vocation mentioned with enthusiasm was the religious vocation, and one Sister, when she became exasperated with a student who had trouble with a translation, would say, "Go learn to beat eggs. That's all you're good for." The implication that housekeeping was for morons and the vocation of wife and mother without any particular distinction was unmistakable. The Sisters seemed to take a personal interest only in those girls who appeared to have religious vocations or who were scholarship material. Otherwise vocational guidance was omitted, and no idea was given to the girls of educational or professional possibilities for women.

The high school gave only an academic course and was proud of the record of its graduates in regional examinations. Studying to get good marks was the focus of interest. The girl's most pleasant experience as far as school-work was concerned was a geometry class taught by a Sister who had an enthusiastic knowledge of her subject and through whom she caught the sheer joy of thinking an original problem through on her own.

The woman, who had not especially liked high school, was delighted to be in college where she quickly made friends who shared her cultural and social interests. From her family she had received a love of music and art and she had always been rather disturbed when the Sisters in grammar school and high school implied that there was something wrong in going to the opera or ballet. It was thus a relief to her, in college, to share her enthusiasm with faculty members and friends who took this kind of interest for granted. The woman soon learned, however, that among these faculty members modern art was taboo and that she could take the course in contemporary literature without reading anything written in the present century. The courses in Dante and Chaucer were fine.

This student found the college religion courses especially disappointing. Although the religion courses in high school had been dry and had seemed to have no relevance to life (no one would dare ask questions or voice any practical difficulties), at least they had had a solid intellectual content. One had to study religion. But in this college the religion courses were practically devoid of intellectual content. The students followed a semester scripture course without ever reading the Bible. The senior course in marriage consisted of learning the impediments to marriage and the grounds for nullity. When this student voiced an objection to a professor about the low level at which the courses in religion were taught, he replied that most of the girls were there simply to mark time until they married, so there was no point in attempting to give them a more exalted knowledge of the faith.

In Senior year there was a class once a week to prepare the graduates for life, but it usually consisted of a reading from an etiquette book with an occasional exhortation from a well-meaning, sweet-faced Sister that the girls should get a good job (one that paid good money) or try to marry well (the meaning of this phrase was not defined). No specific discussions or lectures were sponsored by the college on a woman's place in a changing world. Although there were vague exhortations that "you can change the world," the woman felt at once isolated and protected from the world outside the campus. The one sociology course given was really an expression of the professor's own social philosophy and did not help at all toward an understanding of social reality.

Most of these charges have been made before. Indeed, many of this woman's criticisms—the "ghetto" mentality of the Catholic schools, the spirit of Irish Jansenism in regard to sex, the lack of appreciation of learning for *its own sake* and not simply as a means to a good job and social prestige, the lack of awareness of the lay vocation, the absence of stimulus to independent thinking —have been considered in a number of books and articles. A recent one, *American Catholic Dilemma,*[2] can be recommended to readers interested in pursuing this discussion further and especially to anyone looking for a sociological analysis, in historical perspective, of the present Catholic intellectual scene.

No one, however, has been as critical of education as the educators themselves. Monsignor Henry C. Bezou, Superintendent of Schools in the Archdiocese of New Orleans, when he addressed more than three thousand elementary school teachers of the New York Archdiocese at the annual Teachers Institute on February 4, 1960, exemplified this spirit of earnest, constructive self-criticism. Stressing the importance of developing Catholic leaders who can think independently, Monsignor Bezou said: "The religious teacher should never confuse, or allow the student to confuse, his or her role in the classroom with the awe-inspiring role of a person in the religious state of life. Otherwise he or she may unwittingly foster servile respect and blind obedience to the neglect of student initiative, intellectual curiosity, independent thinking and self-expression."[3]

This self-criticism on the part of a Catholic educator is by no means exceptional. Organizations such as the College Teachers of Sacred Doctrine have made valiant attempts to improve the quality of teaching as well as the content of the courses in Catholic schools. This is especially true of the work of the conferences on Sister Formation, which, over the past ten years, have accomplished in a quiet and unspectacular way some rather spectacular reforms in Catholic education and the preparation of Sister educators. Under the aegis of a group of gifted and devoted Sisters, these conferences have not been afraid to investigate the spiritual, intellectual, and emotional formation of religious teachers, and to suggest a program for improvement. That their criticism of Catholic education has been forthright and incisive will be apparent to anyone who takes a look at the published proceedings of these conferences.[4]

Without any doubt then, there has already been a great improvement in Catholic education; but no one—least of all the persons most active in these organizations—would say that all the problems have been met.

EDUCATION FOR THE FEMININE ROLE

One can insist that it is the job of the home not the school to inculcate basic attitudes towards marriage, sex, family life, and feminine roles. The girl who says that, as long as she can remember, her mother complained to her of the length and intensity of the labor pains which accompanied her entrance into the world, has already been conditioned to fear, if not to reject, the experience of motherhood, and there is probably little the school can do to help her solve her problem. She can be helped to change her irrational attitude toward childbirth, but if her emotional disturbance is deep, psychotherapy is the only solution and this is outside the school's control. Similarly, girls who come from homes in which their mothers provide examples of women who happily accept their roles and lead rich, satisfying lives, will not be markedly influenced by anything a teacher can say to derogate the vocation of wife or mother. Even a teacher's under-evaluation of a housewife's skills will strike them as amusing. But in the case of those girls who come from what may be called the middle-range of families—who have been neither drastically influenced to reject the traditional feminine role or profoundly motivated to look forward to it with great desire—the attitude of the teacher may have an influence which, although difficult to measure, cannot be dismissed as unimportant.

Needless to say, no one argues that the teacher give little ferverinos about marriage and motherhood. This is an area in which the teacher's own emotional reaction to the feminine role is of more importance than what she verbalizes. If she herself is an integrated Christian woman she will quite naturally give a favorable impression of marriage and motherhood without striving to say anything good about them or feeling the need to rise to their defense. Since the integration of femininity must, primarily, be in the person teaching, rather than in the subject taught, it would be pointless to have textbooks rewritten to present a subject specifically for girls. One of the advantages of having separate high schools and colleges for women is the freedom of the teacher and students to explore a topic occasionally as it especially affects or interests women; such discussions to be helpful should arise spontaneously.* If too much planning enters into them they become forced and unnatural, and may interfere with the effective teaching and learning of the subject itself. Thus, a biology course taught with the purpose of stressing the feminine "angle" (like a biology course taught with the purpose of showing how biology can be put to apostolic uses) might not only be a complete failure from this point of view, but it would most likely not give the student what she has the right to expect from it, namely, a knowledge of biology.

Without pretending to answer the question of whether or not the schools should teach domestic science as a regular part of their program, certainly one can say that their minimum obligation is to not encourage snobbery toward running a home. The finest Latin or math students may very well spend the best part of their lives "beating eggs" and doing similar jobs. The argument that domestic arts ought to be taught at home and not at school is often countered by the view that, since so many homes have lost this function by default, the school must therefore take it over. Whether the latter view is so or not, certainly it is im-

* I remember one such digression which took place in a college Shakespeare course. One of the remarks of the professor, a lay woman, was that a girl should not become a nun unless she would have made a good mother. It was an idea which was new to me, and it encouraged the students in a whole fresh line of thinking. Obviously, the professor did not go out of her way to set the students straight on vocational qualifications. It was just the sort of thing which comes about naturally when a subject is taught by a woman whose Christianity and femininity are intrinsic.

perative that teachers of girls by word and attitude should convey the dignity and challenge of the housewife's vocation, and that students are not left with the impression that it is something fit only for those with low IQ's. There is no reason why the academic training of women—especially in the liberal arts tradition which demands the most strenuous mental effort and emotional discipline—should make them unfit to be housewives, unless it is accompanied by an attitude on the part of the educators which fosters intellectual and social snobbery.

Such an attitude, unfortunately, often prevails. Catholic education in general has been frequently criticized for encouraging the tendency of students to think that they know all the answers. Because they have studied apologetics and scholastic philosophy they feel qualified to answer some of the most complex intellectual problems of the modern world. The assumption is, of course, tragic, both on account of its effect on the mental and cultural growth of the individual student and on account of its disastrous hampering of the Christian intellectual apostolate as a whole. And it can safely be said that the only thing worse than a man who thinks he knows all the answers, is a woman who *knows* she knows all the answers. Although there are Catholic college graduates who manifest that sort of attitude in their social contacts, it would be wrong to infer that a college education is damaging to a woman and should therefore not be attempted, just as it would be wrong to infer that because some college men are unbearable pedants we should not attempt the higher education of men.

THE INTELLECTUAL LIFE

There will probably always be an element of risk in giving women higher education, but then, as Professor O'Dea has pointed out,[5] the intellectual life itself involves risk and it is a risk that one must recognise and accept. Undoubtedly intellectual work for a woman involves additional hazards. There is, for instance, the danger that excessive rationality will destroy the sense of wonder that is so important to her as the bearer and educator of children or the danger that it will detract from the spirit of simplicity which she needs for loving response to her husband. Feminine intuition, Father Gerald Vann suggests, can be destroyed by a masculinized, over-rational education.[6]

Risk demands knowing courage, not ignorance or flight. And for a woman, intellectual work has a special function, as Edith Stein, the saintly contemplative and philosopher was quick to remark. Because a woman is so much concerned with the personal, her work so intimately involved with the lives of other people, and her influence upon them so often decisive, the danger of her love and compassion degenerating to mere *meddling* is great. "Instead of offering her husband, her children and all creatures the service of her reverence and love, instead of helping them to their unfolding in God's honor and to their happiness, she will hinder their growth and destroy their lives. If a woman is to avoid these pitfalls, and if her loving care for others is to keep its measure, she must fasten her life to the life of Christ. . . . Like a hand from above, Christ slows to proper speed our affections which, left to themselves and their proper inertia, do not know when to halt. The counterpoise in the natural realm is intellectual work, work with ideas, or creative work with things, or work for the world at large: such concerns will keep a woman from attaching herself to the lives of those entrusted to her, from meddling and immoderate closeness."[7]

That intellectual work and concern with ideas have the balancing effect stressed by Edith Stein many a woman can testify from her own experience. Therefore, it would be a shame if the renewal of emphasis on education for the feminine role should be misconstrued to mean a doing away with all the purely theoretical and speculative studies. Mathematics, philosophy, and logic should be taught to the college woman—to any woman for that matter who has the potentialities to profit from them.

On the subject of a liberal education for women, Jacques Barzun has this to say: "It is true that as a general rule, girls are less interested than boys in theory, in ideas, in the logic of things and events. That is why their minds must not be cluttered up with details which they instinctively prefer—and make no use of. Girls are more conscientious and hard-working, they want to please their teachers more, and they do not want to be bothered by implications. They argue less, and the art of winning which they have been taught since the cradle has given them a respect for convention which makes them unerringly pick out the accepted hokum. At the same time they are practical enough to distrust it, and the distrust ends by tainting all intellectual matters, so that one constantly meets women of fine intelligence who use their brains exclusively about concrete things such as clothes, food, and the persons whom they know. Their imagination about the distant or the abstract is completely atrophied; they are at the mercy of words, and their vehement opinions about war or strikes or politics are little short of brutish. Though it may be hard work, the minds of women students can be forced out of their groove of conventionality and made to cope even with abstractions. If the teacher takes pains to show repeatedly that concrete harm, good, suffering, pleasure, or profit follows from some belief or truth or question, a beginning can be made of substituting reason for memory." (In case this passage should be misinterpreted to mean that Barzun takes a dim view of the female intelligence, I shall quote him again: "After teaching a roughly equal number of men and women, I am certain that the best mind in each group was fully the equal of the other.")[8]

Of course "the learned woman is not the average woman nor does the average woman wish or need to be the learned woman."[9] The point here, however, is not advanced specialized training or graduate work, but the college education of women, and, particularly in middle-class America, college training is not looked upon as something for the rare female genius but as an education for the average intelligent woman who will meet and marry the average college-trained man. Several married women, college graduates, who are fully occupied in their roles of wives and mothers, complained to the author, not that their college gave them too intellectual a training, but one that was half-baked and mediocre.

"In hours of despair when I was a young mother, I regretted

the years I'd spent in learning to use my mind when, I thought, I should have been learning to use my hands. By the time my children were of school age, I regretted that I did not have an M.A. and a Ph.D. as well as a B.A. I had by trial and error acquired sufficient domestic skill, but I could never hope to acquire the background of general information in the sciences and the arts every mother of mentally alert children needs. A liberal-arts education, I realized then, is of more value to a woman in the day-to-day rearing of children than it is to many a man in business. Never too high for her, it was ever too narrow."[10]

Those mothers who have looked glassy-eyed as they tried to carry on an intelligent conversation about rockets to the moon with a thirteen-year-old boy will readily admit that they wish they had had more education. Many graduates of Catholic women's colleges particularly regret that a course in science was not one of their degree requirements even though a basic knowledge of the principles and methods of science would seem indispensable today. Dr. Conant's book, *On Understanding Science,* outlines the kind of course that could be integrated with profit into the curriculum of none-science majors.[11]

Not specialized learning, then, but a broader, more universal knowledge is what women need. And here Chesterton's famous remark that women are universalists rather than specialists is pertinent. A woman who has received a good, solid liberal arts education which has stimulated her mental and imaginative faculties; which has given her a knowledge of the background facts of our culture so that she can always integrate whatever new knowledge she acquires into what she already knows of history, literature and science; which has given her the kind of introduction to a foreign language that is not simply an acquaintance with a new grammar but with a new people, culture, and way of expressing the wonder of life; which has trained her to observe keenly as well as to analyze the reality of what she sees; which has stimulated her to develop whatever talent she herself may have in music or the arts so that she not only can admire but also create—such a woman is truly a universalist. And one is afraid that to produce such a woman several four-year college courses would be required. But the ideal liberal arts education can attempt to do this for a woman, can help her in the universalist attitude she brings to her role as wife and mother.

Relevant in this connection are Diana Trilling's comments: "In closing off experience from themselves (and I do not mean the experience of earning money or entering a profession—which is a separate problem—but simply the experience of exploiting one's imaginative faculties), they close themselves off both from men and from children. By courting a diversity of experience, on the other hand, they allow the fundamental womanly attributes—maternalism, responsiveness and compassion—to flourish over a larger terrain. . . . Why should we believe that intellectuality means a sacrifice of the feminine graces, or that the graces thrive less abundantly when a woman's mind is being exercised than when it stagnates?"[12]

Many people feel that a college education is wasted on a woman who marries because, concerned as she is with her husband and children, she has no time to keep her intellectual interests alive. They would agree with Jacques Barzun that "the men's intellectual interests may have narrowed, but in most cases they have fused into their professional interest. . . . Few college men give up thinking altogether."[13] He does not feel that the same thing can be said of college women.

While this lack of thinking characterizes some married women who are college graduates, one may wonder whether they ever thought in the first place. Were they like the girl mentioned at the beginning of the chapter who went to college because it was the thing to do but who never acquired an intellectual spark? (Needless to say, some men are like this too!) Here one needs to differentiate between the woman who is a genuine intellectual—not, understand, a genius, but a person who thinks—and the woman who is a good student in school. Often the college fails to appeal to the first type of woman because she may be more interested in going off on a tangent, doing reading on her own, than in docilely doing assignments and getting good marks. Her teachers may often underestimate her and overlook her intellectual potentialities. It would seem that the college has a different function to perform for each of these types. The intellectual woman who is not a good student has to learn the self-discipline of doing an assignment, of keeping to a task that is set for her. The good student has to be stimulated to think independently; in her case, perhaps, the professor should throw assignments to the wind and present arguments calculated to make her mad enough to disagree, because even disagreement might be thinking!

The good student, good because she gets good marks because good marks are the thing to get, may at another stage in her life when something else is the good thing to get, drop her supposed intellectual interests completely and never think another thought. The woman who really is intellectually curious will continue to think and continue to read come hell or high-water. Everyone knows busy mothers who, while devoted to their families, somehow or other still find time to read. They often excel men in keeping alive their intellectual interests; certainly they keep them alive on a broader base than many men who seem only able to talk about their professional or business life and can take part in no general conversational topic other than the World Series.

Married couples today are supposed to be companions and it is important to keep them talking to each other. Thus Barzun writes: "There is one conclusive argument for keeping women's college work close to that of men in scope and substance and yet giving them separate and different instructions. This is the fact that men and women live a great part of their lives together. Most men may not be like Milton in demanding intellectual companionship from their wives, but all feel to some degree the need for other conversation than that about groceries and clothes. . . ." He goes on to recommend that married couples cultivate friends "to whom general conversation is not an unknown thing. For ordinary people, intellectual interests need a social base and an easy upkeep or they peter out."[14]

But one cannot consider the education of women only as it affects (or has affected) wives and mothers. Who is to tell looking at a group of girls who will marry and who will stay single?

A strong argument can be made to support the theory that the same sort of education can benefit both, just as mediocre, insufficient, or warped education has, in the past, harmed both. Married or single, a woman should have been trained to think. Married or single, she will have benefitted by an introduction into the broad stream of Christian humanism. Married, single, or nun, it is indispensable that she should have been helped to accept feminine functions, to see the beauty of the role of wife and mother, to see how woman complements man, and how feminine gifts can be used in society. The sort of education which brings out the true meaning and dignity of marriage and motherhood will discourage a girl who remains single against her will only if they are presented as the sole and indispensable goals for a woman. Based on this distorted view of marriage, her adjustment to her single state is bound to be precarious; and it is even more dangerous for a nun to have chosen her state out of *under*-evaluation of the normal feminine role.

The liberal education which has been envisioned should be an excellent background for specialized or professional training, either for the single woman who wants to enter into a career that will provide her personally with satisfaction and enable her to make a social contribution, or for the married woman whose children are grown who looks for work outside the home. Older women who today are taking a year of education courses to prepare themselves to teach are discovering that neither their college education nor their years as wives and mothers are wasted; while the single woman in her late twenties or early thirties who goes on to graduate school very often finds that it is her ability to think, to observe, and to analyze the reality around her which is her greatest asset, even to the extent of dispensing her from the necessity of previous undergraduate work in her field of specialization.

THEOLOGY AND THE SOCIAL SCIENCES

Pope Pius XII called for an education for woman that would provide her with "a culture of not mere imagination and sentiment, but one built on truth and faith, a culture which would mold in woman a wise, strong, active Christian character."[15] Obviously, then, there is no room in the religious education of girls for those sickly-sweet stories of the saints common in past years, nor for those appeals to Our Lady (such as "Our Lady weeps when a girl whistles") which were a favorite means of training in feminine deportment. A culture "built on truth and faith" should imply a solid, serious grasp of the doctrines of faith, a study which naturally is adjusted to the particular level of the student. While this is not the place to decide the question of how theology should be taught to laymen or laywomen, the necessity for such study is undeniable. Courses in liturgy, scripture, the writings of the Fathers of the Church, although when taught in an academic setting their aim is primarily knowledge rather than piety, are part of the culture of which the Pope spoke. They serve the purpose not only of providing background for an intellectual grasp of the faith, but also of refining the Christian imagination, steadying the emotions, and giving to a woman the sturdy foundation on which she can build her personal spiritual life.

In addition to theology, there are two other areas which cannot be neglected in the education of modern Christian women. The one area is that of the social sciences, especially sociology. For too long emphasis in Catholic women's colleges has been placed on social philosophy to the exclusion of sociology. Girls have been taught what the ideal society *should be,* without ever being helped to examine carefully what the society they are living in actually *is.* Since previous chapters have been concerned with stressing the conflicts in our society which are a cause of great tension to women it is not necessary to repeat them here. However, it is to the point to note that cultured women should themselves have been trained to observe and analyze these social conflicts. The study of sociology can perform a function for them the need of which is well-expressed in the following words of Dr. Harding: "If women are to see their personal problems in true perspective, it is absolutely essential that they learn to take things impersonally, while not losing touch with their own feeling. Otherwise, they are hopelessly caught in the network of the personal, and have to suffer as though it were a personal fate, or even a personal fault, things which really belong to the fate of a generation and are rightfully the burden of society."[16]

It seems that the intelligent woman is helped to see her personal problems in their social setting more effectively by the serious study of sociology than by any number of "life-adjustment" courses. These latter, based as they are on consideration of particular problems in a particular setting, are of insufficient value in an age such as our own in which changes are as rapid as they are drastic. Not solutions for her personal problems but the ability to analyze her personal problems in their social setting is what the modern woman needs from education. To do this she needs training in the principles of the social sciences, and not merely an acquaintance with the facts which various social scientists may incidentally have gathered.

3 The third area which needs emphasis in the education of women revolves around acquiring a contemplative spirit. The four years of college have been traditionally four years of leisure to acquaint oneself with the riches of the past, to ponder the truth one has learned, to enjoy the beauty one has seen. It is regrettable if the necessity to work one's way through college, or the social pressure to engage in extra-curricular activity, should make the enjoyment of fruitful leisure during the college years totally impossible. Certainly, all through one's life one should think, but these are the years set aside to have *time* to think, not only time to analyze, but time to reflect, time simply to enjoy.

Most women's colleges are in settings of natural beauty and in all Catholic women's colleges there is a chapel where a girl can enjoy the quiet to meditate. In an increasing number of them the chapel, as well as the classrooms, have become places of beauty, using the best of contemporary art to symbolize to the student the presence of God in a transitory world. All of these externals are good. But in addition it would seem that among the faculty (especially among the administrators) there should be an awareness of the importance of directing education toward the development of a contemplative spirit. Poetry, for example, should be taught not just so that one can unearth and talk about its possible meanings, but primarily so one can read and experience it oneself.

The failure of higher education in America to develop inner resources is critical. Especially is this failure serious in the education of women; it is almost disastrous in the education of Catholic women—for a reason that will be clear presently.

The educated woman who marries and starts keeping house complains that she is utterly bored. She cannot listen to the soap operas which pacify some women, so what is she to do? "I have nothing to think about." No one denies that there are tensions in changing from an active professional life to a quiet domestic scene; there are real difficulties and important readjustments to be made. But there is an underlying problem. Should not education have given this woman and others like her something to think about? Are plays attended, books read, music listened to, aesthetic experiences in general, merely to be dissected verbally, criticized at length, and used to stimulate conversation? Are they not supposed to have an intangible but nonetheless lasting and indelible effect on oneself?

Many people who would scorn studying simply for a degree still acquire an education exclusively for its external effect, perhaps not for its purely monetary value, but for its social, companionable value. Or, at least, whether intended or not, that seems to be the result. One is well-read and keeps the conversation going. One can make endless, apt quotations; one has an opinion on Dylan Thomas and can take either side with ease if there is a debate on the Catholicity of Graham Greene. Conversation is a fine and important thing, but there is the danger that conversational gambits can become merely goods to be displayed. What have these goods done to oneself? Do they help at all when one is alone? Do they deepen, sharpen one's thought, or even give one something to think about? Do they give significance to the ordinary duties one performs? Give a heightened awareness of the reality behind the trivialities of every day? (The breeze rustling the paper, the child's light laughter.) The woman who has studied as literature the Bible, Dante, Chaucer, Bernanos—should she not somehow see the symbolism of the objects involved in her housewifeliness, of bread and meat, water and soap, more than her less educated neighbor? And if she does not, if she cannot, why?

Some failure in her education is indicated. To blame the formal education system alone for this failure is manifestly and grossly unfair. The home as well as the school may have gone along with the spirit of the times, which is a spirit alien to the cultivation of inner resources, to the development of the contemplative spirit.

Catholic education, and especially Catholic education for women, must recognize the importance of encouraging the contemplative spirit. Such a spirit is essential for any profound intellectual life as well as for any serious creative effort. And isn't it possible that neglecting to acquire inner resources and to cultivate quiet meaningful "aloneness," is at least partially responsible for keeping many women from advancing in the spiritual life, the life of prayer? We recognize and credit activity. We recognize and credit prayer. But how does one cross the bridge from the exteriority of action to the interiority of prayer unless there is a deliberate effort to learn to live within? Even the graces of contemplation which are beyond any human effort usually presuppose a personality that is already conditioned to them. Acquiring a contemplative spirit will not inevitably make a contemplative. Nonetheless, God is not easily heard by the soul who has never made the effort to shut her doors and look within.

NOTES

1. Joseph Fichter, *Parochial School: A Sociological Study* (Notre Dame, Ind.: University of Notre Dame Press, 1958), p. 260.
2. Thomas F. O'Dea, *American Catholic Dilemma: An Inquiry into the Intellectual Life* (New York: Sheed and Ward, 1958).
3. As reported in *The New York Times,* February 5, 1960.
4. Sister Ritamary, C.H.M., *The Mind of the Church in the Formation of Sisters* (New York: Fordham University Press, 1956). By the same author and publisher: *Spiritual and Intellectual Elements in the Formation of Sisters* (1957); *The Juniorate in Sister Formation* (1960). Also see Sister Ritamary, C.H.M., "Lavigierie

and the Education of Sisters," *Thought,* Winter 1959-1960, Vol. XXXIV, No. 135, pp. 607-615.

5. O'Dea, *op. cit.*
6. Gerald Vann, O.P., *The Water and the Fire* (New York: Sheed and Ward, 1954), especially the chapter, "The Role of Woman," and *The Paradise Tree* (New York: Sheed and Ward, 1959).
7. John M. Oesterreicher, "Edith Stein on Womanhood," *Integrity,* September 1953, Vol. VII, No. 12, p. 26.
8. Jacques Barzun, *Teacher in America* (Garden City, N. Y.: Doubleday Anchor Books, 1954), p. 219, 212.
9. Ruth Reed, *The Single Woman* (New York: Macmillan, 1942), p. 192.
10. Worth Tuttle Hedden, "People in Skirts," *Women Today,* edited by Elizabeth Bragdon (New York: Bobbs-Merrill, 1953), p. 64.
11. James Bryant Conant, *On Understanding Science* (New Haven: Yale University Press, 1947).
12. Diana Trilling, "Are Women's Colleges Really Necessary?" *Women Today,* p. 270.
13. Jacques Barzun, *op. cit.,* p. 212.
14. *Ibid.,* p. 220.
15. *Woman's Duties in Social and Political Life,* Address given on October 21, 1945.
16. M. Esther Harding, M.D., *The Way of All Women* (New York: Longmans, Green, 1937).

14

Toward a Spirituality for Women

THE young woman was pregnant with her first child. "Just think," she said, "the baby grows without my doing anything about it. There is nothing for me to do but just wait."

This attitude of passivity, of patient waiting, is the attitude preeminently of the expectant mother, who knows, of course, that she must co-operate in the growth of her baby by eating good food, getting adequate rest, and proper exercise, but who also realizes that what she can do in an active way is the least part of the wonder of the child's development. When in her loving surrender to her husband she expresses her "Be it done unto me," she consents to the whole outcome of their union. Her pregnancy, then, is the visible indication of her willing acceptance of her condition of passivity. But whether she desires the child or not, once his conception has taken place she is, in her body, completely given over to him; from her he draws his life. She is, in a sense, his victim; but victim only that she may achieve fulfillment; that she may experience the beatitude of becoming a mother. For, as Gertrud von le Fort has so well expressed it, "The child is not only born by the mother, the mother is also born through the child."

Pregnancy, the supreme, normal, physical experience of passivity (for in the realm of bodily abnormality there is the passivity of being eaten away by disease), has important indications for a woman concerning the supernatural experience of passivity. Various reasons have been advanced to account for the fact that the greater number of mystics in the Church have been women. One telling reason certainly is that a woman is conditioned psychologically for that complete surrender to the Holy Spirit which is the indispensable prerequisite for the mystic's life. In marriage and childbirth she knows what it is to let herself be acted upon, to develop a spirit of patient waiting, of silent expectation. Whether a woman is married or not (for it can be argued that the greater number of mystics were consecrated virgins) the normal feminine biological and cultural preparation for pregnancy has marked her individual psyche to the extent that passivity is natural to her, and she is disposed to let the Holy Spirit form Christ within her.

IS THERE A STRICTLY FEMININE SPIRITUALITY?

The spirit of loving surrender, of self-effacement before the marvel of the divine creative action, of simplicity in waiting until He accomplishes His designs does seem to be especially a woman's way to perfection. It is often said that before God the soul must always assume a feminine role, and in the spiritual life of male saints the same marks of loving surrender are found, just as in the spiritual life of female saints the heroic practice of the active virtues and the manly battle against temptation are never absent. And certainly one can exaggerate the relationship of spirituality to the sex of the person seeking God. An individual, man or woman, has his or her own particular path to God, with his or her individual assets and liabilities. No two persons will become saints in the same way, and we cannot, obviously lay out two paths to holiness. Consequently while in this chapter several points are discussed which may be especially applicable to a modern woman, they are meant to be only suggestions. Respecting God's designs for the individual soul, one recognizes that, just as there can be no clear-cut divisions between the active and contemplative virtues, there can be no nice, final distinctions between masculine and feminine types of spirituality. This chapter, as well as other discussions throughout the book, is not intended to be dogmatic. Anyone seeking to learn what is dogmatic in spiritual development can consult any of the many excellent works in spiritual theology. Here spirituality is simply related to the experience of the average woman in the United States.

Obviously for every sex and for every age and for every culture, the Church offers the same means of grace in her sacraments. The Mass and the liturgical life are for everyone. The infused virtues and the gifts of the Holy Ghost grace every soul. The ten commandments are for all, regardless of sex and culture, as are the counsels of perfection. In the Gospels the beatitudes point out to everyone the same spiritual exigencies, and the parables speak to all. The words of Jesus find an echo in every soul, and in every Christian Baptism has planted the same seed of glory to flower in eternity. For all Our Lord is the Way as well as the Goal, the Truth as well as the Life. Our Lady is Mother of all, and all share the treasures of the Communion of Saints.

But each one has his own gift. In each soul, it seems to please God to leave a particular reflection of Himself. Circumstances and natural aptitudes may go far in explaining personal spiritual "bents" or "leanings," but they still remain mysterious, and it would imply a limit to God's freedom if we questioned the existence of echoes of His goodness in souls where their presence seems naturally inexplicable.

To the general means of grace afforded by the Church and to the special grace which is God's particular gift to each, all of us must be faithful. But we come from Mass into daily life; we arise from our prayer to the day's work. The tensions of earthly existence and the circumstances of life in the world inevitably influence us. As Christ was a Man of Palestine and His spirituality as He lived it was marked by His Jewish culture, the women of America are influenced by the culture which has formed them. The ambiguous position of American women and the confusion they experience over their roles are the background of their spiritual life, as are, for example, the developments in modern medicine and the equalizing of the position of husbands and wives. In this social context we live and grow holy, or we live and grow farther from God. One way or the other, this social context affects us and cannot be overlooked in our approach to God.

PASSIVITY AND THE AMERICAN WOMAN

Take the matter of passivity. Certainly it is not as natural for an American woman as it was for women in the past or is for women of different cultures. The acceptance of pregnancy has been, and is still, easier in other cultures, even when childbirth itself is full of dangers. Modern medicine has removed the hazards of childbirth for American women, but a girl formed by American culture does not accept pregnancy with the simple, unthinking, spontaneous simplicity of the peasant women of two centuries ago or the Indian women of today. The necessity of passivity and patient waiting she may come to accept, but her acceptance is a rational rather than an instinctive one. St. Elizabeth of Hungary went docilely and joyfully into an arranged marriage; St. Bernadette expressed her willingness to be "stuck away in some corner like an old broom that has done its job;" St. Thérèse of Lisieux rejoiced in her littleness and asked Our Lord to make her an elevator so that she would not have the arduous climb up the ladder of perfection. These saints had a docility, a simplicity, a spirit of self-surrender and humble self-effacement which are, naturally-speaking, foreign to American women. They seem to be the accompaniment of cultures where a woman spontaneously and simply fulfilled her role, where she accepted the duties of marriage and the pains of childbirth, where she was trained to be docile and self-sacrificing, where, in a word—despite the paradoxically great activity which marked her daily life—she was passive. St. Teresa of Avila, admonishing her Sisters that they should not complain about their sufferings since many married women had a great deal more to endure and at the same time had to "put on a good face" to their husbands, was pointing to the common lot of women as a spiritual spur for her nuns.

But today in America women do not have a common hard-lot to endure passively, when it cannot be accepted heroically. Pregnancy *is* avoidable, and women are not educated to be docile to their husbands. The spirit of self-surrender and self-sacrifice on the part of women which seemed necessary for the good of society in other ages and cultures is not considered necessary in the mid-twentieth-century United States. To a woman trained to be independent, trained to value her freedom of choice, pregnancy and childbirth and the rearing of children are no longer facts to be accepted without a thought or struggle.

How do these attitudes of independence affect the others, self-surrender to God, acceptance of His holy will, docility to the Holy Spirit and the willingness to remain passive in His hands? Does the social situation of American women make these virtues less necessary? The answer is a decided "No." Even though the social situation has rendered these virtues more difficult, it has not made them less important. Obviously the woman destined to become holy in marriage and motherhood still needs them, and it is axiomatic that they are still as important as ever for the nun who is to become the ever more docile, ever more deeply surrendered bride of Christ. The single woman, too, must cultivate them if she is striving for union with God, but in her life, especially, there is a tension since the emotional independence and the ability to stand on her own two feet which she needs for her work (and which society expects from her) perhaps militate against them.

What is a woman today to do? She has to give conscious consideration to these passive virtues, evaluate them in the presence of Our Lord, and make the *positive* effort to integrate them into her own life. The woman pregnant for the first time, after an active college career and intense professional work, will have to make a deliberate decision to accept the period of waiting for her child. The single woman who all day long makes decisions on her job, who has possibly to defend her point of view or to maintain an independent position, has to meditate on her dependence on God, even while she tries to accept her lack of emotional satisfaction as His will. There has to be conscious cultivation of virtues and attitudes of soul which, to women of other times, might have appeared as a natural part of their being.

Woman today needs to *learn* to wait, to be passive and patient in suffering, to be cheerful of heart in self-sacrifice. Perhaps more than ever before she needs these virtues, since, in the complex civilization in which she finds herself, in the confusion and ever-changing social expectations under which she must live out her life, there is so much beyond her control. So many things she can do nothing about.

"You can't fight City Hall," or "You can't buck the system," may be the words of a cynic or they may be an expression of the philosophy of a cheerful realist. Their truth can be exaggerated, but nevertheless there is truth in these phrases. There are currents in modern life which the individual alone is as unable to fight as he is to resist the stream of traffic of the mob subway-bent during the rush-hour. A woman who works for a mammoth corporation and a girl on the factory assembly line have to accept many things as beyond their personal ability to change. A wife whose husband's job enforces annual moves to another part of the country, or a mother who regrets that the nuclear family is an institution in our society, can express their regret, but they themselves cannot reinstate residential stability or the extended family system. Many factors in the social set-up in which they live they must simply accept. (That is not to say, of course, that one cannot and should not work for social change, but meanwhile one cannot destroy oneself with discontent over the reality that is.)

Besides difficulties that arise from the social system in which the American woman finds herself, there are inevitable problems and sufferings which have always been the human lot. But it is a premise of our scientific society, it would seem, that all problems yield themselves to solution just as diseases can be conquered and human pain destroyed. There are the March of Dimes and the Mother's March on Polio. We are told to "Fight Cancer," "Wipe out MS," "Conquer Heart Disease." The implication sometimes is that, with time, *all* obstacles will be conquered and *all* pain yield itself to a cure. Given this social climate, how is the individual woman to react to the difficulties of her personal life?

Because she has been trained to be "rational," to seek and to find the answers, it is hard for her to learn, and even harder to accept the knowledge, that for some situations there are no answers, no solutions; she must just learn to accept. A woman who is married to a man with a severe emotional disturbance which does not yield to treatment has to accept her predicament. A woman whose husband has deserted her has, as a Catholic, no possibility of remarriage; she must simply accept. An old woman whose life has been prolonged by modern medicine which cannot, however, cure her loneliness, must wait for the good pleasure of God. A single woman who goes through periods of deep unhappiness can and should do all in her power to brighten her life, but most important of all she must be patient and accept her lack of fulfillment. A woman whose husband's sudden death leaves her alone with several children has to try to resign herself to God's will unquestioningly while she waits for time to heal her sorrow. Not that time itself heals anything, but grace works in time and it takes time for her to learn the answer given to Job: that God is God and human beings have no right to demand an explanation of His actions. All they can do is to imitate the Son of God in accepting suffering with love, while they wait for God to heal their wounds.

Sometimes, however, waiting seems to be impossible. Patient endurance is too much for us and silent acceptance seems to us an attitude of soul as unrealistic of achievement as it is desirable in theory. What then are we to do? Unceasing prayer would seem to be the only answer. Unceasing prayer, insistent prayer, if need be, desperate prayer. If Christ said that God is like a benefactor who finally yields himself to his neighbor's importunate entreaties for bread; if He, moreover, told us that our Heavenly Father knows what we need, we have every claim upon His goodness. For the grace to say "yes," to God's will, for the grace to accept the pain we must endure, for the grace to wait in patience through a trial we cannot flee, for the grace to remain passive beneath the action of the Holy Spirit as He purifies us through external circumstances as well as through interior suffering, we have every right to beg.

Sometimes we have received the grace before we know it. The action of God in our soul is imperceptible. It is not necessary that we have the grace to endure this pain forever, but only for *this moment.* It is not necessary that we feel ourselves able to accept these difficult and even wretched circumstances for years, but only for the present. Bolstering as it would be to our pride and to our security to know that we are capable of "enduring all things," it is better if our acceptance and self-surrender appear to us—as indeed they must be if they are to be meritorious in God's sight—the fruit of our response to His grace, rather than the result of a stoic ability to suffer or a stubborn attempt to keep a stiff upper lip.

THE IMPORTANCE OF SELF-ACCEPTANCE

But acceptance of our interior poverty and even the asking of God to give us the grace to accept (or, if such a grace is too high for souls as weak and small as ours, the grace merely to wait patiently until we can accept cheerfully) would presuppose an acceptance of ourselves which is another name for humility. To pray as we ought we need humility, but in order to get humility we need to pray. Here we seem to go round in circles! In a sense in the spiritual life we do; for while we can say that all the virtues are rooted and grounded in charity, we cannot show clearly how one virtue precedes another. They do not form a straight line, but a circle, no point of whose circumference we can designate as its beginning or as its end. This is true of the virtues. Humility leads to self-surrender to God, but surrendering to God we become humble. (This is, just another way of saying what St. Thomas Aquinas put so exactly: that all the virtues grow together like the fingers of one hand.)

Aiming at the true humility which is acceptance of oneself as one is seems particularly important today. We know that the humility which comes from spectacular humiliations is foreign to the circumstances of the average woman and that it could be especially dangerous in an emotionally unbalanced age, but are perhaps unaware of a more common distortion: the conformity which results from social pressure and which appears, on the surface, to be a sort of humility. Pride today for many women does not consist in wanting to be extraordinary but in wanting to be just like everybody else. The "Organization Woman" like the "Organization Man" does not wish to excel; her pride, therefore, consists in a more subtle thing—the refusal to be herself.

The acceptance of oneself involves the acceptance of one's talents as well as one's limitations. It involves being (if one may use the expression) true to one's own grace. It certainly involves accepting one's own disorders. If she is anxious, the humble woman accepts the fact that she is; if she has an overwhelming desire to be loved, she accepts the fact of the existence of this desire. Some things about herself are obvious and perhaps easy to accept. Others are more difficult. And still others she cannot accept because they are hidden from her eyes. The point is that she must strive to accept the reality of herself which she sees. There will be a time for her to accept the deeper and truer reality of herself which God now mercifully keeps hidden from her eyes. For, when He finally presents that reality to her vision, He will simultaneously give her the grace to accept it.

But in case self-acceptance appears too lofty and too subtle, let us relate it to everyday realities. Self-acceptance for a woman means acceptance of the fact that she is not as good a cook as several other ladies, but that she irons clothes well. It may mean acceptance of the fact by a girl that she has little or no artistic talent and should change her major. Self-acceptance may mean continuing to cultivate one's liking for philosophy or poetry even though the other women in the neighborhood spend their spare time playing bridge or growing African violets. For a Catholic woman self-acceptance may mean (dare one say it?) recognizing the fact that emotionally she is unable to cope with ten children, or breast-feed her baby for six months, or give lectures in addition to making a home—even though Mrs. X, Mrs. Y, and other Catholic Mothers of the Year all seem to be able to do all these things.

Acceptance of oneself as one is, is indispensable if one is to grow to be what God desires one to become. One cannot strive for an ideal wisely and well unless one knows the already-existing reality. And the ideal of sanctity will always be phony and unreal to a woman unless she can make it personal to herself, realizable to herself, in terms of what *she herself is.*

It may be objected that self-acceptance sounds a great deal like self-complacency. Unfortunately the two can be mistaken even though they are essentially different. The complacent person only accepts that aspect of herself which is agreeable, while the one who really accepts herself accepts her unpleasant side as well. Emphasis on self-acceptance can be misconstrued to mean a spirit of relaxation which hinders one from striving for an ideal. Self-acceptance thus appears as a lazy toleration of oneself that keeps one from reaching for the heights. Admittedly a certain type of person can twist the idea of accepting herself into meaning this indifference toward ideals, but it seems that this is not the tendency of the ordinary Catholic woman.

Further, American women are under tremendous pressure to measure up to an *ideal*—whether it is the ideal presented by television, advertising, the next-door neighbor, or the one inculcated by their parents or teachers—and this has helped create an excessive feeling of guilt. This *is* the Age of Anxiety. It is true that too often people feel guilty about the wrong things, but to add to their emotional burden of guilt does not help them. (Needless to say the reference here is not to persons who suffer from such intolerable, neurotic guilt-feelings that they need psychiatric help, but to the average, normal individual, who may suffer a certain amount of irrational guilt.) A woman certainly should not be made to feel guilty because she is not measuring up to some vague "ideal woman." Trying to accept herself as she is in God's sight, a woman is freed from the false sense of guilt which she feels when she sees herself as a mirror of other people, and at the same time she liberates herself from her true guilt since, recognizing and accepting it before God, she can atone for it.

Self-acceptance is related to the acceptance of the frustration of some, at least, of our potentialities. The mature person accepts it as a truism that there are very few people in life who are able to do all the things they would like to do and are capable of doing; in other words, very few persons are able to realize all their potentialities. Women, especially today, are aware of all the opportunities they might make use of and have to make a deliberate and conscious effort to accept the frustration and limitations which may be imposed on them by external circumstances or by their vocation itself. Vocation usually spells out God's Will, and while there are some frustrations that can be overcome without interfering with one's vocation, there are others that must be accepted if the vocation is to be followed successfully to its end. The wise Christian woman knowing that she cannot do everything she wishes, just as she cannot have everything she wishes, accepts these frustrations and does not allow them to interfere with the joy with which she follows her vocation and serves Our Lord.

STEPPING STONES

To return for a moment to the passive virtues, it might be suggested that some positive effort can be made to develop the ability for patient waiting and endurance. A culture like ours which stresses the active virtues, such as efficiency and the willingness to work hard and do a good job, does not usually form us in the qualities that mark a more leisurely, contemplative culture. Missing a bus or being kept waiting by a friend, for instance, are not seriously irritating matters in Latin culture. Yet because being kept waiting is an exercise in patience we can, if we wish, use it to positive advantage to form within us dispositions which are not native to us. A slight headache, an appointment not kept, a delayed airplane, a letter delivered late, a long distance telephone call that takes longer than usual to put through—all can be reminders that even in the Age of Efficiency we still have to put up with many things. They are also means of mortification, means of melting down self-will and making ourselves agreeable to the Will of God. They can help to prepare us to endure the *real* hardships that may come into our lives, as well as to keep our spirit of self-sacrifice strong.

For, in the emphasis on passivity, we cannot overlook the positive efforts we must make, if we would become holy, to prepare ourselves for the action of God in our souls. Mortification is our voluntary effort to remove the blocks that sin has put in the way of the Holy Spirit's working in us. Obviously, asceticism is regulated by one's state in life, but there are ways of introducing it into the most crowded life, since mortification, unlike creative writing, does not call for a "room of one's own"! Father François de Sainte-Marie gives a list of "little, intelligent, generous efforts to struggle against slackness and sensuality"; he remarks that "such mortifications are infinite in number, because infinitely small. Thus there are many small matters in connection with meals (which no one but Our Lord can see): drink in little sips when one is thirsty, not avoid portions of unpleasing food, taking little of a favorite dish or not taking a second helping, 'forgetting' to take sugar or wine, not adding salt, etc. Sometimes there is bitter medicine to be taken, and so many other trifles. More generally there is laziness to be shaken off, and love of ease and comfort, compelling oneself to get up at once at the fixed time, not putting things off till tomorrow, accepting the fatigue of household duties, not being rough with inanimate objects, finishing the task undertaken before starting another . . . bearing having to stand the cold or intemperate weather without grumbling and so on."[1] Any imaginative woman could add to this list—finishing up what is left in the babyfood jars, eating the ends of the loaf of bread, not putting off the mending, not entering into competition for a vacant seat in the subway, reading the article her husband calls to her attention rather than letting her eye wander to a more interesting one on the opposite page, refusing a second cocktail, hiding her mood when she feels glum instead of expressing it, letting some other member of the family choose the television program, or going to the play preferred by her friend, not complaining about a wrong telephone number, and so forth.

There is an obvious danger for a woman in these little mortifications and that is that she will get petty or compulsive about them. Before her mind must always be the aim of mortification, and that is the freeing of the spirit to love God. But to introduce voluntarily an element of hardness into her life, especially when her life is going along smoothly and her happiness is unclouded, is a good thing. A woman who had an easy, pampered life as a girl and later finds things too difficult when her husband's income is cut, can justifiably complain, "Why didn't someone, somewhere along the line, warn me that life can be tough?" As another woman, whose bringing up of a large family was complicated by illness and other trials, said to a friend who felt that she should complain more than she did: "But this life is supposed to be hard; whoever said we were going to have Heaven on earth?" In a society of unprecedented prosperity and good health, it is easy to forget that the Christian still lives under the sign of the cross. And the incidents that used to remind women of their call to follow Christ and Mary in their suffering are forgotten when the death of a child is no longer a common occurrence and the pains of childbirth are considerably mitigated.

The cross is all the more difficult to bear when it comes into the life of those who never expected to receive it. In a civilization like our own, dedicated to the pursuit of happiness, suffering seems especially out of place. Yet great suffering persists; we may know about it professionally or merely read about it in the newspaper. We may dedicate our days to relieving it or we may simply contribute an occasional dollar to the victims of famine and war. But since the presence of suffering, in an age which inordinately desires ease and a good time, presents what may become a spiritual crisis for the individual, it is necessarily related to seeking God.

Obviously a woman cannot take *personally* every one of the worries and hardships in the world, yet nothing could be worse than the complete lack of compassion and the brutal curiosity with which many women view the most intimate human sufferings pictured in the tabloids. Confronted with pain, these women may react differently. To the sufferings of someone close to them they respond compassionately. To the sufferings of someone with whom they are in professional contact they may react either with a too emotional identification which renders them useless to the person or the development of a self-protective shell of hardness.

A non-Catholic writer puts well a Christian solution to this problem of coping with suffering. "A supra-personal value has power to rescue a woman from the impasse, on the one hand, of being overwhelmed or, on the other, of becoming hard, when it is accepted as supreme, for then it transcends not only her own personal life and desires but also the personal needs of those whose suffering has so painfully affected her. In by-gone days women found such a supra-personal value in their religion. They found relief from their too great suffering by casting their burden on the Lord or by communing with Our Lady of Sorrows."[2]

THE BALANCE OF THE MORAL VIRTUES

The qualities of gentleness, sympathy and tenderness should particularly mark a woman's approach to fraternal charity. But in order that compassion does not degenerate into emotionalism and love of neighbor deteriorate into a sickly sentimentality, a woman needs to develop the rather stern, unappealing virtues which theologians call the moral virtues. The stereotype of the Lady Bountiful dispensing food baskets to the poor while she ignores the most basic demands of justice may not be truer than the stereotype of Lord Bountiful donating large sums of money to major charities while he continues to underpay his workers. But Lady Bountiful needs to mend her ways whatever Lord Bountiful does, and it is unfortunately true that a great many women who respond to sob stories do not bring to their practice of charity the prudence and the strength of character which it demands. How many Catholic women, for example, while they sit around sewing for the missions express the most uncharitable sentiments regarding Negroes or Jews, or argue against foreign aid for needy nations? Perhaps this kind of seeming hypocrisy is the result of ignorance or misinformation rather than of any lack of development in the moral virtues in the life of the individual woman. However, it seems that too often in practice charity is the unthinking response to a play on her emotions. If she had developed prudence it would be the result of the thoughtful consideration of what means should be chosen for the end in view after the end has been assessed in the light of Christian faith and principle. What does love of neighbor demand? More basic still, who is my neighbor? And if my neighbor is everyone in the whole world, what are the best means I can take to help him, granting the limitations under which I labor? These are questions prudence proposes.

Perhaps prudence—which is an exalted form of common sense and emotional balance on the supernatural level—should be especially easy for a woman to practice, since, proverbially, a woman is supposed to be overflowing with common sense and practicality. This may be so in relationship to her own affairs and those of her family, but she must learn to cultivate prudence in relationship to those outside her immediate emotional concern. Love for neighbor, if it is to be effective, needs all the means a woman can place at its disposal.

The other moral virtues are as necessary to a woman as are prudence and justice. She needs fortitude to prevent her docility from becoming compliance with evil, her self-surrender the result of her refusal to fight for what is good. She needs temperance to curb a generosity which might drive her to excess and allow sensuality to overcome her spirit.* To her practice of charity, which is at once the chief means and the end of her Christian life, a woman must bring all the virtues. This is simply another way of saying that she must put all she has and is at the service of love. Love of God is the purpose of her existence and is inextricably tied to love of neighbor. And in her love, a woman seeks to follow Christ. In Him, is the balance of all virtue.

For, "Christ is the ideal of human perfection: in Him there is

* In this connection St. Thomas wrote: "Sobriety is most requisite in women because in women there is not sufficient strength of mind to resist concupiscence."[3] Many women may react indignantly to this statement. It would be better if they saw the root problem. It is not so much that women are weak in the face of concupiscence (or the direct appeal of the sexual or sensual), but that they can be so easily led by their love for a man. Therefore, as their guard they need to develop the virtues of sobriety, chastity, and modesty, all of which St. Thomas includes under temperance.

no one-sidedness, no want; in Him there is the excellence of all that is manly and womanly, and none of the weakness. His faithful followers then, becoming more and more like Him, will more and more be carried beyond the limits of their natures . . . What no denial of nature, no human power or determination, can ever do, grace brings about in those who humble themselves under God. Thus saintly men often show true tenderness, womanly goodness, motherly care for souls, and holy women show unconquerable will and manly daring."[4]

In her active striving to follow Christ, woman learns to put into practice all the virtues. Yet strive as she will, act as she will, she knows that her own efforts are the least part of her way to holiness. It remains true that it is God who makes saints.

The woman who surrenders herself completely to the Holy Spirit lives in a constant state of receptivity. But lest her passivity degenerate into quietism, and receptivity into mere inertia, she must keep herself vivified by *hope*. In lively confidence that what He has promised will come to pass, in fervent expectation that the Holy Spirit will form Christ within her, in silent, joyful waiting she looks forward to His coming.

There is a beautiful German expression to describe a pregnant woman: she is referred to as being "full of good hope." Hope is expectancy, and, it would seem, is pre-eminently a woman's virtue. Full of good hope, then, she awaits His coming, knowing that the darkness of this life will soon be over and that in the morning she shall see His glory.

NOTES

1. *Chastity,* edited by A. Plé, O.P. (Westminster, Maryland: Newman Press, 1955), p. 237.
2. M. Esther Harding, M.D., *The Way of All Women* (New York: Longmans, Green, 1937), p. 100.
3. *Summa Theologica,* II, II, Q. 149, a. 4.
4. John M. Oesterreicher, "Edith Stein on Womanhood," *Integrity,* Vol. VII, No. 12 (September 1953), p. 28.